The Role of Old Testament Theology in Old Testament Interpretation

The Role of Old Testament Theology in Old Testament Interpretation

And Other Essays

Walter Brueggemann

Edited by
K.C. Hanson

James Clarke & Co

James Clarke & Co
P.O. Box 60
Cambridge
CB1 2NT
United Kingdom

www.jamesclarke.co
publishing@jamesclarke.co

ISBN: 978 0 227 17545 3

British Library Cataloguing in Publication Data
A record is available from the British Library

First published by James Clarke & Co, 2015

Published by arrangement
with Cascade Books

Contents

Acknowledgments

The author and publisher gratefully acknowledge the publications where earlier versions of these essays first appeared.

Chapter 1: "The Role of Old Testament Theology in Old Testament Interpretation" first appeared in *In Search of True Wisdom: Essays in Old Testament Interpretation in Honour of Ronald E. Clements,* edited by Edward Ball, 70–88. Journal for the Study of the Old Testament Supplements 300. Sheffield: Sheffield Academic, 1999. Used by permission.

Chapter 2: "The Travail of Pardon: Reflections on *slḥ*" first appeared in *A God So Near: Essays on Old Testament Theology in Honor of Patrick D. Miller,* edited by Brent A. Strawn and Nancy R. Bowen, 283–97. Winona Lake, IN: Eisenbrauns, 2003. Used by permission.

Chapter 3: "The Defining Utterance on the Lips of the Tishbite: Pondering 'The Centrality of the Word'" first appeared in *In Essentials Unity: Reflections on the Nature and Purpose of the Church: In Honor of Frederick R. Trost,* edited by M. Douglas Meeks and Robert D. Mutton, 141–50. Minneapolis: Kirk House, 2001. Used by permission.

Chapter 4: "Texts that Linger, Not Yet Overcome" first appeared in *Shall Not the Judge of All the Earth Do What Is Right? Studies on the Nature of God in Tribute to James L. Crenshaw,* edited by David Penchansky and Paul L. Redditt, 21–41. Winona Lake, IN: Eisenbrauns, 2000. Used by permission.

Chapter 5: "A 'Characteristic' Reflection on What Comes Next (Jer 32:16–44)" first appeared in *Prophets and Paradigms: Essays in Honor of Gene M. Tucker,* edited by Stephen Breck Reid, 15–32. Journal for the Study of the Old Testament Supplements 229. Sheffield: Sheffield Academic, 1996. Used by permission.

Chapter 6: "A Shattered Transcendence? Exile and Restoration" first appeared in *Biblical Theology: Problems and Perspectives, Essays in Honor of J. Christiaan Beker,* edited by Steven J. Kraftchick et al., 169–82. Nashville: Abingdon, 1995. Used by permission.

Chapter 7: "The Epistemological Crisis of Israel's Two Histories (Jer 9:22–23)" first appeared in *Israelite Wisdom: Theological and Literary Essays in Honor of Samuel Terrien*, edited by John G. Gammie et al., 85–105. Homage Series 3. Missoula, MT: Scholars, 1978. Used by permission.

Chapter 8: "'Exodus' in the Plural (Amos 9:7)" first appeared in *Many Voices, One God: Being Faithful in a Pluralistic World: In Honor of Shirley Guthrie*, edited by Walter Brueggemann and George W. Stroup, 15–34. Louisville: Westminster John Knox, 1998. Used by permission.

Chapter 9: "Theology of the Old Testament: A Prompt Retrospect" first appeared in *God in the Fray: A Tribute to Walter Brueggemann*, edited by Todd Linafelt and Timothy K. Beal, 307–20. Minneapolis: Fortress, 1998. Used by permission.

Abbreviations

AB	Anchor Bible
AnBib	Analecta Biblica
BASOR	*Bulletin of the American Schools of Oriental Research*
BDB	F. Brown, S. R. Driver, and C. A. Briggs, *A Hebrew and English Lexicon of the Old Testament*
BHT	Beiträge zur historischen Theologie
Bib	*Biblica*
BTB	*Biblical Theology Bulletin*
BWANT	Beiträge zur Wissenschaft vom Alten und Neuen Testament
BZAW	Beihefte zur Zeitschrift für die alttestamentliche Wissenschaft
CBQ	*Catholic Biblical Quarterly*
ET	English translation
EvTh	*Evangelische Theologie*
FCBS	Fortress Classics in Biblical Studies
HBT	*Horizons in Biblical Theology*
HSM	Harvard Semitic Monographs
HUCA	*Hebrew Union College Annual*
Int	*Interpretation*
IRT	Issues in Religion and Theology
ISBL	Indiana Studies in Biblical Literature
JAAR	*Journal of the American Academy of Religion*

JBL	*Journal of Biblical Literature*
JNES	*Journal of Near Eastern Studies*
JSOT	*Journal for Study of the Old Testament*
JSOTSup	Journal for the Study of the Old Testament Supplement Series
JTS	*Journal of Theological Studies*
LAI	Library of Ancient Israel
LXX	Septuagint
NRSV	New Revised Standard Version
OBT	Overtures to Biblical Theology
OTL	Old Testament Library
SBLDS	Society of Biblical Literature Dissertation Series
SBLMS	Society of Biblical Literature Monograph Series
SBT	Studies in Biblical Theology
ThBü	Theologische Bücherei
ThTo	*Theology Today*
TLZ	*Theologische Literaturzeitung*
USQR	*Union Seminary Quarterly Review*
VT	*Vetus Testamentum*
VTSup	Vetus Tesamentum Supplements
WMANT	Wissenschaftliche Monographien zum Alten und Neuen Testament
ZAW	*Zeitschrift für die alttestamentliche Wissenschaft*
ZTK	*Zeitschrift für Theologie und Kirche*

Foreword

THE ESSAYS IN THIS VOLUME comprise the first of three volumes of Walter Brueggemann's contributions to *Festschriften*. These hidden gems are an important component to his oeuvre because they allow the reader to see him take on very brief passages (chapters 7 and 8), longer passages (chapters 3 and 5), biblical themes (chapters 2, 4, 6), as well as methodological issues (see chapters 1 and 9)—all at the highest level.

What continually intrigues me in reading Brueggemann's books, articles, and essays are not only his detailed analyses and clarity of writing, but also his broad interests and his ability to cut through all the distractions to the meat of the matter. My experience of reading Brueggemann is that I am always getting a fresh take—an angle of vision that challenges, broadens, and provokes me. One will find a excellent entry-point into his approach to exegesis in his *A Pathway of Interpretation*.[1] Furthermore, I recommend Davis Hankins's essay that provides a provocative analysis of Brueggemann's work in relation to contemporary philosophers and theorists.[2]

As one reads these essays one is acutely aware that all of these essays are interconnected with Brueggemann's Old Testament theology both leading up to it and flowing out it.[3] Perhaps my biggest professional disappointment is that I began as biblical studies editor at Fortress Press a few months too late to edit that volume.

1. Brueggemann, *A Pathway of Interpretation: The Old Testament for Pastors and Students* (Eugene, OR: Cascade Books, 2008).

2. Hankins, "Introduction," in Brueggemann, *Ice Axes for Frozen Seas: A Biblical Theology of Provocation*, edited by Davis Hankins (Waco: Baylor University Press, 2014), 1–18.

3. Brueggemann, *Theology of the Old Testament: Testimony, Dispute, Advocacy* (Minnesota: Fortress, 1997).

Preface

THERE ARE AS MANY ways of doing theological interpretation of the Old Testament as there are people who take up the task. Only a few years ago one could not have anticipated the present ferment and energy in Old Testament theological interpretation, because we had arrived at something of a stalemate between the major German models of the twentieth century that dominated the field. In the wake of that stalemate, however, came a variety of fresh initiatives that have evoked new interpretive possibilities. Among the new initiatives have been the fresh importance of social-scientific methods, the emergence of new voices from beyond the old guild of white males, a turn from the critical to the canonical, and a new engagement between Jewish and Gentile readers.

These essays reflect over time my effort to make a contribution to the ongoing conversation. Because these articles have been generated ad hoc over time, it will not surprise that there is some repetition of the accents of my work. Each of these essays was a contribution to a *Festschrift* volume. For readers who may not know the term *Festschrift*, it is a combination of two German words, *Fest* meaning "festive celebration" and *Schrift*, "writing." Thus such a volume is a celebrative writing, characteristically offered as a tribute to a senior scholar on his/her sixtieth, sixty-fifth, or seventieth birthday as a salute from other colleagues in the field. One does not initiate a contribution to such a volume, but is on occasion invited to participate. I have been fortunate to be invited to make such contributions, the substance of which is evident here. I have been glad to have been invited to join in honoring such senior, major scholars, each of whom has made a formative contribution to our common work and has been a generative influence on my own work. The warrant for reprinting such articles is that a volume that is a *Festschrift* is usually quite expensive and so has only limited circulation. Consequently such articles are often unnoticed or "buried" in such a volume. In each case I have tried to offer a contribution that is congruent with the major interests of the honoree of the volume. It is a distinct honor to travel in the train of such distinguished scholars who have shaped our discipline and my own work in the discipline. Such an assignment provides occasion to make a programmatic statement; or more often it is an opportunity to focus on a more narrow subject and to give it more leisurely attention. It is also an opportunity to reflect on one's academic rootage and the great debts owed to predecessors.

It is impossible for me to overstate the heavy lifting that K. C. Hanson at Cascade Books has done on this collection of essays (as with other of my publications) to make it useful and coherent. I am grateful to him and his colleagues at Wipf and Stock for their continuing attentiveness to my work.

Walter Brueggemann
Columbia Theological Seminary
November 17, 2014

1

The Role of Old Testament Theology in Old Testament Interpretation

Four Interpretive Phases

IN A SUMMARY WAY, it is possible to distinguish in scholarship four rather distinctive phases of critical study, each of which hosted theological interpretation in a way peculiar to its horizon.

The Reformation Period

IT WAS IN THE Reformation that "biblical theology" became a distinct enterprise, as theological interpretation was undertaken apart from the sacramental system of the church, and to some extent outside the conventional categories of the dogmatic tradition.[1] In that context, "biblical theology" had as its role the attempt to voice the fresh, free, live word of gospel, completely uncontained and unfettered by any hegemonic categories of established church tradition. Different traditions in the Reformation, of course, gave different accents to this newly "evangelical"

---

1. It was Luther's intention to interpret the Bible and its Gospel apart from the interpretive controls of the church. Thus "biblical theology" became an enterprise distinct from church theology. It is instructive that Kraus, *Geschichte der historisch-kritischen Erforschung des Alten Testaments*, 6–24, begins his study of biblical criticism with the rubric *sola scriptura*.

interpretation, best known in Lutheran *grace* and Calvinistic *sovereignty*. In all these cases, however, the effort was made to deal directly with "the things of God" in the text, without mediating forms and structures that worked toward domestication and containment. Thus "biblical theology" had a distinctly "evangelical" impetus.

Enlightenment Historicism

WHILE THE FORMS AND cadences of Reformation "biblical theology" persisted into the seventeenth century, the notion of unfettered witness to the things of God was exceedingly difficult to maintain. In both Lutheran and Calvinist circles (not to speak at all of Trent), the great claims of unfettered gospel were eventually reduced to new scholastic formulation, surely as domesticated as the scholastic formulations against which the primal Reformers had worked.[2]

In that context, the move from *dogmatic* to *historical* questions was an attempt to emancipate biblical interpretation from the deep domestication of Scripture. It is exceedingly important to recall that the emergence and appropriation of "the historical" was an effort to maintain the free availability of scriptural claims against the new theological scholasticism. It is common to cite the lecture of Johann Philip Gabler in 1787 as the decisive articulation of this new approach, whereby Gabler insisted that Old Testament study was primally an historical and not dogmatic enterprise.[3] As Ben Ollenburger has shown, however, Gabler's intention is more subtle than the simple categories of dogmatic–historical may indicate.[4]

Focus upon "the historical" brought with it the subsequently developed notion of "God acts in history." But the primary energy released by this new category was devoted to historical criticism and the effort to situate every text according to its date and recoverable context. This movement culminated in Wellhausen's great synthesis that is aptly titled *Prolegomena to the History of Israel*.[5] That is, the documentary hypothesis,

---

2. See Reventlow, *The Authority of the Bible and the Rise of the Modern World*.

3. Gabler's decisive lecture is available in its pertinent parts in English by Sandys-Wunsch and Eldredge, "J. P. Gabler and the Distinction between Biblical and Dogmatic Theology."

4. Ollenburger, "Biblical Theology." See also Knierim, "On Gabler."

5. Wellhausen, *Prolegomena to the History of Israel*.

for which Wellhausen is widely credited and blamed, is a preparation for doing *history*.

Historical criticism, perhaps inevitably, focused upon the history of Israelite religion, thus situating each religious practice and implied theological claim in a specific context, understanding each practice and claim as context specific. The outcome was to relativize every practice and claim, to permit a developmental scheme by which every practice and claim was eventually displaced (superseded!) by another. As a consequence, every practice and claim is pertinent only to its immediate historical context. In that enterprise that stretches, as we conveniently put it, from Gabler to Wellhausen, the study of the history of Israelite religion almost completely displaced Old Testament theology, and the latter continued only in a subdued way as a rearguard action to maintain the "constancies" of "orthodoxy." It is of particular interest that whereas "biblical theology" in the Reformation period was emancipatory, in the period of high Enlightenment it was, where it was undertaken at all, not so much emancipatory as conserving and consolidating, an attempt to resist the vigorous enterprise of relativizing historicism. Such an approach to the text was distinctly against "the spirit of the times."

The Barthian Alternative

The dominance of a history-of-religion approach, with its relativizing consequences, inevitably evoked a response. But no one could have imagined that the response would be as forceful, bold, and demanding as that offered by Karl Barth in his *Römerbrief* in 1919.[6] Barth's effort was to interpret the text in a boldly and unembarrassedly theological, normative way, without yielding anything to historical relativism and without reducing faithful practice and theological claim to contextual explanation.

It is difficult to overstate the decisive contribution of Barth in turning the interpretive enterprise and in freshly legitimating theological interpretation that dared to treat theological claim in the text as constant and normative. Barth enlivened and legitimated nearly a century of theological interpretation, including the most important work in Old Testament theology; but of course from the perspective of scholars who, for personal or intellectual reasons, fear and resist such claims of the "normative," Barth is to be regarded as an unfortunate digression in the discipline.

6. It was presented in English translation as *The Epistle to the Romans* (1933).

While Barth's theological eruption already in 1919 is taken as a de-cisive break in Enlightenment historicism, it is not possible to appreciate the impact of Barth apart from the later context of his work, with par-ticular reference to the challenge of National Socialism in Germany and the articulation of the Barmen Declaration in 1934. The mood and tenor of the work is profoundly *confessional*, an assertion of *normative* truth that had practical consequences and that implied personal and concrete risk. That mood and tenor of confession did not bother to make itself persuasive to "cultural despisers," who, by historical criticism, managed to tone down "evangelical claims" for God, to make matters compat-ible with Enlightenment reason. The daring claims made in a Barthian posture stand in deep contrast with the consolidating, even reactionary function of biblical theology in the earlier period of historicism. Barth's dominance is a primal example of the ways in which context presents questions and challenges that push biblical theology in one direction rather than another. It is unmistakable that the crisis of the twentieth century both required and permitted biblical theology in ways neither permitted nor required in the earlier period of high historicism.

The legacy of Barth may be said to have dominated the field of biblical theology until about 1970. In the center of that period is the magisterial work of Walther Eichrodt who took *covenant* as his mode of normativeness, and the even more influential work of Gerhard von Rad, whose definitive essay of 1938 surely echoes the credo-orientation of Barmen.[7] While the normativeness and constancy of Barth's perspective can take different forms, both Eichrodt and von Rad sought to provide a place of normativeness in which to stand in the face of the huge barba-risms of the twentieth century, for it was clear that the domestications of historical criticism provided no standing ground at all. More than Eich-rodt, von Rad continued to attend to and be puzzled by the unmistakable dynamic of historical change reflected in the faith of Israel, but he finally does not yield to it. In the United States, moreover, the odd juxtaposi-tion of normative theological claim and historical vagary was handled

---

7. The pivotal essay for von Rad, surely reflecting the confessional crisis of Barmen, is "The Form-Critical Problem of the Hexateuch." The belated English translations of the more comprehensive works are Eichrodt, *Theology of the Old Testament* (2 vols.); von Rad, *Old Testament Theology* (2 vols.). See Brueggemann, "Introduction," as an overview and critique of von Rad's contribution.

with remarkable finesse and, for the moment, in a compelling way by G. Ernest Wright in his influential *God Who Acts*.[8]

It is to be noticed that while this essentially Barthian enterprise of "the Short Century" might provide credible ground for faith midst the brutalities of history, it is also the case that the interpretive movement out of Barth was vigorously hegemonic, providing in various ways a summary account of the faith of ancient Israel that was exclusionary in its claims and allowing little room for alternative reading.[9] While such an assertiveness can well be understood in the context of brutality whereby interpretation was an emergency activity, it is also important to recognize that such a hegemonic posture evokes an inescapable response at the end of its domination, a response of considerable force and authority.

The Coming of Post-Modernity

It is now common to cite 1970 as the break point of what came to be called (pejoratively) "the Biblical Theology Movement," that interpretive enterprise propelled by Barth and especially voiced by von Rad and Wright. The "ending" of that monopolistic interpretive effort was occasioned by many factors. It is conventional to cite the work of Brevard Childs and James Barr as the decisive voices of the ending, even though it is clear that Barr and Childs come from very different directions and agree on almost nothing except their critique.[10] Also to be fully appreciated, from inside the movement itself, are the insistence of Frank Moore Cross (a colleague of Wright) that Israel is enmeshed in ancient Near Eastern culture and is not as distinctive as had been urged, and Claus Westermann's (a colleague

---

8. Wright, *God Who Acts*. See also Wright, *The Old Testament against Its Environment*.

9. On "the short century" see Hobsbawm, *The Age of Extremes*. The "short century" refers to the time from the outbreak of World War I to the fall of the Soviet Union. The nomenclature is pertinent for our topic that was dominated by a certain set of assumptions growing from Barth. The exclusion practiced by what became "the Biblical Theology Movement" is easy to spot in retrospect. On the positivism related to the enterprise, see now Long, *Planting and Reaping Albright*.

10. See especially Childs, *Biblical Theology in Crisis*; and Barr, "Revelation through History in the Old Testament and Modern Theology"; Barr, "The Old Testament and the New Crisis of Biblical Authority"; Barr, *The Bible in the Modern World*; and Barr, *Holy Scripture*. In addition, it is important to mention Gilkey, "Cosmology, Ontology, and the Travail of Biblical Language."

of von Rad) urging that the horizon of creation was as important as the "historical recital" for the faith of Israel.[11]

More broadly the rise of feminist and liberation hermeneutics and the failure of mono-interpretation have produced, since 1970, an interpretive context that is by many styled "postmodern," that is, after the hegemony that had dominated the twentieth century.[12] Coming to the more important features of this development of scholarship that has put the work of Old Testament theology in some disarray, we may notice three.

Pluralism. Von Rad has already taken seriously the pluralism of the theological claims of the Old Testament text. But now the awareness of pluralism is much deeper and more seriously noticed, so that the text seems to admit of no single, grand formulation. Indeed the text not only offers a plurality of God-claims, but when read closely, the several texts themselves are plurivocal, open to a variety of readings. The quality and character of the text, moreover, is matched increasingly by a plurality of readers, reflecting a diverse community of interests, so that no single synthetic reading is any longer possible.[13]

Ideology. It follows from a full-faced acknowledgment of pluralism, that one can readily see that every offer of normativeness is in some sense ideology. Most benignly this means it is an advocacy for a certain perspective and not a given. Thus, even the hegemonic approach held in common by Barth, Eichrodt, von Rad, and Wright is seen to be not a stable foundation, but rather an advocacy on offer to the larger interpretive community that must be received and adjudicated by interpreters who occupy other ideological perspectives.[14] Behind this collage of interpretive adjudications among advocacies, we are able to see more clearly that the pluralism in the text itself concerns the things of God, a collage of competing advocacies

11. See Brueggemann, "The Loss and Recovery of Creation in Old Testament Theology," and the references there to Cross, Westermann, and Schmid.

12. I have no special concern for the label "postmodern," except that it is a convenient way to reference the quite new interpretive context in which we are now placed. See Brueggemann, *Texts Under Negotiation*. For a vigorous and important resistance to postmodernity, see Watson, *Text and Truth*.

13. For an insistence upon a unified reading that resists pluralism in faithful reading, see Watson, *Text and Truth*, and his earlier *Text, Church and World*.

14. It seems evident that long-standing theological hegemony turns out to be ideological advocacy, as does skepticism that assumes the ideological claims of Enlightenment rationality. None is immune from an ideological insistence, so that we must work midst our competing advocacies.

that made it into the text, advocacies that are not done (we may assume) in bad faith, but that are not easily or quietly compatible.

Speech as Constitutive. Emphasis upon the`` power of rhetoric, when considered in the context of pluralism and ideology, makes clear that speech about God is not simply reportage on "what happened" in history or "what is" in ontology, but the speech itself is powerfully constitutive of theological claim as it is of historical "past."[15] Thus the new, postmodern world of theological interpretation is powerfully focused on utterance, a concrete utterance offered in the text, and on *interpretive utterance* offered in contemporary conversation. Insofar as utterance is taken as mere utterance, it may indeed be shaped either by the dogmatic claims of the ecclesial community or by the requirements of Enlightenment reason. But it is also in the very character of utterance that it may be a novum, that can be recognized in some quarters as a claim of truth beyond the fetters of church or academy.[16] Thus it is the *appropriation and reception of utterance* and *the critique of utterance* that I take to be the work of Old Testament theology. In our present context, this reception, appreciation, and critique of utterance takes place in the loud and dissonant presence of many voices. But this accent on utterance as the offer of new truth also has important continuities with the Reformation accent upon the word, and with the insistence of Barth, even though that reception, appreciation, and critique must now be done in a quite different form.

The Marks of Old Testament Theology

The location of Old Testament theology in a postmodern situation sets some severe limits on what is possible, but also yields some legitimate place for such demanding, important work. Both the severe limits and the legitimate place, however, are freshly situated in a new cultural, interpretive context in which old practices must indeed be relinquished. Indeed, the case is readily made that from our present vantage point (that also must not be absolutized, as has been a recurring temptation for every vantage point), Old Testament theology has been much too often imperialistically

15. On the constitutive power of public speech, see Brueggemann, *Israel's Praise*, 1–28. A more rigorous discussion of mine would appeal to the work of Foucault.

16. Steiner, "A Preface to the Hebrew Bible," luminously makes the case for the ways in which the discourse of the Bible is originary. See also Kort, *"Take, Read."*

Christian, coercively moralistic, and vigorously anti-Semitic.[17] These critiques of past work must be taken seriously and count much more, in my judgment, than the easier contention that theological interpretation does not honor Enlightenment rationality and is therefore fideistic.

Old Testament theology in such a context, I propose, may have the following marks.[18]

1. *"Theo-logy"* is "speech about God." That is, it does not concern, in any primary sense, all that might be said of Israel's religion, but it is an attempt to pay attention to the God who emerges in the utterance of these texts, a God marked by some constancy, but a God given in a peculiar, even scandalous characterization. What ever else may be said of this God, it is clear that the God of the Old Testament conforms neither to conventional monotheism nor to flat dogmatic categories, nor to usual philosophical Enlightenment assumptions of the West, though it is equally clear that a monotheizing tendency is at work.[19]

2. *Speech about God* is given by human persons, reflected in human institutions, in human contexts, serving human, political agendas. This is no new insight and no threat to the enterprise. All the efforts to minimize "the historical," moreover, cannot eliminate the fact that human persons have made these utterances. Thus the God of Israel is given us *on the lips of Israel*, constituted through utterance, utterance no doubt deeply driven and informed by lived experience but in the end shaped by artistic, imaginative utterance.

3. Such speech about God is not idle chatter but is characteristically *intentional speech* and is so treated in the canonizing process. More specifically, we may say that *intentional human speech about God is testimony*, an attempt to give a particular account of reality with this God as agent and as character at its center.[20] And while we may notice the great pluralism in the text in God-utterances, we may also, perhaps more importantly, observe a family kinship of all these utterances when set over against alternative accounts of reality, ancient or modern. While close theological reading will attend to the differences in utterance, Old Testa-

---

17. See Levenson, "Why Jews Are not Interested in Biblical Theology."

18. For what follows, my more extended treatment is given in Brueggemann, *Theology of the Old Testament*.

19. See Sanders, "Adaptable for Life."; and most recently Sanders, *The Monotheizing Process*.

20. On "testimony" as the decisive genre for biblical theology, see Brueggemann, *Theology of the Old Testament*, 117–44.

ment theology in the end has a propensity toward that shared kinship, to see what is recurring midst the vagaries of testimony.

4. Old Testament theology treats of the text of canon and so takes human testimony as *revelation*.[21] One need not so take it, and many scholars preoccupied with "historical questions" would not make that move, even though what is claimed to be "history" turns out almost every time to be advocacy. Be that as it may, Old Testament theology, in its attention to what is recurring and constant in Israel's God-utterance, takes that God-utterance to be disclosing. I understand, of course, that the history of Christian revelation, with its deposit of dogmatic truth, has been profoundly coercive; here I use "revelatory" and "disclosing" to mean that the God-utterance of Israel seeks to *un-close* lived reality that without the generative force of Yahweh as character and agent is characteristically *closed* in ways of denial, despair, and/or oppression.

5. To take Israel's God-speech as revelatory means that it is utterance that seeks to speak about a *mystery* that attends to and indwells the world in which Israel lives. That mystery, according to Israel's utterance, is on the loose, wild and dangerous, often crude, inaccessible, unattractive, capable of violence, equally capable of positive transformation.[22] In its God-speech Israel does not set out everywhere to give us an attractive or appealing God, the stable God of church catechism or the winsome God of therapeutic culture. But it does seek to give an account of an agency of otherness who operates with intentional purpose and who refuses to be captive either to slogans of self-sufficiency or in the terminology of despair.[23] Israel's God-speech seeks to give an account of restless holiness that decisively redefines and resituates everything else about life.

6. Israel's God-speech, moreover, in a rich variety of ways, offers that this Other is *provisionally identifiable*. "God" in the Old Testament is

21. It is especially Brevard Childs who has insisted that when the text is studied as "Scripture," as the holy book of the ecclesial community, the shape and claims of canon are decisive for interpretation. Childs has rightly linked "Scripture" to theological intentionality of a quite specific kind. But whereas Childs's notion of Scripture tends to be stable and consolidating, Kort, *"Take, Read,"* offers a much more radical, lively, and serious notion of the reading of Scripture.

22. On the defining dimensions of violence in the text that is assigned to God, see Blumenthal, *Facing the Abusing God*; and Schwartz, *The Curse of Cain*.

23. It was, of course, Barth who focused on the "Wholly Other." The notion of alterity has been more fully and helpfully developed in Jewish interpretation, stemming from Martin Buber and given classic formulation by Lévinas, *Totality and Infinity: An Essay on Exteriority*. See also Steiner, *Real Presences*.

identifiable, known by characteristic actions that are recognizable from one context to another, known by direct utterance treasured and passed on, known by moves that can be placed in the text and on the lips of the witnesses. Because that Other is genuinely *other*, however, Israel itself knows that all such identification is provisional and not final or certain.[24] And so there are "many names," many metaphors and images, many songs, poems, and narratives, all of which attest differently.[25] There are crises of naming when the name is displaced (Exod 3:14; 6:2), and there is a withholding of the name (Gen 32:29).[26] In the end, moreover, there is the inscrutability of the Tetragrammaton (YHWH), Israel's final resistance to idolatry and Israel's defiant notice to check both church theologians who know too much about this Other and academic theologians who work apart from this Other.

7. In a postmodern context, it is important to accept that these voices of God-talk are all advocates in the debate about how to voice provisional identity of the undoubted, unaccommodating Other. Thus "J," Second Isaiah, Job, and Ezra each advocate differently. At the most they advocate but they do not finally know. They are witnesses and neither judge nor jury.[27] They propose and offer, but do not finally comprehend. Insofar as all these witnesses agree (which is not very far), their shared utterance is also advocacy and not certitude. In our postmodern context, it can hardly be more than advocacy.

I am, however, quick to insist that there are many scholars who discount the God-speech of Israel in the name of "disinterested" scholarship, who refuse theological questions on the ground of "history," who are themselves advocates and not more than advocates.[28] We have arrived at the odd situation in which the *resisters* to the God-utterances of Israel posture themselves as more certain than the *practitioners* of Old Testament theol-

---

24. On the problematic of God's name, see the representative, rather conventional discussion in Braaten, ed., *Our Naming of God*. Kort, *"Take, Read,"* 133–38, has important suggestions about the scriptural deconstruction of patriarchy that dominates Scripture.

25. See Wren, *What Language Shall I Borrow?*, especially ch. 6.

26. As is often remarked, it is important that the name of YHWH is withheld in the long poetic exchange of the book of Job until chapter 38. Such a withholding is surely intentional and strategic for the book.

27. On the witness and counter-witness, see Brueggemann, "Life-Or-Death."

28. Skepticism is not particularly high ground in intellectual activity. It simply advocates Enlightenment rationality, an increasingly doubtful stance for interpretation. See, e.g., the odd use of the term "disinterested" by Davies, *Whose Bible Is It Anyway?*, 1.

ogy dare to be; but in fact the resisters also are only advocates of Enlightenment rationality, bespeaking old and long wounds from ancient theological coerciveness, preferring a self-contained, self-explanatory world to one of hurt-producing theological authoritarianism. A postmodern Old Testament theology, so it seems to me, dare not be coercive and need not be coercive. For in our present context, Old Testament theology is proposal and not conclusion, offer and not certainty. Interpretation stands always in front of our deciding and not after. For the *otherness* of reality given us on the lips of Israel makes our deciding always penultimate and provisional, always yet again unsettled by new disclosings.

Attending to the Testimony

Given the history of the discipline, and given a postmodern situation with no agreed-upon "meta-narrative,"[29] we may now consider the role of Old Testament theology in the discipline, a role that must respect both the critical foundations of the discipline and the postmodern options that at the same time limit and permit.

I purpose that the primal role of Old Testament theology is to attend to the testimony out of which lived reality was then and may now be reimagined with reference to a Holy Character who is given us on the lips of Israel, who exhibits some constancy, but whose constancy is regularly marked by disjunction and tension.[30] The act of imagining alternatively is what these witnesses are doing in the text-world itself, and the ongoing option of imagining alternatively is kept alive by continual attentiveness to this testimony.[31] That Holy Character on the lips of the

29. On this characterization of postmodenity, see Lyotard, *The Postmodern Condition*.

30. On such a characterization of God, see Patrick, *The Rendering of God in the Old Testament*.

31. To *imagine alternatively* seems to me a fair notion of what biblical theology is about. Brevard Childs is frequently worried that my emphasis on imagination is to assign too much to human initiative. It is surely the case, however, that any fruitful, faithful interpretation is indeed an act of imagination. See van Wijk-Bos, *Reimagining God*; Davis, *Imagination Shaped*; and Green, *Imagining God*. And even such a conservative perspective as that of Watson, *Text and Truth*, 325, yields the verdict: "At the very least, the interpretative tradition that is here in process of formation is an expression of a *creative theological imgination* that has learned to see the scriptural texts in the light of Christ, and Christ in the light of the scriptural texts" (my emphasis). One must of course make differentiations, but to resist imagination in principle is impossible.

witnesses through whom lived reality is construed differently is often given as a characteristic assurance; but on many other occasions this same Character is rather a deconstructive force who moves against every settlement, every certitude and every assurance. Or, as Jürgen Moltmann has said of more belated, Christian claims for faith, the God given on the lips of witnesses is both "foundation" and "criticism," both *the power for life* who is profoundly generative and authorizing, as well as summoning and dispatching, but who is also *a critical principle* who stands as a check upon what these witnesses may say against this Charcter.[32] Or more summarily, this testimony to God is a claim that at the core of lived reality there is a mystery invested with transformative energy and with durable purposiveness. The witnessing community endlessly relearns, however, that embrace of that transformative energy and durable purposiveness does nothing to minimize the inscrutable Otherness of the Character who inhabits such mystery.

The role of Old Testament theology as attendance upon the testimony concerning this Character varies as we consider the various "publics" addressed by such study. We may be guided by David Tracy's identification of three publics that concern us—the academic, the ecclesial, and the civic.[33] Of any work in Old Testament studies, it may be especially Old Testament theology that reaches beyond the limits of the discipline of Old Testament study itself to address those other publics.

Old Testament Theology within the Academic Community[34]

There is no doubt that Old Testament theology is related to and much informed by many different kinds of critical study, literary and historical.[35] It no longer pertains, moreover, that these several modes of critical study are conducted in the service of theology, as might have been the case when theology could claim to be the "queen of the sciences." In a

32. The subtitle of Moltmann, *The Crucified God* is *The Cross of Christ as the Foundation and Criticism of Christian Theology*.

33. Tracy, *The Analogical Imagination*, 3–46.

34. I am aware that by "The Public of the Academy" Tracy refers to the entire university community. Here, because of my particular topic, I refer more explicitly to the guild of Old Testament studies.

35. I take "historical" here broadly to include more recent developments of "social-scientific" methods.

postmodern setting, it is clear that very much critical study is taken as an end in itself, without any reference to theological issues, or in some quarters critical study is undertaken precisely to defeat theological interpretation and eliminate the questions it purports to address.

Old Testament theology, in the present context of scholarship, has no leverage or need to be taken seriously by the guild of scholarship, and has no mandate to insist upon its own claims. Nonetheless, those of us in the field who take up the work of theological interpretation sense that critical study that is singularly preoccupied with historical or literary questions, or that proceeds according to positivistic rationality that in principle nullifies Israel's testimony to God, has in fact failed to pay attention to the text or to the claims that are expressed and that invite the hearer's engagement. In the end, it seems clear that the Old Testament text is not preoccupied with historical questions nor even with literary finesse-though both historical and literary issues are fully present—but with the strange, sometimes violent, sometimes hidden, often unwelcome ways of this Holy Agent in the midst of life.

Very much historical and literary study, taken in and of itself, while perfectly legitimate, is conducted in a way that is "tone deaf" to the voice of the text. Thus Old Testament theology, if conducted in a way that is not reductive or coercive, may be an invitation that could keep the academic discipline from being turned in upon itself, preoccupied with greater and greater intensity on issues that matter less and less. In the end, so it seems to me, the history of ancient Israel that can be recovered by positivistic categories does not seem to go anywhere that would interest the witnesses themselves, for when the Holy Character is deleted from the calculus of meaning, not much that matters remains.[36] In the same way, attentiveness to literary and rhetorical elements of the text seems to indicate the artistry of the sort of folk who are always pointing beyond the artistry itself to the true Subject of the artistry who defies critical decoding. It seems to me inevitable that the core claim of Old Testament theology, witness to the Character, will continue to live in discomfort with a kind of positivistic criticism that resists its very subject. Nonetheless, its work is

---

36. On the limits and inadequacy of positivistic history for our purposes, see Yerushalmi, *Zakhor*. Said another way, what concerns Old Testament theology must to some extent be concerned with an "emic" approach to the text in distinction from a more conventional "etic" approach. On the distinction, see briefly Gottwald, *The Tribes of Yahweh*.

to keep before the more general discipline the central Character without whom much of the rest of our study ends up being trivial.

Old Testament Theology in the Context of Ecclesial Communities[37]

Because Old Testament theology is here defined as speech about God, it is inevitable that reference will be made to those communities that intentionally engage in and attend to serious speech about God. There is, I take it, an unresolvable tension between academic study and ecclesial study, if the former is defined in positivistic categories. But to define academic study in positivistic categories is itself an advocacy of special pleading and is not a necessary assumption. How the interplay of academic and ecclesial references is adjudicated seems largely to depend upon the interpreter, but to begin with an assumption of total separation is a premise that in my judgment is not readily persuasive.[38]

But the more important ecclesial question concerns the tension and interplay between faith communities, Jewish and Christian, both of which look to these texts as Scripture.[39] It is now completely clear, especially through the work of Jon Levenson, that Old Testament theology historically has been an unashamedly Christian enterprise, or even more specifically, a Protestant enterprise. Such study, moreover, has been deeply marked by unthinking anti-Jewish interpretation, an outcome that is inescapable, I suggest, as long as work is done in isolation.

Moreover, Brevard Childs has made a powerful case that Jews and Christians read different Bibles, so that the theological interpretation among Christians and among Jews is different from the ground up.[40] This

---

37. By speaking of such communities in the plural, I refer to both synagogue and church. It is evident that my way of speaking concerns the church; but, mutatis mufflndis, the same issues pertain to the synagogue.

38. This large and important point is well urged by Marsden, *The Soul of the American University*.

39. The interplay of Jews and Christians concerning Scripture is as important as it is vexed. The problematic is already reflected in the different nomenclature for the texts, names that bespeak important issues. See Brooks and Collins, eds., *Hebrew Bible or Old Testament?*

40. Childs, *Biblical Theology of the Old and New Testaments*. Clearly Watson, *Text and Truth*, agrees with Childs on this point. See Watson, *Text and Truth*, 209–19, for a reflection on the work of Childs.

same view is reiterated from the Jewish side by Jon Levenson.[41] While the argument has much to commend it, it is not one by which I am persuaded. It is my judgment, rather, that theological interpretation of these Scriptures can be and is better done by Jews and Christians together, who may part company in their reading only late, if at all. The ground for common reading is partly moral and historical, that Christian supersessionism and its consequent brutality require an alternative approach.[42] Beyond that and more important, however, is the generative, evocative character of the text and the Character dominant within it. It is evident that the Old Testament imagines toward the New, but it manifestly does not imagine exclusively toward the New. It is evident that Hebrew Scripture imagines toward the Talmud, but it does not imagine exclusively toward the Talmud.[43]

Rather the Old Testament/Hebrew Scriptures imagine vigorously, in pronouncedly polyvalent ways, an offer addressed to and received by both Jewish and Christian faith communities as authoritative for a life faith. But because the imaginative thrust of the text is richly generative beyond every interpretive domestication, it will not do for a subsequent faith community to construe itself as the exclusive receiver of that generativity. Thus it seems to me that it is not a mistake to see this text toward the New Testament, but it is a deep, substantive mistake to see this text *exclusively* toward the New Testament (and mistaken in a similar way to see it only toward the synagogue).[44]

The truth is that the ecclesial communities are summoned precisely to host this Character marked, on the lips of the witnesses, by inscrutable mystery, assertive will and energy, and inviolable purpose. And while that mystery, will, energy, and purpose may be provisionally linked to the Jewish community (in the claims of election and covenant) or to the Christian community (in the claims of Christology), the linkages are ideed provisional and contingent. As Old Testament theology may have

41. Levenson, *The Hebrew Bible*, 80–81 and passim. He concludes: "There is no non-particularistic access to these larger contexts" (80).

42. See Soulen, *The God of Israel and Christian Theology*.

43. Holmgren, *The Old Testament and the Significance of Jesus*, has shown how the communities of Judaism, Christianity, and Qumran all engaged in the same "creative/ depth" interpretation of scriptural texts.

44. Clearly to move from the nonnative text to any of the emergent texts requires an immense act of imagination, surely imagination that is informed by the canonical community. On this kind of freedom and discipline in interpretation, see Campbell, *Preaching Jesus*.

as its work to summon academic scholarship away from trivialization and preoccupation with marginal matters, so Old Testament theology may summon ecclesial communities from certitudes that are excessive and exclusions that are idolatrous, by witnessing to the elusive but insistent reality of this Holy Character.

Old Testament Theology in Public Discourse

If Old Testament theology is *a practice of reimagining lived reality with reference to this odd core Character*, then Old Testament theology, in its furthest stretch, may speak past academic and ecclesial communities to be concerned for public discourse.

I do not imagine that Old Testament theology can contribute specifically and concretely to questions of public policy and public morality, as interfaces between old text and public issues are exceedingly complicated. But if the emerging dominant construal of reality in the global economy is the unfettered pursuit of private power by the manipulation of the "money government," then Old Testament theology as a witness to this Holy Character can indeed provide materials for an alternative imagination.[45] It seems evident that the more recent construal of the world in terms of privatized global economy is not one that will enhance our common life. Such a construal of the world, so it appears, ends either in self-sufficiency or in despair. In either case it offers a huge potential for brutality, either to fend off in active ways those who impinge and threaten, or simply by neglect to allow the disappearance of the non-competitive.

It may be that from some other source can come an alternative to this dominant construal of reality, perhaps from what Robert Bellah terms the "republican" tradition.[46] It can hardly be doubted that some alternative construal of social reality is urgent among us. And if we work from the ground up, it is entirely plausible that *lived reality reimagined out from this Character who lives on the lips of these witnesses* could offer such a wholesale and compelling alternative.

---

45. The phrase "money government" is from Reich, *Opposing the System*. See also Daly and Cobb, *For the Common Good*; Greider, *One World*; and Kuttner, *Everything for Sale*.

46. Bellah et al., *Habits of the Heart*.

Naïve Realism

There is no doubt that Old Testament theology, in converstaion with any of these three publics, proceeds with something of a "naïve realism," prepared to take the utterance of the witnessing text as a serious offer.[47] Such "naïveté" may be only provisional and instrumental, as the interpreter withholds a serious personal commitment, or that "naïve realism" may reflect (as in my case) the primal inclination of the practitioner. Either way, so it seems to me, the practitioner of Old Testament theology must move between a credulous fideism and a knowing, suspicious skepticism, wherein the former does not pay sufficient attention to *the problematic* of the witness, and the latter is *tone deaf* to the core claim of the witnesses.

At the moment and perhaps for the foreseeable future, Old Testament theology must work its way between two determined challenges. On the one hand are those whom I would term "children of innocence," who are excessively credulous but who do not remain long with the elusive quality of the text, but immediately push the testimony along to the more reified claims of the ecclesial community—for example, in Christian parlance, to reduce the testimony to doctrinal categories. It appears to me that such innocence is so much powered by *anxiety* that old truths are in jeopardy and the world does not hold. The reduction of the testimony turns out to be a strategy for the recovery of a "lost coherence."

On the other hand, there are those whom I would term "children of coercion," who are exceedingly skeptical, but who do not linger long enough with the playful disjunctive quality of the Character, but immediately push the testimony to reified formulation that they then immediately are obligated to combat. It appears to me that such skepticism is rooted in *great rage*, not really rage at the text or even its claims, but rage rooted in old, hidden histories of coerciveness whose wounds remain endlessly painful.

Both such anxiety-rooted-in-innocence and such rage-rooted-in-coercion are serious, endlessly powerful postures that are not easily overcome. It seems equally clear, however, that neither *anxiety* over a world that is passing nor *rage* about a world that has injured is an adequate place from which to engage the Character who lives on the lips of the witnesses.

In a postmodern context where hegemonic claims of any sort are doubtful, Old Testament theology must play a modest role, not claim too much for itself, but stand in some interpretive continuity with ancient

47. It is, to be sure, a "second naïveté": see Wallace, *The Second Naiveté*.

witnesses who imagined and uttered with radical difference. While embracing an appropriate modesty, however, Old Testament theology must have its own say, voice its own offer that claims no privilege but is not to be confused with any other claim. It could be that, if done with authority but without any streak of arrogance, Old Testament theology could invite

- *the academic community* away from self-preoccupied triviality that is such a waste;

- *the ecclesial communities* away from excessive certitude that is idolatry; and

- *the civic community* away from brutality rooted in autonomy long enongh to engage this summoning mystery.

Anxiety and rage are real and legitimate. It remains to see if reading through them and past them is possible. The offer of these witnesses is sometimes as definite as "a God so near and a Torah so just" (Deut 4:7–8). Sometimes the witness is as open and inviting as a question, "Where shall wisdom be found?" (Job 28:12). Either way, the witnesses invite beyond anxiety and beyond rage to a mystery whose name we know provisionally.

Bibliography

Barr, James. *The Bible in the Modern World*. The Croall Lectures 1970. London: SCM, 1973.

———. *Holy Scripture: Canon, Authority, Criticism*. Philadelphia: Westminster, 1983

———. "The Old Testament and the New Crisis of Biblical Authority." *Int* 25 (1971) 24–40.

———. "Revelation through History in the Old Testament and Modern Theology." *Int* 17 (1963) 193–205.

Barth, Karl. *The Epistle to the Romans*. Translated by Edwyn C. Hoskyns. London: Oxford University Press, 1933.

Bellah, Robert N. et al. *Habits of the Heart: Individualism and Commitment in American Life*. Berkeley: University of California Press, 1985.

Blumenthal, David R. *Facing the Abusing God: A Theology of Protest*. Louisville: Westminster John Knox, 1993.

Braaten, Carl E., editor. *Our Naming of God: Problems and Prospects of God-Talk Today*. Minneapolis: Fortress, 1989.

Brooks, Roger, and John J. Collins, eds. *Hebrew Bible or Old Testament?: Studying the Bible in Judaism and Christianity*. Notre Dame: University of Notre Dame Press, 1990.

Brueggemann, Walter. "Introduction." In Gerhard von Rad, *Old Testament Theology*, ix–xxxi. OTL. Louisville: Westminster John Knox, 2001.

————. *Israel's Praise: Doxology agaist Idolatry and Ideology.* Philadelphia: Fortress, 1988.

————. "Life-Or-Death: De-Privileged Communication." *Journal for Preachers* 21.4 (1998) 22–29. Reprinted in Brueggemann, *Deep Memory Exuberant Hope: Contested Truth in a Post-Christian World*, edited by Patrick D. Miller, 19–27. Minneapolis: Fortress, 2000.

————. "The Loss and Recovery of Creation in Old Testament Theology." *ThTo* 53 (1996) 177–90.

————. *Texts Under Negotiation: The Bible and Postmodern Imagination.* Minneapolis: Fortress, 1993.

————. *Theology of the Old Testament: Testimony, Dispute, Advocacy.* Minneapolis: Fortress, 1997.

Campbell, Charles L. *Preaching Jesus: New Directions for Homiletics in Hans Frei's Postliberal Theology.* Grand Rapids: Eerdmans, 1997.

Childs, Brevard S. *Biblical Theology in Crisis.* Philadelphia: Westminster, 1970.

————. *Biblical Theology of the Old and New Testaments: Theological Reflection on the Christian Bible.* Minneapolis: Fortress, 1992.

Daly, Herman F., and John B. Cobb Jr. *For the Common Good: Redirecting the Economy toward Community, the Environment, and a Sustainable Future.* Boston: Beacon, 1994.

Davies, Philip R. *Whose Bible Is It Anyway?* JSOTSup 204. Sheffield, Sheffield Academic, 1995.

Davis, Ellen F. *Imagination Shaped: Old Testament Preaching in the Anglican Tradition.* Valley Forge, PA: Trinity, 1995.

Eichrodt, Walter. *Theology of the Old Testament.* 2 vols. Translated by J. A. Baker. OTL. Philadelphia: Westminster, 1961, 1967.

Gilkey, Langdon. "Cosmology, Ontology, and the Travail of Biblical Language." *Journal of Religion* 41 (1961) 194–205.

Gottwald, Norman K. *The Tribes of Yahweh: A Sociology of the Religion of Liberated Israel, 1250–1050 B.C.E.* Maryknoll, NY: Orbis, 1979.

Green, Garrett. *Imagining God: Theology and the Religious Imagination.* San Francisco: Harper & Row, 1989.

Greider, William. *One World, Ready or Not: The Manic Logic of Global Capitalism.* New York: Simon & Schuster, 1997.

Hobsbawm, Eric. *The Age of Extremes: A History of the World, 1914–1991.* New York: Pantheon, 1994.

Holmgren, Fredrick C. *The Old Testament and the Significance of Jesus: Embracing Change—Maintaining Christian Identity: The Emerging Center in Biblical Scholarship.* Grand Rapids: Eerdmans, 1999.

Knierim, Rolf. "On Gabler." In *The Task of Old Testament Theology: Substance, Method, and Cases*, 495–556. Grand Rapids: Eerdmans, 1995.

Kort, W. A. *"Take, Read": Scripture, Textuality, and Cultural Practice.* University Park: Pennsylvania State University Press, 1996.

Kraus, Hans-Joachim. *Geschichte der historisch-kritischen Erforschung des Alten Testaments.* 3rd ed. Neukirchen-Vluyn: Neukirchener, 1982.

Kuttner, Robert. *Everything for Sale: The Virtues and Limits of Markets.* New York: Knopf, 1997.

Levenson, Jon D. *The Hebrew Bible, the Old Testament, and Historical Criticism: Jews and Christians in Biblical Studies*. Louisville: Westminster John Knox, 1993.

———. "Why Jews Are not Interested in Biblical Theology." In *The Hebrew Bible, the Old Testament, and Historical Criticism: Jews and Christians in Biblical Studies*, 33–61. Louisville: Westminster John Knox, 1993.

Lévinas, Emmanuel. *Totality and Infinity: An Essay on Exteriority*. Translated by Alphonso Lingis. Duquesne Studies: Philosophical Series 24. Pittsburgh: Duquesne University Press, 1969.

Long, Burke O. *Planting and Reaping Albright: Politics, Ideology, and Interpreting the Bible*. University Park: Pennsylvania State University Press, 1997.

Lyotard, Jean-François. *The Postmodern Condition: A Report on Knowledge*. Translated by Geoff Bennington and Brian Massumi. Minneapolis: University of Minnesota Press, 1984.

Marsden, George M. *The Soul of the American University: From Protestant Establishment to Established Non-Belief*. Oxford: Oxford University Press, 1994.

Moltmann, Jürgen. *The Crucified God: The Cross of Christ as the Foundation and Criticism of Christian Theology*. Translated by R. A. Wilson and John Bowden. San Francisco: Harper & Row, 1974.

Ollenburger, Ben C. "Biblical Theology: Situating the Discipline." In *Understanding the Word: Essays in Honor of Bernhard W. Anderson*, edited by James T. Butler, Edgar W. Conrad, and Ben C. Ollenburger, 37–62. JSOTSup 37. Sheffield: JSOT Press, 1985.

Patrick, Dale. *The Rendering of God in the Old Testament*. OBT. Philadelphia: Fortress, 1981.

Rad, Gerhard von. "The Form-Critical Problem of the Hexateuch." In *The Problem of the Hexateuch and Other Essays*, 1–78. Translated by E. W. Trueman Dicken. New York: McGraw-Hill, 1966.

———. *Old Testament Theology*. 2 vols. Translated by D. M. G. Stalker. New York: Harper & Brothers, 1962, 1965.

Reich, Charles A. *Opposing the System*. New York: Crown, 1995.

Reventlow, H. Graf. *The Authority of the Bible and the Rise of the Modem World*. Translated by John Bowden. Philadelphia: Fortress, 1985.

Sanders, James A. "Adaptable for Life: The Nature and Function of Canon." In *Magnalia Dei: The Mighty Acts of God: Essays on the Bible and Archaeology in Memory of G. Ernest Wright*, edited by Frank Moore Cross et al., 531–60. Garden City, NY: Doubleday, 1976.

———. *The Monotheizing Process*. Eugene, OR: Cascade Books, 2014.

Sandys-Wunsch, John, and Laurence Eldredge. "J. P. Gabler and the Distinction between Biblical and Dogmatic Theology: Translation, Commentary and Discussion of His Originality." *Scottish Journal of Theology* 33 (1980) 133–58.

Schwartz, Regina M. *The Curse of Cain: the Violent Legacy of Monotheism*. Chicago: University of Chicago Press, 1997.

Soulen, R. Kendall. *The God of Israel and Christian Theology*. Minneapolis: Fortress, 1996.

Steiner, George. "A Preface to the Hebrew Bible." In *No Passion Spent: Essays 1978–1995*, 40–87. New Haven: Yale University Press, 1996.

———. *Real Presences*. Chicago: University of Chicago Press, 1989.

Tracy, David. *The Analogical Imgination: Christian Theology and the Culture Pluralism.* New York: Crossroad, 1981.

Van Wijk-Bos, Johanna W. H. *Reimagining God: The Case for Scriptural Diversity.* Louisville: Westminster John Knox, 1995.

Wallace, M. I. *The Second Naiveté: Barth, Ricoeur, and the New Yale Theology.* Studies in American Biblical Hermeneutics 6. Macon, GA: Mercer University Press, 1990.

Watson, Francis. *Text and Truth: Redefining Biblical Theology.* Grand Rapids: Eerdmans, 1997.

———. *Text, Church and World: Biblical Interpretation in Theological Perspective.* Grand Rapids: Eerdmans, 1994.

Wellhausen, Julius. *Prolegomena to the History of Israel.* Translated by J. Sutherland Black and Allan Menzies. Edinburgh: A. & C. Black, 1885.

Wren, Brian. *What Language Shall I Borrow? God-Talk in Worship: A Male Response to Feminist Theology.* New York: Crossroads, 1989.

Wright, G. Ernest. *God Who Acts: Biblical Theology as Recital.* SBT 1/8. London: SCM, 1952.

———. *The Old Testament against Its Environment.* SBT 1/2. London: SCM, 1950.

Yerushalmi, Yosef Hayim. *Zakhor: Jewish History and Jewish Memory.* The Samuel and Althea Stroum Lectures in Jewish Studies. Seattle: University of Washington Press, 1982.

2

The Travail of Pardon
Reflections on *slḥ*

Introduction

THE BOOK OF DEUTERONOMY offers the normative statement of covenantal theology in ancient Israel. In that covenantal theology, deriving
from Moses but situated a long time later, Israel is set in a Torah-relation
of command and obedience. That relationship of command and obedience, moreover, carries with it non-negotiable sanctions, so that the
rhetoric of "if . . . then" is definitional for this presentation of faith.

The rigorous requirements of Torah obedience are indeed doable
(Deut 30:11–14). However, in the life of Israel, the doable is in actuality not done, at least according to the Deuteronomistic History. Here,
the not-done Torah evokes the negative sanctions of curse, causing the
destruction of Jerusalem, the dislocation of many of the faithful, and the
eventual exilic situation of the sixth century. This sequence of negativi-
ties, in the purview of Deuteronomy, is fully explained and justified in
terms of covenant requirements, failures, and sanctions. Such a construal
of lived experience is clear enough and fully understandable.

And yet, given the air-tight logic of covenant, the most important question remains—namely, what next? The future of Israel with
its God depends upon reentry into the covenant. That reentry is to be
premised on "repentance" whereby Israel, now failed, re-engages the

commandments of covenant. That notion of repentance is clear enough and fits the uncompromising expectation of the Torah. But in this paper I want to push beyond the return of repentance, to see if initiative from God's side—forgiveness—is a working theme in the covenant theology of exilic Israel. I will consider specifically the term *slḥ* ("pardon") as a clue to the developing pastoral possibility for restoration in an alienated community that seems only partially able to undertake repentance. While the theme of "pardon" seems to move beyond the primary assumptions of the covenantal theology of Deuteronomy, I shall consider whether such a motif actually emerges from that covenant theology.

Yahweh—A God Who Pardons

It is notoriously difficult now to suggest an early dating for any text; we may begin, nonetheless, with the claim that Israel's oldest theological understanding of Yahweh includes a glad affirmation of a readiness and capacity to pardon. We may consider the creedal response to the violation of covenant in Exod 34:6–7 as a source for Israelite theology.[1] In that stylized assertion, Yahweh's capacity for pardon is explicit, even as it is crucial in context:

> Yahweh, Yahweh,
>> a God merciful and gracious,
> slow to anger,
>> and abounding in steadfast love and faithfulness,
> keeping steadfast love for the thousandth generation,
>> forgiving iniquity and transgression and sin.

That readiness to pardon is deeply qualified by the provision of v. 7b, suggesting that pardon is not a facile matter for this God who takes covenant requirements seriously:

> Yet by no means clearing the guilty,
>> but visiting the iniquity of the parents
> upon the children and the children's children,
>> to the third and the fourth generations.

---

1. On this text, see Brueggemann, *Theology of the Old Testament*, 215–28.

In the reuse and quotation of the text in Num 14:18, the same two-sided characterization of Yahweh is given.[2] In both cases, the confessional formulation of forgiveness is with the verb *nś'*. In both cases, Moses petitions Yahweh to "pardon" (*slḥ*) the iniquity of the people (Exod 34:9; Num 14:19). In Exod 34:10, Yahweh's response to the petition to pardon is to provide a covenant; in Num 14:20–23, Yahweh's response is a readiness to pardon, with deep and brutal qualification. "Pardon" is thus one of Yahweh's available responses, but it is not lightly or readily granted. Still, in these early texts, the capacity for pardon with the verb *slḥ* is nevertheless available in the character of Yahweh. It remains to see what is made of that available dimension of Yahweh in the trajectory of Deuteronomy.

The Problem of Pardon in Deuteronomy

In the book of Deuteronomy, the issue of forgiveness and pardon is not a primary agendum. We may suppose that it is only in the late, emerging parts of the book of Deuteronomy—late and emerging in the sixth century—that the crisis of pardon even surfaces. Prior to that, in the primary tradition of Deuteronomy, perhaps linked to the hopeful act of reform, obedience to Torah is seen as fully possible and therefore there is no need to ponder pardon. However, in the later part of Deuteronomy, specifically in 29:20—30:20, Patrick D. Miller detects three themes in sequence:[3]

1. Curse (29:20–28);

2. Preaching of Repentance and Restoration (29:29—30:14); and

3. Covenantal Decision (30:15–20).

Three comments seem appropriate regarding the text and Miller's rendering. First, of the second element on "Preaching of Repentance and Restoration," Miller writes:

> The marvelous thing about this text is that it arises out of the harsh realities of disobedience, judgment, and exile and yet dares to assert the new possibilities not only of God's mercy and pardon but of the people's full obedience to the Lord's way. The church has called this justification of the unrighteous and sanctification. In the covenant at Moab, it is blessing for those who have been judged and obedience. Either set of categories

2. See also Jonah 4:2; Pss 86:15; 103:8; 145:8; Neh 9:17.

3. Miller, *Deuteronomy*, 211–15.

confronts us with the powerful grace of God and the transformation of life that it can effect.[4]

While Miller rightly sees grace offered here, the trajectory from these
texts moves well beyond this way of affirming God's grace. That is, the
"powerful grace of God" offered in 29:29—30:14 turned out not to be
an adequate formulation for the circumstance of exile and needed to be
developed in the tradition beyond this formulation.

Second, the urgency of a covenantal decision in 30:15–20 is yet
again a return to a tight, symmetrical "if . . . then" conditional statement
in which the offer of grace is simply a permit to reenter into the demand
of the "as . . . if" relationship. This is a characteristic Deuteronomic affirmation, but one that is deeply circumscribed in comparison with more
belated interpretations of grace.

Third, the "curse" of 29:20–28 is handled by Miller as "language typical of the treaty curses . . . a stereotyped question and answer schema."[5]
This is surely correct, and yet this "typical/stereotyped" curse seems to
not take account of the remarkable negation stated concerning Yahweh
in the only passage that employs *slḥ* in the book of Deuteronomy:

> Yahweh will be unwilling to *pardon* them,
>> for Yahweh's anger and passion will smoke against them. (29:20)

The negative verdict is upon the Israel that turns away from Yahweh to
serve other gods and that went in "our own stubborn ways" (29:18–19).
This is presumably the generation that disobeyed Torah and evoked the
distortion that produced exile. The accent for that generation is on "unwilling to pardon."

My point is to notice that: (a) the force of the negation in 29:20 is as
strong as the positive in 29:29—30:14; and (b) the connection between
the negation and the affirmation is made by the "after all these things"
(30:1), presumably referring to the destruction and exile, when Israel is
to turn and repent. It is clear that the "powerful grace of God" consists in
receptivity to repentance for the coming generation, but not in any forgiveness or pardon for the disaster-evoking generation that precedes. It is
clear that receptivity to repentance is indeed powerful grace. The severe
negative of 29:20, however, even if stereotypical, set me to wondering
about "pardon" in Deuteronomy, and how rigorous and uncompromising

4. Ibid., 213.
5. Ibid., 211–12.

the "if . . . then" of the covenant is, even in the restored covenant of
30:15–20.

Solomon's *slḥ*: Kings vs. Chronicles

Out of that strong denial of pardon in Deut 29:20, I want to consider uses
of *slḥ* in other materials that I consider closely linked to and perhaps derivative of the problem posed by that denial. There are only two programmatic uses of the term *slḥ* in the Deuteronomistic History.[6] The first of
these is the prayer of Solomon in 1 Kings 8 that is strategically important
to the larger narrative of the history.[7] Whereas the earlier material in this
chapter, especially vv. 12–13, offers the temple as a place of presence, the
later Deuteronomistic material resists the claim of presence (see v. 27)
and instead offers the temple as the access point to Yahweh's forgiveness.
In 1 Kgs 8:30, 34, 36, 39, and 50 (see parallels in 2 Chr 6:21, 25, 27, 30, 39),
the term *slḥ* is used to designate the temple as the proper place of petition
and pardon even, we should note, for those "carried away captive to the
land of the enemy" (v. 46). In vv. 34, 36, and most elaborately v. 50, the
petition to pardon is preceded by an anticipation of repentance, "if they
turn (*šub*)" (vv. 33, 35, 47–48). Such anticipation of repentance does not
precede vv. 30 and 39, but the implication is apparently the same.[8] The
prayer in the mouth of Solomon is a bold and confident one, counting
on Yahweh's readiness to accept repentance and to grant pardon to those
who turn. The assumption is the same as that made in Deut 30:1–10, with
the same term *šub*.[9] Two observations are in order. First, the premise of
forgiveness is the repentance of Israel. Yahweh's grace consists in a readiness to accept Israel's return to obedience. Second, the use of the term
"pardon" is on the lips of Solomon as a petitionary imperative. It is not

6. I exclude 2 Kgs 5:18, which I take to be incidental and not programmatic for the
larger narrative.

7. See McCarthy, "II Samuel 7 and the Structure of the Deuteronomic History."
Even though McCarthy focuses on 2 Samuel 7, his analysis appreciates the decisive
placement and function of 1 Kings 8 in the larger narrative.

8. Wolff, "The Kerygma of the Deuteronomic Historical Work," has fully appreciated the theme of "turn" (*šub*) for the shape and theology of the larger narrative. It is
worth noting, in passing, that Wolff regards Deut 4:29–31 along with Deut 30:1–10
and 1 Kgs 8:46ff. as later elements in the narrative. Such a critical distinction is not
especially pertinent to the point made here.

9. See also Jer 36:3, also a Deuteronomistic formulation.

an assurance given by God. Thus it makes a claim that contradicts the negation of Deut 29:20, but does so in an act of Israelite hope, apparently in the conviction that the efficaciousness of the temple as access point to Yahweh more than overrides the rejection based on Torah. I suggest that the positive possibility affirmed by Solomon reflects temple theology, wherein the conditionality of Yahweh is less stringent than in the Torah traditions. Temple is here offered as a more receptive vehicle for forgiveness.[10]

Immediately upon the conclusion of the temple dedication in 1 Kings 8, the text of 1 Kgs 9:1–9 reiterates the rigorous "if . . . then" of the Torah, as though to counter the offer of temple forgiveness. The relation of 8:31–54 to 9:1–9 is not unlike Deut 30:1–10 and 30:15–20, an invitation to turn, followed by an "if . . . then" assertion of life. The positive "if . . . then" of 1 Kgs 9:4–5 and its negative counterpart in vv. 6–9—culminating in the explanation of why has Yahweh done such a thing "to this land and to this house" (vv. 8–9)—is preceded by an oracle of assurance in v. 3. The divine oracle would seem to be a direct response to the "prayer and plea" of Solomon in 1 Kings 8; we might thereby expect an assurance of the pardon for which Solomon prays. What is odd is that there is no offer of pardon here, but only a stringent "if . . . then" that culminates in a heavy threat. That is, the temple offer of pardon is recontextualized in Torah theology so that there is no offer of pardon, but only yet another insistence upon obedience.

The absence of an assurance of pardon that might be commensurate with the petition is made more obvious by the contrast in the parallel statement of 2 Chr 7:12–14. The response of Yahweh to Solomon's prayer is formally the same in 2 Chronicles 7, and concludes in vv. 17–22 with a formula of "if . . . then." But between the assurance of hearing in v. 12 and the "if . . . then" of vv. 17–22, the Chronicler has the following:

> If my people who are called by my name humble themselves, pray, and seek my face, and turn from their wicked ways, then I will hear from heaven, and will forgive [slḥ] their sin and heal their land. (2 Chr 7:14)

The condition of turning is the same, but the assurance of pardon is explicit with the use of slḥ that the Deuteronomistic presentation seems unwilling or unable to utter. Whereas 1 Kings 8 has slḥ as a petition on

10. On the ways in which 1 Kings 8 both voices and moves beyond temple theology, see Levenson, "From Temple to Synagogue."

the lips of Solomon, the Chronicler is able to have the same term as an as-surance on the lips of Yahweh. This later theological development in the Chronicler flies in the face of the negation of Deut 29:20. The conditional "turn" persists, but now there is an explicit readiness on the part of Yah-weh, albeit qualified, to pardon. That readiness, however, comes outside of and after the Deuteronomic and the Deuteronomistic. Thus the temple prayer, a petition and a hope, is the only time in the Deuteronomistic History that "pardon" (*slḥ*) is continued as a sustained, positive theme.[11]

The Failure (and Transformation) of Repentance

It turns out that the hope of Solomon, who staked everything on the tem-ple, was only an interim possibility in the royal narrative. The only other use of *slḥ* in the books of Kings is the verdict rendered on Manasseh.[12] It is clear that Manasseh and Josiah are paradigmatic figures in the royal narrative.[13] Josiah is the "turner" par excellence:

> . . . because your heart was penitent, and you humbled yourself before Yahweh . . . and because you have torn your clothes and wept before me, I also have heard you, says Yahweh. (2 Kgs 22:19)

> Before him there was no king like him, who turned to Yahweh with all his heart, with all his soul, and with all his might, ac-cording to all the law of Moses; nor did any like him arise after him. (2 Kgs 23:25)

Josiah is the perfect Torah-keeper who enacts the "if" of Torah and is entitled to the "then" of covenant blessing. Josiah is the one who fully enacts the repentance of Deut 30:1–10, who should therefore make pos-sible a way of life in Jerusalem.

But whereas Josiah enacts Deut 30:1–10 and is a "turner" to life, his positive generativity is countered, according to this presentation, by Manasseh who embodies the fickleness of Deut 29:18–20. In the end-game of royal narrative, the negation of Deut 29:20 is reiterated concern-ing Manasseh as a warrant for the final destruction of the city:

11. See the vexed usage of the term "pardon" in Jer 5:1, 7, in the same broad tradition.

12. Again excepting 2 Kgs 5:18.

13. The paradigmatic quality of the contrast between the two kings is not unlike that of Ahaz and Hezekiah in the book of Isaiah, on which see Seitz, *Zion's Final Des-tiny*, 195–202 and passim.

> Surely this came upon Judah at the command of Yahweh, to re-
> move them out of his sight, for the sins of Manasseh, for all that
> he had committed, and also for the innocent blood that he had
> shed; for he filled Jerusalem with innocent blood, and Yahweh
> was not willing to pardon. (2 Kgs 24:3–4)

Indeed, 2 Kgs 24:4 directly matches Deut 29:20, both passages use *slḥ* governed by *lo' 'abah*—Yahweh unwilling to pardon.

The story of king and temple thus winds down in a failure to par-don. There had been repentance . . . on the part of Josiah. The repentance of Josiah, however, coming after the disobedience of Manasseh, was not enough. Indeed, in this telling of the royal tale, there is *not enough repentance* to evoke *pardon*. Repentance, even that of Josiah, is an inadequate antidote to the systemic, long-term disobedience of royal Israel epito-mized by Manasseh. The question that arises is anticipated by Moses:

> they and indeed all the nations will wonder, "Why has Yahweh
> done this to this land? What caused this great display of anger?"
> (Deut 29:24)

The question is reiterated in 1 Kgs 9:8, after the interim offer of the temple. The question haunts the narrative, as it haunted the generation of Israel that lived in the wake of the events of 587 BCE. Why? Because repentance did not avail. Because repentance, even of the deepest kind—from Josiah—could not counter the evil that had evoked the curse.

Given that deep negative, we may notice one more use of *slḥ* that is akin to 2 Kgs 24:4. In Lam 3:40–45 the themes of "return" and "pardon" are taken up:

> Let us test and examine our ways,
>   and return (*šub*) to Yahweh.
> Let us lift our hearts as well as our hands
>   to God of heaven.
> We have transgressed and rebelled,
>   and you have not forgiven (*slḥ*).
> You have wrapped yourself with anger and pursued us,
>   killing without pity;
> you have wrapped yourself with a cloud
>   so that no prayer can pass through.
> You have made us filth and rubbish
>   among the peoples.

This generation must still live in an unpardoned state. One can, however, see the beginning of movement in the poem beyond that forlorn state in which devastated Israel has no recourse. For as the poem moves beyond Yahweh's anger in vv. 43–45, the "enemy" begins to appear as the perpetrator of the trouble. In response to Israel's "I am lost" (v. 54), there is now from Yahweh "Do not fear" (v. 57). There is not yet rescue; but it is already clear here that Yahweh is now repositioned vis-à-vis Israel after v. 45. The ground for the repositioning would seem to be Israel's humiliation at the hands of the enemy and Israel's daring capacity to speak the trouble to Yahweh in ways that move Yahweh to response. In the movement of the poetry from v. 40 to v. 60, the divine subject has been changed by the Israel that speaks. What had evoked Yahweh's *rage* now makes Israel subject to Yahweh's *pity*. Now it is Israel's *need* and not Israel's *failure* that matters to Yahweh. This is not at all what Deut 30:1–10 means by "turning." This is a turn *on the part of Yahweh* rather than on the part of Israel; this makes newness possible.[14] Israel turns not in order to admit failure but to plead for help (v. 40). The news of v. 57 is that help is on the way, the help an unpardoning God had not until now been willing to give.

Pardon as Yahweh's Unilateral Act

No more is heard elsewhere in Scripture of the "not pardoning" expressed in Deut 29:20 and 2 Kgs 24:4. Now, finally, I will consider the announcement of pardon that takes repentance into account but that does not wait for repentance on the part of Israel. It is not clear that the texts I cite are directly linked to the tradition of Deuteronomy; but I take it as plausible that they are derived from and represent movement that can be understood as part of the same trajectory. It turns out that the absolute negation of Deut 29:20, voiced in 2 Kgs 24:4 with particular reference to Manasseh but with the entire Jerusalem enterprise in purview, was not the last word. Miller has already seen that it is not the last word in Deuteronomy, since Deut 29:20 is followed by 29:29—30:20. Here I will explore other evidence that the absolute negative of 29:20 is actually penultimate and therefore not as absolute as it was intended to be heard in its utterance.

It is commonly noticed that Second Isaiah begins (Isa 40:8) and ends (55:10–11) with reference to Yahweh's decisive word that fulfills its own

---

14. Reference might usefully be made to the same turn in Ps 90:13, where the verb is parallel to *nḥm*, a term also important for the offer of grace in Second Isaiah.

purpose. It is not so often noticed that the framing of Second Isaiah is not only by "the word" but by an announcement of *pardon*. In 40:1–2, there is a declaration of pardon, or at least an assertion that enough has been suffered for sin by those displaced from Jerusalem. This is clearly not the same as repentance, but rather a sense that the punishment has run it course. In 55:6–9, where *slḥ* occurs in parallel to *rḥm* ("mercy"), there is an offer of pardon to which exilic Israel is summoned. The ground of the offer is that Yahweh's "thoughts" and "ways" are beyond the thoughts and ways of Israel. Presumably the thoughts and ways of Israel in exile are that the exile is to perpetuity (as voiced in Deut 29:20 and 2 Kgs 24:4), but Yahweh's "otherwise" is for homecoming (Isa 55:12–13). The appropriation of "pardon and mercy," however, is indicated by the imperatives, "seek" (Isa 55:6a), "call" (v. 6b), and "turn" (v. 7b). The first two imperative verbs simply reinforce "turn," which brings this text into complete alignment with Deut 30:1–10 where repentance is the condition of restoration. This Deuteronomy-like invitation is a move beyond the harsh judgment of First Isaiah in the same way that Deut 30:1–10 follows after the harshness of 29:20.[15] In both cases, the harshness is overcome by a willingness to offer pardon.

Beyond the affirmation of pardon-*cum*-repentance in Isa 55:6–9, there are three texts in the tradition of Jeremiah that seem to be a later development in the same trajectory, given the close connection between Deuteronomy and the tradition of Jeremiah. The best known of these is Jer 31:31–34. The offer of a new (renewed?) covenant is cast as a remarkable prophetic oracle of promise. The single matter that is of interest here is that in v. 34, the conclusion and ground of the newness is precisely pardon:

> For I will *forgive* (*slḥ*) their iniquity,
> and remember their sin no more.

The assurance of pardon and the forgetting of sin are voiced as a unilateral act by Yahweh, without any seeking, calling, or turning—that is, without any repentance on the part of Israel. Pardon is a genuine *novum* on the part of Yahweh, the breaking of all vicious cycles of alienation that permits a new start with Yahweh.[16] The connection to Deuteronomy is well articulated by Robert Carroll:

15. On the connections between Second Isaiah and the Deuteronomic traditions, see Brueggemann, "Isaiah 55 and Deuteronomic Theology"; and more recently, Sweeney, "The Book of Isaiah as a Prophetic Torah."

16. See Raitt, *A Theology of Exile*, for an extended treatment.

> I would regard the relation between 31.31–34 and the Deuter-
> onomistic strand in the tradition to be one of critical dialogue
> . . . The Deuteronomists believed that the covenant had been
> broken and therefore had become inoperable. Late additions
> to their work allow for the possibility of Yahweh's restoration
> of the nation and the divine circumcision of its mind after it
> has turned back to him (Deut 30.1–10). But of a new covenant
> the Deuteronomists know nothing . . . The author of 31.31–34
> transcends that limitation by asserting the divine initiative
> beyond human turning and the making of a new *berit*. It is a
> post-Deuteronomistic hope but one which has learned its theol-
> ogy from Deuteronomism and made the leap of hope into the
> utopian future.[17]

I shall return to this "leap of hope" in a moment. Here I only note that it
is a leap beyond the repentance that is the ground of pardon even in the
most generous parts of Deuteronomy.

In what is likely an even later oracle in the Jeremian tradition, Jer
33:4–9 makes an abrupt and heretofore unknown turn. Jeremiah 33:4–5
announces Yahweh's word concerning Jerusalem, which is about to be
filled with the dead due to Yahweh's hidden face. After this announcement of destruction, the fresh assertion of vv. 6–9 is staggering in its
form. The series of first person verbs, grounded in nothing from Israel's
side, amounts to a total offer of pardon:

> I will heal,
>   I will reveal,
>   I will restore,
>   I will build,
>   I will cleanse,
>   I will pardon.

The outcome is "prosperity and security." By v. 6, nothing is recalled or
operative from vv. 4–5.

Finally, in Jer 50:17–20, in a prose promise in the midst of the oracle
against Babylon, another promise from Yahweh is offered that begins in
punishment for Babylon and ends in pardon for Israel (v. 20). Nothing is
made of it, but the report in v. 17 may suggest that Yahweh's new initiative
toward Israel is a response to and compensation for the victimization
of Israel by the enemies. Here the work of Assyria and Babylon is not

---

17. Carroll, *Jeremiah*, 613–14.

regarded as an outcome of Yahweh's authorization but is simply brutaliz-
ing imperial activity, in the face of which pardon by Yahweh is a welcome,
transformative alternative. It should be noted that here the promise of
pardon is to "the remnant," that is, the community of survivors after the
deportation. This use of "remnant" does not, however, refer to the reli-
giously privileged, but simply to those fortunate enough to survive the
ordeal of imperial aggression.

Adjudicating Pardon

Our survey of the material concerning pardon (*slḥ*) traverses a broad
sweep from *absolute rejection* (Deut 29:20; 2 Kgs 24:4; Lam 3:42) to a *bid
for repentance* (1 Kgs 8:30–51; Jer 33:6; Isa 55:7), through an *insistence on
the cruciality of obedience without pardon* (1 Kgs 9:4–9; made clear by the
variation in 2 Chr 7:14), to *a full, unilateral pardon without reference to
repentance* (Jer 31:31–34; 33:8; 50:20). From this sequencing of material,
we may consider three questions:

1. Is this trajectory of pardon a legitimate extrapolation from Deuteronomy? Obviously I think so. Miller's judgment about Deut 29:20—
30:20 is that this material is an assertion of "the powerful grace of God."
In the confines of Deuteronomy, however, the offer of Yahweh's pardon
does not move outside the limits of covenantal symmetry within a condition of obedience.[18] That is, pardon depends on becoming fully obedient,
probably fully obedient before pardon. It is an act of grace on the part of
Yahweh to leave open a return to full obedience, but it is a limited offer,
an offer also sounded in Deut 4:29–31 and 1 Kings 8.

But because the tradition of Deuteronomy is covenantal and genuinely interactionist, it is clear that the absolute negation of Deut 29:20
(and 2 Kgs 24:4) or the limited offer via repentance is not sufficient (Deut
30:1–10; Isa 55:6–9). I suggest that because, already in Deuteronomy,
this is a God whose "heart is set" (*ḥšq*) on Israel (Deut 7:7; 10:15), this
deep emotional, passionate yearning on the part of Yahweh for Israel is
operative in Deuteronomy in a way that will not let absolute negation be
the last word. Thus the "not pardon" and the negative use of the term *slḥ*
in Deut 29:20 already inchoately introduce questions, constraints, and

18. Miller, *Deuteronomy*, 213, shows himself to be a discerning Calvinist theo-
logian by seeing the interface in the text of "justification of the unrighteous and
sanctification."

challenges beyond "not pardon," and raise questions about other options from the God "whose heart is set."

The trajectory beyond "not pardon" to "pardon" is accomplished in two theological maneuvers. The first, on which Miller eloquently comments, is that Yahweh will permit recalcitrant Israel back into a covenant of obedience. This is no small matter after what appears to be termination. But the second move, surely also propelled by ḥšq, is a free pardon in which past affronts are not mentioned and no summons to repentance is even issued. Whether this second move, perhaps hinted at in Isaiah 55 but made explicit in the traditions of Jeremiah, is genuinely rooted in Deuteronomy is open to question. But there can be no doubt that the tradition of Jeremiah is deeply situated in the world of the Deuteronomistic History.

Beyond that, however, it may be suggested that the crisis of pardon, seeded in Deuteronomy, is not one among many such traditions, but it is the central tradition that poses the entire problem of the future in an exilic context of covenant canon-making. Thus these several traditions, I propose, all converge around this emergency question. The lived experience of destruction and dislocation required a rhetoric of severity. The severity of absolute negation could hardly be avoided. Deeply rooted in Yahweh's own covenant embracing character, however, is the theological force that causes the theme of slḥ to admit of no single assertion; the term, reflective of a theological emergency, becomes an arena for dangerous interpretive play in which the strictures of Torah, the vagaries of lived experience, an Israelite capacity for candor and hope, plus Yahweh's own ḥšq all converge in a suggestive spectrum of interpretive conviction.

2. Does this spectrum of interpretive opinion have a theological coherence to it? By identifying two theological maneuvers, (a) conditional pardon via repentance and (b) unilateral pardon without a call to repentance, I may seem to suggest a kind of developmental sequence to these texts. While such a development is not impossible, given the lived crisis of the sixth century, it is not definitional to my argument. I mean rather to insist that the covenantal symmetry of obedience is the defining rubric in all of these traditions. That symmetry of obedience can produce either an absolute negative or it can result in a summons to repentance.

What is odd and curious is the "leap" to a third posture of pardon—unconditional forgiveness—that seems provisionally to violate the symmetry of obedience. Along with Carroll, however, I suggest that the "leap" that goes beyond the symmetry of obedience is inchoately already given in the texts of symmetry. This relationship of Yahweh and Israel is not strictly contractual, but it is grounded in passion and commitment, the very factors that require genuine interpersonal interaction that goes beyond technical or juridical guidelines. Thus whatever may be said about the historical-critical relation of these several texts to each other, their theological coherence evidences Israel's daring traditionists struggling, once the notion of *slḥ* has been uttered, to discern what the tension, the severity of punishment, and the asymmetry of pardon may preclude or permit.

3. We may move into a more speculative realm to ask about the reasons why the "leap" in pardon eventuated in these traditions. A "suspicious" response might be that such an assertion of pardon met a pastoral need of a community in crisis, so that the oracles are made to say what needs to be said. A more "transcendent" view might say simply that in the mystery of God's way with God's people, the oracles of God disclose great depth to God's grace.[19]

I suggest we need not choose between the pastorally pragmatic and the theologically inscrutable justifications. Within that matrix, however, we may suggest two other matters that are to some extent obvious in the text. First, the judgment of "not pardon" has run its course and expired its claim. In the older assertion of Exod 34:6–7, the resolve to "visit iniquity" upon the parents is qualified by "the third and fourth generations." That is, the punishment may last a long time, but eventually it reaches its statute of limitation. We may also suggest that the remarkable assertions of Jer 31:34; 33:8; and 50:20 are made possible at the limit of the fourth generation, a recognition perhaps also evident in Isa 40:2.

Second, there is an inclination to identify Israel first as *perpetrator*, but then as *victim*.[20] As long as Israel is the guilty perpetrator, as with Manasseh, pardon is not easily forthcoming. It is, however, hinted in Jer 50:17–28 that Israel is victim, with no hint of any role as perpetrator. This sort of statement, surely with reference to 587 BCE, is astonishing, for it completely disregards the earlier prophetic notion that Nebuchadnezzar (and before him the Assyrians) had moved against Israel only

---

19. On a later exposition of this aspect of the issue see Johnson, *The Mystery of God*. There is no doubt that Karl Barth locates the possibility of forgiveness deep in the mystery of God.

20. I have learned of the interface of the categories of "perpetrator" and "victim" from Ricoeur, *The Symbolism of Evil*, 232–78, even though Ricoeur focuses upon matters other than those that concern me here. His mention of Jer 31:31–34 (ibid., 241) indicates that Ricoeur is not only reading Genesis 2–3, but is concerned with the "dialectic of judgment and mercy" as it permeates Israel's articulation of its faith.

at the behest of Yahweh as punishment from Yahweh (see Isa 10:5–11; 47:6; Jer 25:9; 27:6).

The point is perhaps even more clear in Lam 3:40–66. I began my treatment of that poem above with the stanza of vv. 40–42, because that is where the term *slḥ* occurs. In v. 42, Israel's guilt is acknowledged and is taken as the proper ground for God's anger. But then in v. 52, the poem turns. Israel's enemies are "without cause." The prayer of petition (vv. 55–56) evokes Yahweh's "Do not fear" (v. 57). From that point on in the poem, Israel's role of abused victim is explicated. To be sure, the term "pardon" does not recur in the poem, but the salvation oracle of v. 57 indicates a glad, attentive response on the part of Yahweh. The guilt of v. 42 is completely overridden by the sense of victimization. Clearly, Yahweh will come in fresh ways to this people that is now not perpetrator but victim. How this poetic maneuver is accomplished in the ongoing reflection of exile is not obvious. Still, it is apparent that the deep sense of guilt has run its course, a fact that makes the idea of free pardon by Yahweh more credible.

These possible responses to the questions of legitimacy, extrapolation, coherence, and theological rationale (all considered above) suggest that the tradition of pardon, rooted in Deuteronomy, is a major theological agenda that receives a great deal of Israel's continued and belated interpretive energy.

Present-Day Crises of Pardon

Finally, given that Patrick Miller is a deeply committed churchman, let me reflect briefly on the ways in which this convergence of *absolute negation*, summons to *the symmetry of obedience*, and *unconditional pardon* continues to be pertinent to the church. I identify three "crises of pardon" that continue to haunt in deep ways the church in the United States and its society:

1. The barbarism of slavery and the ensuing racism evident in every facet and dimension of our common life;

2. The unparalleled act of barbarism in Hiroshima and Nagasaki that bespeaks Western savagery toward Asia in a most particular way, but more largely epitomizes U.S. hegemony as the "last superpower";

3. The durable shame of Vietnam, the untold costs of which continue in visible and in hidden ways among us.

Other such "crises of pardon" could readily be added to this list. These are representative and typical of the deep theological crises that mark our society where raw power has become utterly separated from God's will in the world. I suggest that the taxonomy of pardon that I have traced from the trajectory of Deuteronomy is a way in which such "crises of pardon" bear upon long-term interpretive tasks. In each of these cases, as with many others we could add, it is too easy, as is our wont, to imagine easy, free pardon. It is excessively bourgeois, I suspect, to imagine a credible repentance that promptly "puts all this behind us." It is thinkable, but hardly bearable, to imagine that any of these acts might place us permanently beyond pardon from God. Yet the interpretive task is not to select one of these options. It is rather to recognize that such a lived, visible fissure as 587 BCE along with its desolation-like moral fissure, requires long term interpretive staying power. By noting the use of the term sib and its several uses in the trajectory, we are able to see how Israel, in its desolation, understood and stayed at such an interpretive task that was unavoidable, but that admitted of no easy or obvious resolution.

To conclude: It is clear that the theological notion of "pardon" entailed an immense field of interpretive imagination for Israel. That field of imagination included: (a) harsh judgment, (b) *quid pro quo* reconciliation on the basis of repentance, and (c) a free offer of a new start by Yahweh, the offended party. In contemporary social transactions, in both the church and larger society, it is clear that this "immense field of interpretive imagination" is still at work, or at least potentially available. The maintenance of community requires ordered, accountable relationships with firm sanctions. Israel, however, discovered that in the end the future is only possible by a large gesture of compassion on the part of the offended party. In contemporary imagination, that same discernment surfaces here and there yet again, as theological models sometimes inform social relationships.

Bibliography

Brueggemann, Walter. "Isaiah 55 and Deuteronomic Theology." *ZAW* 80 (1968) 191–203.

———. *Theology of the Old Testament: Testimony, Dispute, Advocacy.* Minneapolis: Fortress, 1997.

Carroll, Robert P. *Jeremiah: A Commentary.* OTL. Philadelphia: Westminster, 1986

Johnson, William Stacy. *The Mystery of God: Karl Barth and the Postmodern Foundations of Theology.* Columbia Series in Reformed Theology. Louisville: Westminster John Knox, 1997.

Levenson, Jon D. "From Temple to Synagogue: I Kings 8." In *Traditions in Transformation: Turning Points in Biblical Faith,* edited by Baruch Halpern and Jon D. Levenson, 143–66. Winona Lake, IN: Eisenbrauns, 1981.

McCarthy, Dennis J. "II Samuel 7 and the Structure of the Deuteronomic History." *JBL* 84 (1965) 131–38. Reprinted in *Institution and Narrative: Collected Essays,* 127–34. AnBib 108. Rome: Biblical Institute Press, 1985.

Miller, Patrick D. *Deuteronomy.* Interpretation. Louisville: Westminster John Knox, 1990.

Raitt, Thomas M. *A Theology of Exile: Judgment/Deliverance in Jeremiah and Ezekiel.* Philadelphia: Fortress, 1977.

Ricoeur, Paul. *The Symbolism of Evil.* Translated by Emerson Buchanan. Religious Perspectives 17. New York: Harper & Row, 1967.

Seitz, Christopher R. *Zion's Final Destiny: The Development of the Book of Isaiah. A Reassessment of Isaiah 36–39.* Minneapolis: Fortress, 1991.

Sweeney, Marvin A. "The Book of Isaiah as a Prophetic Torah." In *New Visions of Isaiah,* edited by Roy F. Melugin and Marvin A. Sweeney, 50–67. JSOTSup 214. Sheffield: Sheffield Academic, 1996.

Wolff, Hans Walter. "The Kerygma of the Deuteronomic Historical Work." In *The Vitality of Old Testament Traditions,* Walter Brueggemann and Hans Walter Wolff, 83–100. 2nd ed. Atlanta: John Knox, 1982.

3

A Defining Utterance on the
Lips of the Tishbite Pondering
"The Centrality of the Word"

KARL BARTH HAS PROVIDED the definitive statement concerning the Word of God—preached, written, revealed.[1] None has shown so closely as Barth what it means that "the Word is central." An Old Testament teacher, however, may have a much more modest sense of the theme of "the Word" before it is overlaid with all of the christological freight that it has come to carry. In the Old Testament, the "word of Yahweh" is characteristically taken to mean direct utterance that is efficacious and performative, that causes to be by the authority of the one who utters. When one moves in a christological direction, the one who utters becomes the utterance.[2] Here, however, I shall consider the utterance of Elijah the Tishbite who did indeed, according to the tradition, give utterance from God that made all things new. There is no doubt that his utterance is understood as central to every episode of his narrative and to the larger narrative of Israel in which his stories are embedded. The narrative ac-

---

1. Barth, *Church Dogmatics*, I/1, 88–124.

2. By such formulation I allude to the dictum of Bultmann, *Theology of the New Testament*, vol. 1, 33, "The proclaimer became the proclaimed." I am grateful to my colleague, Charles Cousar, for helping me locate this formula. Cousar notes, moreover, that in English translation Bultmann did not use capital letters on "proclaimer" and "proclaimed," thus making the parallel with Elijah more accessible.

count of Elijah attests to the conviction that in the horizon of faith, the Word is indeed central in redefining and transforming the world of death into an arena for life.

The Widow of Zarephath

The word is central to the widow of Zarephath who has no other resource for life (1 Kgs 17:8–24). Indeed the life-giving, life-restoring Word is a perfect counterpoint precisely for those who have no other hope in the world. The Tishbite is sent by "the word of Yahweh" to this woman about to die of starvation (vv. 8–16). By his utterance, Elijah asserts a supply of plenty in a world of scarcity, declaring the economics of scarcity to be null and void:

> For thus says Yahweh the God of Israel: The jar of meal will not be emptied and the jug of oil will not fail until the day that Yahweh sends rain on the earth. (v. 14)

Elijah's greater utterance, however, is in his second encounter with the widow, whereby he restores her dead son to life (vv. 17–24). In this case his utterance is a powerful prayer addressed to the God of all life. We are told that "Yahweh listened to the voice of Elijah." His utterance evokes a response from God as God impinges upon the world of deathliness. Elijah has summoned Yahweh to action in that world of death. In both episodes, the concluding formula acknowledges the centrality of the word:

> The jar of meal was not emptied, neither did the jug of oil fail, according to the word of Yahweh that he spoke by Elijah. (v. 16)

> Now I know that you are a man of God, and that the word of Yahweh in your mouth is true. (v. 24)

The narrative knows that we are in the presence of an utterance and an utterer who decisively reshapes the world.

Naboth

The word is central to the memory and identity of Naboth (1 Kgs 21:1–24). In the first sixteen verses of the narrative, Naboth, Jezebel, and Ahab manage without the word. Life managed without the word, so the narrative makes clear, is short, brutish, and ugly, filled with rapaciousness, mendacity, and finally death. This real-life episode features the big ones eating the little ones, characteristically manipulating the powers of governance and the law for the sake of land advantage. Long before Karl Marx, this narrator knows that the powerful will manage the processes of governance for their ruthless advantage.

As we have it, however, the narrative does not end—as it otherwise would—with the execution of Naboth and the new royal success. It would have ended there if the Word were not central. But in v. 17 comes the Word, insisting that no earthly transaction is finished or proper if it is void of the relentless utterance that keeps the story of the world from shriveling into death. So speaks Elijah. First he utters a speech of judgment with its characteristic indictment and sentence of the king (vv. 17–19). Elijah is properly and correctly acknowledged by the king as "troubler," for the Word that is central is always a trouble for the shut-down royal world that wants to operate without the disruption of transformative utterance. In this account, however, the royal shut-down is not finally permitted.

Second, in vv. 20–24 Elijah offers a long, formal, devastating utterance against the house of Omri. As in 14:7–14 and 16:2–4, this narrative specializes in prophetic oracles that terminate royal dynasties. What an odd portrayal of public power: *oracles* terminating *dynasties*, speech upsetting power! That is what Elijah does in this encounter with Ahab, threatening every heir of the royal family, with a special notice of the much despised queen. The oracle makes clear that royal power is at best penultimate, is always at the behest of what is ultimate, namely, the uncompromising will of the one who authorizes the utterer.[3] This word from Elijah has two identifiable features. First in vv. 27–28, even Ahab accepts the prophetic verdict and repents, willing to accept the demanding conditions whereby he retains power for a little while. But second, the repentance gives only a deferral of the Word, not its nullification. For in 2 Kgs 9:36–37, the Word that causes powers to "rise and fall" comes to fruition in the termination of the dynasty (see also 1 Sam 2:6–8).

These two utterances, in turn to a powerless widow and to a powerful king, are surely twinned. Together they exhibit the capacity of this God-sent utterer to intervene decisively in closed power arrangements that pertain to both economics and politics. This is the utterance that brings fullness midst scarcity, life midst death, and death midst life.

---

3. Reference might usefully be made to Dan 4:25, 32, "until you have learned that the Most High has sovereignty over the kingdom of mortals, and gives it to whom he will." The same learning is so urgent and difficult for the House of Omri.

Elijah's utterance is his own; it comes from his lips in understandable human coding. Nobody has trouble understanding him. At the same time, however, the narrative insists that the formula "the Word of Yahweh" makes clear to all parties that this utterance so central to the deployment of economic, political power is not "merely" a Tishbite utterance. The narrator displays no curiosity about this odd juxtaposition of the Word so central that belongs to the Tishbite and yet belongs beyond the Tishbite to the central Utterer of life in the world.

The House of Omri

The Word is central to the dynasty of Ornri. The house of Omri featured four kings, Omri its founder (1 Kgs 16:23–28), Ahab its star performer (1 Kgs 16:29—22:40), and his two relatively inconsequential sons, Ahaziah (1 Kgs 22:51) and Jehoram (2 Kgs 3:1–3). We know from ancient Near Eastern records that the house of Omri was a major political-military force to be noticed and reckoned with in the world of international posturing. What interests us, however, is that the narrative of the books of Kings pauses over the House of Omri so long. We may be astonished by that fact because, in the ideology of the narrator, all Northern kings are in principle condemned and dismissed out of hand, precisely because they are non-Davidic or anti-Davidic.

Given that angle of assessment, the coverage given the Omri dynasty amazes. The reason, of course, is that the Omri dynasty that lasted thirty-four years, is the launching pad and arena for the utterance of Elijah and his disciple Elisha. This extended narrative is precisely a study in the centrality of the Word, a meditation on how it is that something as elusive, "non-substantive," and fleeting as utterance can impinge decisively upon the royal world of ideology, management, technology, and ruthlessness. One would know beforehand that the Word stands no chance in such a managed environment. And yet it does! That is the purpose of the narrative that cannot tum its attention away from this inexplicable wonder. As a consequence, we are offered an exposé of Niebuhrian proportion about the penultimate character of worldly power in the face of such utterance. Indeed, the dynasty is, in the end, defined by this utterance that it can neither withstand nor administer.

The presenting problem for the dynasty is a drought. The dynasty lives in an an arid climate where water is always a preoccupation. Like every goverment, this one is in the end legitimated and consented to by its capacity to provide adequate resources for viable life and a viable economy. Obviously, if the royal government cannot supply water, it cannot endure. What the royal house may know but cannot acknowledge is instigated, beyond royal control, by the Holy Utterer who operates on the lips of Elijah. Indeed, in 1 Kgs 17:1 when Elijah first abruptly appears in the narrative the very first utterance, not even framed by a conventional "messenger formula," is a declaration of drought. This is a divine resolve to threaten the government in Samaria by withholding rain:

> As Yahweh the God of Israel lives, before whom I stand, there
> shall be neither dew nor rain these years, except by my word.
> (1 Kgs 17:1)[4]

It is the drought that creates disaster for the widow. It is, moreover, the drought that generates the decisive confrontation at Mt. Carmel in chapters 18–19. In 18:1–6, we are offered a sketch of the pitiful, helpless Ahab traversing the land in a "research and development" venture to find water. But of course he will not find water, because water has been denied at a "higher level" of government to which the king has no access.

That sketch of royal impotence at the beginning of the narrative report on the drought is matched in the conclusion with a report of heavy rain (1 Kgs 18:41–46). The drought ends, not by any royal maneuver but by the Word of Elijah, who has secured public allegiance to Yahweh and who now prays for rain as he prayed for the life of the boy. The narrator adds laconically:

> But the hand of Yahweh was on Elijah; he girded up his loins
> and ran in front of Ahab to the entrance of Jezreel. (1 Kgs 18:46)

The power of Yahweh is upon Elijah. He precedes the king in triumphant royal procession. There is no doubt that this utterer and his utterance— his own, yet not his own—is the decisive, concrete reality of the Omride house. Characteristically, these kings who hold the appearance of power are slow to notice that the realities of power lie beyond them. These kings, who manage the levers of government, late if ever notice that what is central is utterance and not their royal appearance.[5]

---

4. The drought is readily understood in that ancient world as a curse authorized by Yahweh who will brook no disobedience (see Deut 28:23–24; Lev 26:19–20).

5. The same interface is nicely narrated in Luke 3:1–2. There the full pedigree of kings and priests is offered, only to be tersely contrasted with "the Word of God."

The Royal Narrative

The word is central to the royal narrative of 1 and 2 Kings. Gerhard von Rad has perceptively noticed that the editors of 1 and 2 Kings juxtaposed *prophetic utterance* and *narrative fulfillment* as a central organizing principle of the narrative.[6] By this arrangement, von Rad nicely understood that prophetic utterance is not incidental to the narrative; it is rather the decisive constitutive feature of this theory of public power.[7] Von Rad's exquisite exposition, however, could leave the impression that such a narrative device is an editorial imposition upon the royal narrative.

But that, of course, is not the case. For the fact is that kings in Israel and Judah are characteristically confronted with prophetic utterance that judges and condemns, that summons to repentance or that legitimates in office. Kings in Israel and Judah characteristically must exercise their royal authority in a context of confrontive utterance that stands outside royal legitimacy and that has of itself no visible authorization beyond its self-proclaimed "messenger formula." That utterance, however, is, in the horizon of the narrative, recognized to be a valid utterance that cannot be safely disregarded. That is, the management of earthly power, so this material attests, always takes place in the presence of inconvenient, disruptive, unaccommodating utterance. If we consider this claim "from above," it is to be concluded through the "messenger formula" that such inescapable utterance is a recurrent vehicle for the will of the Holy God who stands outside royal orbit and addresses royal power. This is the intent of the narrative that by the messenger formula makes a Yahwistic claim. If, however, we consider the matter "from below," it is characteristically the case, as this regime learned and as every self-contained concentration of power learns, that the human yearning for well-being is irreducible and finally not silencable, not by ideological manipulation nor even by the use of techniques of intimidation or torture.[8] Human voices of protest and hope will sound and have social force.[9] Thus when we say "the Word

6. Von Rad, *Studies in Deuteronomy*, 74–91.

7. This theory of history is nicely phrased by Koch, *The Prophets: The Assyrian Period*, 5, 73, 8, 99, 121, 155, and especially his schematic presentation on 156.

8. On the remarkable juxtaposition of speech and torture, see Scarry, *The Body in Pain*.

9. Wilson, *Prophecy and Society in Ancient Israel*, has provided a suggestive analysis of the way in which social forces generate speech that turns out to be the prophetic word of Yahweh; see especially 192–206.

is central," we are able to see a convergence: Elijah is *sent by Yahweh* with a word; Elijah arises midst a population of *deprivation* and will speak with and for that population. There is no contradiction in the narrative, for the theological claim and the sociological reality completely converge. His is a word bestowed "from above," arising "from below."

That is, the speech–fulfillment pattern offered in the narrative and discerned by von Rad is indeed intrinsic to the human process when that process is known to be more than the manipulation of images and the arrangements of power. That fragile, vulnerable reality of human entitlement, entitlement God-given in creation, will come to speech. And when it speaks, it is offered, in this case as in other cases, as the Word of Yahweh.

The Word is central to this narrative because Yahweh of covenant is committed to the raw reality of human life. The books of Kings are introduced by a cunning report on Solomon (1 Kings 1–11) and conclude with a celebrative but sobered recognition of the reforms of Hezekiah (2 Kings 18–20) and Josiah (2 Kings 22–23). Between Solomon and the belated royal reforms sit the Elijah–Elisha materials, with 1 Kings 12–15 and 2 Kings 11–17 as materials that connect these accent points. Solomon is "top down," interrupted only belatedly by Ahijah (1 Kgs 11:29–39); in parallel Hezekiah and Josiah deal respectively with Isaiah and Huldah. Both the long introduction and the extended conclusion are royal accounts that are only interrupted by prophetic voices. In our long central section, however, the kings are bit-players and the drama is completely concerned for prophetic utterance. This central section shows the Word to be so central that kings count for very little. Indeed the books of Kings are arranged for radical subversion of royal power, a subversion that suggests that where Holy intention and human vulnerability converge, there is the truth of the matter.[10]

Elijah's Legacy

It is no wonder that this Elijah, who did not die but "ascended," continued to haunt Israel (2 Kgs 2:9–12). Utterance authorized by Yahweh has staying power. It keeps uttering. It is not finished in its "original," historical-critical context. It keeps reuttering, so that the face-to-face utterances of Elijah to the woman and to the king become a force vis-à-vis the dynasty. Beyond

---

10. On such subversion that undermines established power, see Lehmann, *The Transfiguration of Politics*, 48–70 and passim.

the dynasty this Word stays central to the larger narrative and to an entire theory of power expressed in the narrative, a theory that depends upon remembered utterance made in quite locatable, concrete circumstance.

Beyond all of that in the books of Kings, however, this odd utterer continues to loom very large in the imagination, hope, and therefore text of Israel. Thus in the Christian Old Testament, Elijah has the last word in the book of Malachi, as we witness not a remembered Elijah but an expected Elijah:

> Lo, I will send you the prophet Elijah before the great and ter-
> rible day of Yahweh comes. He will turn the hearts of parents to
> their children and the hearts of children to their parents, so that
> I will not come and strike the land with a curse. (Mal 4:5–6)

The Elijah that ascended into heaven will, at the right time, descend into the earth again. And when he comes again, he will enact "family values," reconciling children and parents, in order to avoid the curse, the sort of curse Elijah found inevitable upon the house of Omri.

The concrete, uttered Word—its precise cadences known, treasured, and reiterated in Israel—keeps ringing in the ears of the faithful, keeps reassuring widows (see Luke 4:25–26), keeps terminating kings (see Luke 3:18–20), keeps supplying water in many lands of drought (see John 4:14). It is this utterer, with utterances that have inexplicable futures, who remains engaged in the imagination and expectation of the faithful. It is precisely because the Word is central, because this particular concrete utterance is durable and keeps respeaking, that the Gospel narrative surrounds its account of Jesus with Elijah references:

- John is drawn into the orbit of Elijah (Matt 14:14);
- Jesus is seen to be not unlike Elijah (Matt 16:14; 17:10–12);
- Elijah is one of the "old ones" who comes to legitimate and identify Jesus (Matt 17:3–4);
- The cry of Jesus on the cross is taken to be a petition for the coming again of Elijah (Matt 27:47–49).

It is clear that this remembered utterer is central to the Jesus narrative and to the imagination of the earliest circles of his followers. While there is no doubt that Elijah is engaged precisely to attest to Jesus as the Word, it is equally clear that the Jesus narrative could not be fully told and that Jesus as the Word could not be adequately recognized except in the world of Elijah's utterance that persists.

Narrative Framing

The narrative in Kings spends little time pondering how it is that this human utterer could offer a Word so central that is Holy Utterance. We may, however, notice the way in which the Elijah narrative is framed. At the outset Elijah is commanded to the wilderness, outside the royal aegis, where he lives on the food of the land apart from royal offers of food that would soften his utterance (1 Kgs 17:3–6; see Daniel 1; Mark 8:15). From the outset Elijah is an utterer who is unencumbered by the gifts of those who would like to undermine the power, authority, and force of hts utterance. He is nurtured in a way to protect the force and credibility of his unfettered utterance.

At the conclusion of his narrative when he is "taken up," Elisha asks for a "double share of your spirit" (2 Kgs 2:9). Nowhere have we been told that the spirit had come upon Elijah. That reality, however, may be inferred from Elisha's petition as from Elijah's own performance. He is indeed a man beyond himself in authority. He is seen to have such unencumbered power precisely because he is powered singularly by the spirit of God that made him bold, fearless, and fully capable of transformative action. This framing of an introduction in unencumbered nurture (1 Kgs 17:3–6) and this conclusion in underived power (2 Kgs 2:9) provides context and definition for the narratives of utterance in between. The narrative is deftly arranged in order to show that this utterer is fully engaged in the life of the world with all its risks, but he is not of that royal world. It is his "in, but not of" that makes his word so central.

Words Faithfully Uttered

No doubt this notion of the word as central does not fully come up to Karl Barth's christological notion of the centrality of the Word, nor does the narrative intend such a claim for the utterance of Elijah. It is correct, nonetheless, to see that the utterance on the lips of Elijah, in Barth's categories:

a. is indeed "Word preached":

It is the miracle of revelation and faith . . . when proclamation is for us not just human willing and doing characterised in some way but also and primarily and decisively God's own act, when human talk about God is for us not just that, but also and primarily and decisively God's own speech;[11]

b. is indeed "Word written":

This consists in the fact that in Holy Scripture, too, the writing is obviously not primary, but secondary. It is itself the deposit of what was once proclamation by human lips. In its form as Scripture, however, it does not seek to be a historical monument but rather a Church document, written proclamation;[12]

c. is indeed "Word of God revealed":

The Bible is God's Word as it really bears witness to revelation, and proclamation is God's Word as it really promises revelation. The promise in proclamation, however, rests on the attestation in the Bible. The hope of future revelation rests on faith in that which has taken place once and for all. Thus the decisive relation of the church to revelation is its attestation by the Bible. Its attestation![13]

I have no wish to push Elijah in an excessively christological direction; that, moreover, is not necessary in order to see in this lingering text that the concrete Word of the Tishbite is and remains central. Rather my concern, as it was early on with Barth, is not to make a christological connection, but to notice, with and for other preachers, that words faithfully uttered from these words have long-time, enduring, transformative potential. Entrusted as we are with such remembered, expected utterance, it matters what and how we say words that are more than our own. It matters acutely, moreover, because in the world of technological consumerism, there is immense pressure to silence serious, revelatory, subversive utterance. A purpose of our technology of imagery, as Jacques Ellul has seen so clearly, is to preclude utterance wherein the irreducibly human and the irresistibly Holy converge.[14] It belongs to the heirs and children of this text to stand outside such killing of the human and such trivializing of the Holy. To stand outside for the sake of utterance depends, in some way, on refusing royal junk food (as in 1 Kgs 17:3–6), and being powered by the Spirit (as in 2 Kgs 2:9). Where such refusal

11. Barth, *Church Dogmatics*, I/1, 93.

12. Ibid., 102.

13. Ibid., 111.

14. Ellul, *The Humiliation of the Word.*

and empowerment happen, there is a chance that widows will live, that powers will notice, and that water will abound.

It is a deep delight to salute Frederick Trost who has understood so well and worked so tenaciously that the Word be central in all its life-giving freedom in the ministry of the church. Would that his mantle were to be thrown over a host of his followers who know him to be a "chariot of Israel."

Bibliography

Barth, Karl. *Church Dogmatics*, I/1, *The Doctrine of the Word of God, Part 1*. Translated by G. T. Thomson. Edinburgh: T. & T. Clark, 1936.

Bultmann, Rudolf. *Theology of the New Testament*. Vol. 1. Translated by Kendrick Grobel. New York: Scribner, 1951.

Ellul, Jacques Ellul. *The Humiliation of the Word*. Translated by Joyce Main Hanks. Grand Rapids: Eerdmans, 1985.

Koch, Klaus. *The Prophets: The Assyrian Period*. Translated by Margaret Kohl. Philadelphia: Fortress, 1982.

Lehmann, Paul. *The Transfiguration of Politics: The Presence and Power of Jesus of Nazareth in and over Human Affairs*. New York: Harper & Row, 1975.

Rad, Gerhard von. *Studies in Deuteronomy*. Translated by David Stalker. SBT 1/9. Chicago: Regnery, 1953.

Scarry, Elaine. *The Body in Pain: The Making and Unmaking of the World*. New York: Oxford University Press, 1985.

Wilson, Robert R. *Prophecy and Society in Ancient Israel*. Philadelphia: Fortress, 1980.

4

Texts that Linger, Not Yet Overcome

IT IS CLEAR THAT God, as rendered in the Bible, is a continually unsettled character and consequently an unending problem for theology, as theology has been conventionally done in the Christian West. The profound tension between the textual rendering of God and conventional theological settlements constitutes an on-going interpretive problem for any who move between text and a Christian interpretive community.[1] No one has written more passionately or effectively on this issue than has James Crenshaw, and I have come to believe that his careful, critical work has an intentional thrust against reductionist theological conventions.[2] The problematic character of God in the text may be treated variously under the topics of wrath, anger, capriciousness, hiddenness, and so on. Here I shall seek to advance the direction of Crenshaw's acute interest in the issue in one small way by addressing the question of God's abandoning absence.[3]

1. I regard this as especially a problem for Christians and will so discuss the matter. This is partly because there is an inherent propensity in Christianity to give closure to its thought and partly because of the long history of Christianity as a dominant cultural power. It is not, however, a peculiarly Christian problem. Thus, for example, see Levenson, *Creation and the Persistence of Evil*, 3, and his reference to Yehezkel Kaufmann, who exhibits something like the same propensity to closure.

2. On this aspect of Crenshaw's work, see Brueggemann, "James L. Crenshaw: Faith Lingering at the Edges." See Crenshaw's comments in the same issue, which agree with this assessment.

3. This problem has received much more attention from Jewish thinkers than from Christian, no doubt because of the Christian eagerness to give closure, as

Four Texts on God's Absence

We may begin our discussion by focusing on four texts, all of which ponder the absence of God by the strong use of the verb *'azab*.

1. Perhaps the obvious place to begin is Ps 22:2:[4]

> My God, my God, why have you forsaken me?
>> Why are you so far from helping me, from the words of my groaning?

This characteristic complaint voices an accusation against God, suggesting that God's (seeming?) absence is unreasonable, unexpected, and inexcusable, and in fact reflects God's untrustworthiness. As is well known this psalm, with a series of "motivations," expresses a series of petitions that urge Yahweh's presence and active intervention (vv. 11, 19–21a) and culminates in a celebration of rescue.[5] That is, by the end of the poem this abandoning absence of God is overcome and God is decisively present. We cannot, however, permit the resolution at the end of the poem to nullify the experience and expression of absence at the beginning.[6] Moreover, no hint of fault, blame, or sin on the part of the speaker is expressed, as though the speaker's conduct justified the absence of God. It is clear that God is culpable in the intention of the speaker.

The accusation of v. 1, because it is a complaint, is of course in the mouth of the human (Israelite) speaker. Thus it is possible to say that the human voice has it wrong, that God is not absent but "seems" to be absent (on which see below). For Christians, of course, this accusation against God takes on additional gravity when it occurs on the lips of Jesus (Matt 27:46; Mark 15:34). It is a common theological strategy among Christians to explain away the abrasion of the opening lines of the psalm by observing that the line quoted in the Gospel narratives only introduces

---

acknowledged in n. 1. Thus, for example, we may refer to Martin Buber's "Eclipse," André Neher's "exile" and "silence," and the several articulations of Emil Fackenheim.

4. The English and Hebrew versification differ in this psalm. I will be using the English versification throughout the rest of this essay.

5. There is of course a vast literature on Psalm 22. Among the more recent and most helpful are Davis, "Exploding the Limits"; and Kselman, "'Why Have You Abandoned Me?'"

6. For the phrase "experience and expression," I refer to Ricoeur, "Biblical Hermeneutics," and his notions of "limit experience" and "limit expression." These texts of unsettling dimension are "limit expressions" that give Israel access to its "limit experiences."

the whole implied psalm, again as though the implied ending nullifies the expressed beginning. In an important exception to this conventional Christian strategy, Jürgen Moltmann takes the Gospel reiteration of Ps 22:1 with theological seriousness.[7] God is absent and is said to be absent. The narrative of the crucifixion of Jesus is a Christian articulation of that absence of God that causes the world to revert to chaos.[8]

2. The capacity to explain Ps 22:1 away, because it is a human articulation of absence that may be a misperception of God, is an equally possible strategy in Lam 5:20:

> Why have you forgotten (*šakaḥ*) us completely?
> Why have you forsaken (*ʿazab*) us these many days?

Whereas Psalm 22 deals with an unspecified situation, Lam 5:20 is context specific. The verse pertains to the collapse of the symbolic (as well as political) world of Jerusalem (and of Judaism) over which Judah grieved massively.[9] The physical loss entailed by Judeans in the crisis of 587 BCE is matched by the powerful sense of intimate, personal, religious loss. The destruction of Jerusalem signifies God's absence and happens as a consequence of God's (unwarranted?) absence.[10] The interrogative form of v. 20 is the same as in Ps 22:1 with *lamah*. The speaker does not question that God has abandoned. The abandonment by Yahweh is taken as a given. In asking "why," the speaker does not seek an explanation from God but seeks to assert that the absence of God is inexplicable and inexcusable.

Verse 20 is framed in the last strophe of vv. 19–22 by three striking assertions, each of which functions in relation to the desperate accusation of v. 20. In v. 19, the speaker utters a wondrous doxology, appealing to the enthronement liturgies, acknowledging God's sovereign power. The effect of this verse is to make the absence of v. 20 all the more scandalous, for the one who "reigns forever" can hardly be absent. Verse 21 looks

---

7. Moltmann, *The Crucified God*, 146–51, 207, 218, and passim.

8. On the cross of Jesus as an enactment of the unsettling dimension, see the powerful statement of Hall, *Toward an Indigenous Theology of the Cross*. Moltmann (*The Crucified God*, 243) has a very nice phrase for the significance of the cross: "The Fatherlessness of the Son is matched by the Sonlessness of the Father . . ."

9. On grief over the destruction of Jerusalem as paradigmatic grief for Jews, see Mintz, *Hurban*. See especially his programmatic statement on 2.

10. This sense of God's absence is very different from the conventional Deuteronomistic notion that God's absence is a result of Israel's sin. On the tension Lamentations has with both Deuteronomistic and Zion traditions, see the discussion of Albrektson, *Studies in the Text and Theology of the Book of Lamentations*.

behind v. 20 to v. 19, and on the basis of the doxology issues an urgent imperative for God's action, thus characteristically following complaint with petition.[11] In spite of the doxology and petition, however, the final verse (v. 22) returns to and reasserts the conclusion of v. 20:

> But instead you have completely rejected us;
>> you have been very angry with us.[12]

And thus the poem ends. The accusatory verbs of v. 20 ("forget, abandon") are reinforced by "reject, be angry" (v. 22). Unlike Ps 22:1, there is no resolution in this dread-filled complaint. The poem ends abruptly and without any response from God. The effect is to confirm God's absence, a fickle absence, and to leave the words "forget, abandon" ringing in Israel's exilic ears.

3. The enduring echo of "forget, abandon" in the exilic literature apparently takes on liturgic form as evidenced in Isa 49:15. This verse is introduced by the rubric "But Zion said . . ." This is presumably a stylized, often reiterated liturgic complaint. Indeed, this usage is plausibly a reference back to and quotation of Lam 5:20, given the propensity of exilic Isaiah to be a response to Lamentations.[13] To be sure, the two defining terms, *'azab* and *šakaḥ*, are here in reverse order, but the intention is the same. The complaint, which we have seen already in Lam 5:20 as well as Ps 22:1, is that Yahweh is unfaithful and neglectful. Moreover, it is Yahweh's failure to be faithfully present in Israel that results in the suffering and shame of the exile.

The statement of v. 14, however, is lodged in the midst of a proclamation of salvation, whereby the assurance of Yahweh intends to dispute and overcome the accusatory claim of Israel. Thus, in v. 13 Yahweh is assigned two recurring words of assurance, "comfort" (*nhm*) and "compassion" (*rhm*). In direct response to the complaint of v. 14, Yahweh now speaks in the first person, using the term "compassion" and three times "not forget" by way of denying the accusation of v. 13. It is worth noting, though perhaps not important, that Yahweh's response does not use

11. On complaint and petition, see Gerstenberger, *Der bittende Mensch*.

12. The translation is that of Hillers, *Lamentations*, 96. See his comments on 100–101.

13. See Mintz, *Hurban*, 41–46, on the relation of Lamentations and Second Isaiah. My student, Tod Linafelt, has begun important work on this connection; see Linafelt, *Surviving Lamentations*.

a word to negate the accusation of *'azab*. The accent is placed on "not forget" in the denial of Yahweh.

Given the assurance of Yahweh in the third person (v. 13) and in the first person (v. 15), it is not completely clear how the assurances are related to the complaint. It is easiest to take the assurance as a refutation and denial of the complaint. That is, Israel seemed to be forgotten and forsaken but was not. On this reading, the complaint of Lam 5:20 was mistaken. A possible alternative is that Israel is momentarily forgotten by Yahweh, but finally, in the end, Yahweh does not forget. Such a reading points us to our fourth and final text.

4. Thus far, all three texts (Ps 22:1; Lam 5:20; Isa 49:14) have been on the lips of Israel. This fact still allows for the claim that Yahweh "seemed" to Israel to abandon, that Israel "experienced" abandonment, but in fact Israel had it wrong and was not abandoned by Yahweh. Such a reading is of course possible, but it goes well beyond the plain sense of the text, which offers no qualification or ambiguity about the accusation. In our fourth text, Isa 54:7–8, that possible "protection" of Yahweh from the accusation of Israel is excluded, for now the word *'azab* is on the lips of Yahweh.[14] The poetry utilizes the image of barren wife, abandoned wife, and widow.[15] Already in v. 6, the term *'azab* is used parallel to "cast off" (*ma'as*), both terms as passive participles, affirming that Yahweh has taken the disruptive actions.

In vv. 7–8, Yahweh continues to speak in the first person:

> For a brief moment I abandoned you (*'azabtik*) . . .
> In overflowing wrath, for a moment I hid my face (*histarti*) from you.

The two terms ("abandoned, hid") are straightforward and unambiguous. Yahweh did abandon! Yahweh has abandoned Israel and readily admits it. In these verses, moreover, no blame is assigned to Israel as cause of the abandonment, though Yahweh says, "in overflowing wrath." From the text itself, this "wrath" could as well be capriciousness on the part of Yahweh as righteous, warranted indignation.

To be sure, these two admissions whereby Yahweh concedes that Israel has been abandoned are promptly countered by two assurances:

14. On this text, see Brueggemann, "Shattered Transcendence?"

15. Mintz (*Hurban*, 23–25) suggests that the use of the image of raped, dying woman rather than dead woman is used in order that the suffering, pain, and grief may be on-going and not yet (or ever) terminated. "The raped and defiled woman who survives . . . is a living witness to a pain that knows no release."

with great compassion (*raḥamim*) I will gather you . . .

with everlasting love (*ḥesed 'olam*) I will have compassion
on you (*riḥamtik*).

It is profoundly important that the two positives do not nullify the two
negatives, as the positive may nullify the negative in 49:14–15. Here the
statements refer to a sequence of actions and experiences, whereby compassion comes after an acknowledged abandonment. This is reinforced by
the term "again" (*'od*) in v. 9 which admits one abandonment but assures
that there will not be a second one. This use of *'od* is closely paralleled to
its use in Gen 8:21 and 9:11, which admits that there has indeed been one
angry flood, but there will not be another (cf. Isa 54:10).

This fourth text, Isa 54:7–8, belongs in the same theological horizon
as Ps 22:1; Lam 5:20; and Isa 49:14—all of which are preoccupied with
Israel's experience of bereftment caused by Yahweh's unwarranted inat-
tentiveness. This fourth text, however, is of another sort, because it is in
Yahweh's own mouth and because Yahweh concedes that compassion and
everlasting love come *after* the abandonment.

Now all of this is commonplace and well established in Crenshaw's
work. My intent is not to establish an exegetical point that is already
amply recognized by readers of Israel's text. It is rather to inquire about
what to do with such texts in reading communities that want to override
them with sweeping assurances about Yahweh's presence, fidelity, and
graciousness. Thus my study is an exercise in adjudicating the tension
between large theological claims and the awkward specificity of texts.

Five Unworkable Strategies

There is no doubt that these assertions about Yahweh's abandoning activity are problematic for any theology that wants finally to assert the unambiguous fidelity of God. A variety of interpretive strategies are available
and much practiced whereby these troublesome texts can be overcome,
but in each case the alternative strategy does not appear to take the direct
statement of the text with full seriousness. They may be regarded as adequate resolutions of the problem, unless one is intensely committed to
facing the concreteness of the text, a commitment that we may take to be
important for any responsible reading of the text.

We may identify five such strategies that are frequently employed:

1. It is easiest and most common simply to *disregard such texts*. It is for the most part impossible to make use of all texts in any interpretive reading, or all texts at once, and surely impossible to attend to all of them if one wants to present a "seamless" reading, for the text itself is disjointed and disruptive and filled with contradictions, ambiguities, and incongruities. They render the text as a whole "unreadable" on our usual theological readings.[16]

On the basis of that "unreadable" textual reality, reading communities of every kind, including church communities (but also academic communities), tend to be selective. Indeed, it is my judgment that serious readers tend to be "selective fundamentalists," whether theological readers liberal or conservative, or critical readers. That is, readers pick out texts on the basis of hidden or explicit criteria, take those texts with great attentiveness or even urgency, and let the other texts drop out of the working repertoire. An easy example, of course, is the church's lectionary, which operates around such principles that even some verses in the chosen texts are habitually silenced. Part of recent hermeneutical activity is the insistence that those silenced, dismissed texts must be sounded again.

2. The unsettling character of Yahweh is justified by *the sin of Israel*, thus suggesting that God's silence, absence, wrath, or infidelity is warranted in light of Israel's sin and disobedience.[17] This interpretive posture posits a tight moral structure, so that Yahweh responds with precision to moral affront.[18] There are of course many texts that support such a view.

There are other texts, however, including those that we have cited, that do not claim such an exact calculus or even suggest Israel's culpability. Moreover, there are texts (such as Job) that voice an unsettling response of Yahweh that is disproportionate to any available affront. There are sufficient texts to warrant the judgment that there is a wild dimension

16. On our "usual theological readings" that render texts "unreadable," see Handelman, *The Slayers of Moses*. Handelman's study informs much of the argument of my paper.

17. This is, for example, the affirmation of the hymn "Holy, Holy, Holy" by R. Heber:

> Holy, holy, holy! though the darkness hide thee,
> Though the eye of sinful man thy glory may not see . . .

On that assumption, God is not absent but only unseen because of sin.

18. On such a "tight moral structure," see Koch, "Gibt es ein Vergeltungsdogma im Alten Testament?"; and an abridged English translation, "Is There a Doctrine of Retribution in the Old Testament?"; and the more nuanced discussion of Miller, *Sin and Judgment in the Prophets*.

to Yahweh's unsettled character that runs well beyond any tight moral equation. Israel's experience of Yahweh's unsettled character runs well beyond moral justification when the texts are taken seriously.

3. There is a great propensity to explain away the unsettling aspect of Yahweh (in our case, abandonment) by claiming that the accusation made against Yahweh and the desperate plea for presence addressed to God are a case of *human misperception and mistakenness*. That is, God "seems" to be abandoning but in truth is not. Such a human "experience" is asserted by Israel in good faith, and there may be a "subjective" dimension of reality to this claim, but it is theologically not true. It is only in the eyes of the beholder.

This is, of course, not as difficult to claim in our first three cases (Ps 22:1; Lam 5:20; Isa 49:14) because the statements are all on the lips of Israel, and no data is offered beyond the "sense" of the speaker. Thus resort is often taken to the stratagem that claims that this is only "human speech," which is not finally reliable. The case is more difficult in Isa 54:7–8, where the utterance is Yahweh's own—that is, an oracle that purports to be God's utterance. Even here, of course, critical awareness can readily claim that this speech is "human speech," done by a human author, in this case "Second Isaiah," so that even this more insistent affirmation is explained away as not theologically reliable.[19]

This common interpretive procedure, however, is deeply problematic. It appeals to theological-dogmatic convictions nowhere grounded in the particular texts but imposed upon the text in order to dismiss a reading that on the face of it is not in doubt. Moreover, if one explains away as "human and mistaken" such self-assertions made by Yahweh, one is hard put to draw the line and treat with seriousness the textual self-disclosures of Yahweh that one prefers. It may be claimed that the dismissal of the assertion is "canonical"—that is, read in relation to many

---

19. This is from time to time the strategy of John Calvin. On these verses, Calvin (*Commentary on the Book of the Prophet Isaiah*, 140) writes:

When he says that he forsook his people, it is a sort of admission of the fact. We are adopted by God in such a manner that we cannot be rejected by him on account of the treachery of men; for he is faithful, so that he will not cast off or abandon his people. What the Prophet says in this passage must therefore refer to our feelings and to outward appearance, because we seem to be rejected by God when we do not perceive his presence and protection. And it is necessary that we should thus feel God's wrath . . . But we must also perceive his mercy; and because it is infinite and eternal, we shall find that all afflictions in comparison of it are light and momentary.

other texts that say otherwise and are judged to be more central.[20] Such a claim, however, is characteristically reductionist and flattens the dialectic that, in my judgment, belongs properly to canonical reading.[21]

4. A more subtle approach to this same "subjective" verdict voiced in the text is the logical, philosophical claim that even though Yahweh is genuinely "experienced" as one who abandons, the experience of God's abandoning contains within it an assumption of cosmic, primordial presence, thus giving us *a dialectical notion of "presence in absence" or "absence in presence."*[22] That is, even speculation about God's abandoning absence (which never posits God's non-existence) affirms God's "background" presence even in experienced absence. This is, I take it, a quite sophisticated form of a "subjective–objective" distincion, which seeks to honor fully the *lived experience* of Israel, while at the same time guarding against an *ontological* dismissal of God that Israel would not countenance. This strategy is based upon the theological affirmation that there would be no world without God, no world in which to issue compaint and accusation against God, for the world is "held into existence" by God.

This is a powerful and logically coherent position, and I have no desire to combat it. I sugggest only that: a) that it is a way of reasoning that is subtle in ways that Israel would not entertain; and b) it requires a judgment that is against the clear, uncomplicated, and unreserved statement of the text. As a result, even after this argument, we are still left with our guiding question, What shall one do with texts such as these?

5. Finally, a popular stratagem is an appeal to the "evolution" of "the religion of Israel" that includes *the "evolution" of Yahweh,* the subject of that religion. That hypothesis proposes that Israel's religion and Israel's God "developed" from primitivism to the nobility of "ethical monotheism," culminating, perhaps, in Second Isaiah. Thus, there may have been a time when Yahwism (and Yahweh) were understood in quite primitive terms.

---

20. This is the perspective of Childs, *Biblical Theology of the Old and New Testaments.*

21. The whole matter of a "canonical reading" is not obvious in its meaning. Childs himself has, over time, suggested a variety of different dimensions to the notion of "canonical" and, as far as I am aware, only in his most recent book, *Biblical Theology of the Old and New Testaments,* has he concluded that "canonical" means according to a theological "rule of faith."

22. I am grateful to my colleague, Shirley Guthrie, for clarifying this point for me. He and I have had fruitful exchanges about this matter. In the end, I suspect we do not agree. Nonetheless, I have come to understand better because of his instruction, and I am able to rethink matters in ways reflective of his persuasive and gentle influence.

There may have been a time when Yahweh was excessively "dark" in terms of capriciousness, infidelity, violence, absence, and silence. But Yahweh has "evolved" toward fidelity, peaceable generosity, justice, and forgiveness.

That hypothesis of course has been duly critiqued as a reflection of Hegelianism or a reflection of a nineteenth-century milieu dominated by something like Darwinism.[23] Nonetheless, there is, of course, something substantive to the hypothesis, as there regularly is in any hypothesis that captures scholarly imagination over a long period of time. It is the case that there are important changes in the character of Yahweh. Moreover, given a certain literary analysis, one can insist upon a directional inclination to that change. It is the most standard critique of the hypothesis that the change is said to be progressive and unilaterally developmental. In addition to that claim, the critique that is most important for our purpose is the correlative of progressive developmentalism, that as each *novum* appears in the character of Yahweh, the previous portrayals of the character of Yahweh may be sloughed off as now irrelevant and "superceded."

I shall want to insist in what follows that textually, there is no supersessionism, but that what has transpired in the life of Yahweh endures as text, and therefore as data for theological understanding. This remembered character of Yahweh continues to exercise important influence over the whole of Israel's articulation of Yahweh. Specifically, because Israel has texts of God's abandoning, which it evidently has, the character of Yahweh never outgrows or supersedes that remembered reality, which continues to be present textually and therefore substantively both for Yahweh and the community of Yahweh. As a consequence, neither Yahweh nor the interpreters of Yahweh may pretend that such behavior has no happened in the ongoing life of Yahweh with Israel, and may not act as though these textual markings do not continue to be present and available to Yahweh in Yahweh's life with Israel.

Thus I suggest that all five strategies—disregard of such texts, justification through sin, judgment that it only "seems so," philosophical subtlety, and evolutionary supersessionism—are unpersuasive approaches to the problem. Each of these attempts arises from a theological impetus that lies outside the horizon of the text itself, and each of them imports a conviction that is contrary to the unmistakable claim of the text itself. All of these inadequate strategies seek to protect the character of Yahweh from the passionate experience and conviction of Israel with Yahweh.

23. For a recent assessment of Wellhausen, see Knight, ed., *Julius Wellhausen and His Prolegomena to the History of Israel.*

Israel is clear that Yahweh need not and cannot be protected; Yahweh must run the risks that belong to Yahweh's way of being present/absent in the memory and life of Israel.[24]

An Alternative Interpretive Response

I propose now to suggest an alternative interpretive response to these texts of abandonment and, by implication, to all texts that testify to Yahweh's unsettling character.

1. An alternative approach to these unsettling texts will need to move from a metaphysical to a dramatic approach to interpretation. A conventional approach to Christian theology that posits a "nature of God" with which to challenge these texts apparently operates with a notion of a God "out there" who exists independent of these texts.[25] Such a view may be plausible from some other perspective, but it is of little help in taking the specificity of the biblical text seriously. Such a posited "nature" outside of the text stands as a criterion with which to justify or explain away a text without facing its concrete claim seriously. Indeed, such an approach cannot take such texts with theological seriousness, because matters are settled on grounds other than the text and in other arenas.

A consequence of such an approach is that we are still left with the problem: what to do with the text. An alternative approach that shuns the escape of a metaphysical criterion is to take the texts in a dramatic way, as a script for a drama.[26] The biblical text then becomes "the real thing" in terms of plot and character, and there is no appeal behind the text or elsewhere. On such a perspective, when God asserts, "For a brief moment I have abandoned you," we have a God who abandons Israel for a brief moment. That is what Yahweh says, what Yahweh does, and who Yahweh is.

The move toward a dramatic sense of the text permits the reading community to stay with the terms of the text, even with its contradictions,

24. For a dramatic understanding of Yahweh that moves in a postcritical direction, see Patrick, *The Rendering of God in the Old Testament*.

25. It is my impression that in his most recent work, *Biblical Theology of the Old and New Testaments*, Childs attends to the problem of referentiality in a way that results in a God "out there."

26. On a dramatic mode of theological interpretation, see, in addition to Patrick, the work of Hans Frei, and Brueggemann, *Texts under Negotiation*. Most broadly, see von Balthasar, *Theo-Drama* (2 vols.).

incongruities, and unwelcome lines. Thus the text is "unreadable," not because of a poor redactional outcome, but because the subject and character who dominates the plot does not conform to our flattened reading propensity, theological or critical. The character who has once uttered these lines and committed these acts remains always the character who has once uttered these lines and committed these acts. There is more to this character than these particular lines, but these lines become inescapably part of who this character is, no matter what other renderings, actions, and utterances may follow. That is, this approach comes to the text prepared to treat the text "realistically" and "literally," if "literal" means not "factual," not canonically reduced, but according to the concrete utterance of the text.[27]

2. But consider what it means to take the text "realistically." I have found Richard Lanham's distinction between *homo seriosus* and *homo rhetoricus* enormously helpful.[28] Lanham characterizes the model interpreter in this way: "The serious man possesses a central self, an irreducible identity. These selves combine into a single, homogeneously real society which constitutes a referent reality . . . This referent society is in turn contained in a physical nature itself referential, standing 'out there,' independent of man."[29] By contrast, "Rhetorical man is an actor; his reality public, dramatic. His sense of identity, his self, depends on the reassurance of daily histrionic reenactment. He is thus centered in time and concrete local event. The lowest common denominator of his life is a social situation. And his motivations must be characteristically lucid, agonistic . . . He is thus committed to no single construction of the world; much rather, to prevailing in the game at hand."[30] The important difference is that the "serious man" appeals to an "out there" reference. It is a curious fact that common cause in this category includes those who grasp at metaphysics and the "historical critics" who assess the rhetoric of the text in terms of an outside historical reference. Both metaphysicians and historical critics trim and shave the rhetoric of the text to fit some other criterion. By contrast, those who value rhetoric in a central way recognize that speech constitutes reality in some decisive way. The world of "Rhetorical man" is

27. Childs ("The *Sensus Literalis* of Scripture") has offered a most provocative understanding of "literal sense." Childs, of course, knows that his view is not without problem and is not uncontested.

28. Lanham, *The Motives of Eloquence*.

29. Ibid., 1.

30. Ibid., 4.

"teeming with roles, situations, strategies, interventions, but . . . no master role, no situation of situations, no strategy for outflanking all strategies . . . no neutral point of rationality from the vantage point of which the 'merely rhetorical' can be identified and held in check."[31]

It is clear that this dispute is as old as Plato's and Aristotle's dispute with the Sophists. And it is clear that our dominant educational, intellectual tradition is a powerful advocacy toward Plato and Aristotle and a facile dismissal of the Sophists, without attending to the powerful ways in which even Plato and Aristotle are rhetoricians.[32] Thus the critique of Fish goes further than that of Lanham. It suggests that even the "serious man" in fact makes a claim for reality in terms of the effectiveness of utterance.

What to do with the "unsettling texts" depends on where one is in this dispute between rhetoric and "seriousness." If one seriously assumes a reference out there, then these texts must be disregarded, toned down, justified, or explained away in order to suit that outside reference. If we take rhetoric as constitutive, however, then the reference "inside the drama" must yield to these texts and take them with defining seriousness. Richard Rorty makes this distinction:

> There are two ways of thinking about various things . . . The first . . . thinks of truth as a vertical relationship between representations and what is represented. The second . . . thinks of truth horizontally—as the culminating reinterpretation of our predecessors' reinterpretation of their predecessors' reinterpretation . . . It is the difference between regarding truth, goodness, and beauty as eternal objects which we try to locate and reveal, and regarding them as artifacts whose fundamental design we often have to alter.[33]

Fish concludes, of Rorty's verdict, "It is the difference between serious and rhetorical man. It is the difference that remains."[34]

My argument here, which seems to me inescapable if the texts are to be taken seriously, and if Crenshaw is correct about the persuasive intentionality of speech, is that rhetoric constitutes the character of Yahweh.[35]

31. Fish, "Rhetoric," 215.

32. For a recent reconsideration of the Sophists, see Jarratt, *Rereading the Sophists.* I am grateful to Perky Daniel for this reference and for suggesting this line of reflection to me.

33. Rorty, *Consequences of Pragmatism*, 92; quoted by Fish, "Rhetoric," 221.

34. Fish, "Rhetoric," 222.

35. Crenshaw, "Wisdom and Authority." On the constitutive power of speech, see

And so the Yahweh of the Bible is indeed an unsettling character who does abandon and who acts sometimes in unfaithfulness. Focus on the text rather than on a reference "out there" gives us no character other than this one.

3. But we are not yet agreed on what it means to take the text seriously or how to take the text seriously. I cite two interpreters who well articulate what I regard as two quite distinct alternative approaches.

In his "canonical approach" to the text, Brevard Childs is a "serious" reader who does indeed take the text seriously. That is beyond question. In a series of books, Childs has pondered "canonical" reading.[36] In his most recent and most mature book, it is now clearer than in his earlier work, that Childs means by "canonical" reading the text according to Christian doctrinal norms and categories.[37]

> It is one thing to suggest that biblical scholars have not adequately resolved the problem of biblical referentiality; it is quite another to suggest that it is a non-issue. Moreover, I would argue that the attempt of many literary critics to by-pass the problem of biblical reality and refuse to distinguish between text and the reality of its subject matter severely cripples the theological enterprise of Biblical Theology. It is basic to Christian theology to reckon with an extra-biblical reality, namely with the resurrected Christ who evoked the New Testament Witness. When H. Frei, in one of his last essays, spoke of "midrash" as a text-creating reality, he moved in a direction, in my opinion, which for Christian theology can only end in failure.[38]

In his response to Stanley Hauerwas and James Barr, Childs concludes that "'narrative interpretation' avoids for a time the difficult problems of referentiality involved in the term history . . . In a word, the term 'story' is not strong enough to support the function assigned to the Bible. Indeed Christians have always believed that we are not saved by a text or

---

Brueggemann, *Israel's Praise*, 1–53.

36. Childs, *Biblical Theology in Crisis*; Childs, *The Book of Exodus*; Childs, *Old Testament Theology in a Canonical Context*; and Childs, *Biblical Theology of the Old Testament and New Testament*.

37. Childs, *Biblical Theology of the Old Testament and New Testament*, 20, 67, 724.

38. Ibid., 20. On the problem of "reference" with particular attention to Frei, *The Eclipse of Biblical Narrative*; and Frei, "The 'Literal Reading' of Biblical Narrative in the Christian Tradition." On Frei's work vis-à-vis Childs, see Sheppard, *The Future of the Bible*, 41–42; and Campbell, *Preaching Jesus*.

by a narrative, but by the life, death, and resurrection of Jesus Christ in time and space."[39]

It becomes clear that Childs's understanding of God in the text, an "extrabiblical reality," is not construed or nuanced according to the deail of the text but is a reference that is known apart from and at times over against the text. This theological reference must move "from a decription of the biblical witnesses to the object toward which these wittesses point, that is, to their subject matter, substance, or res."[40] Childs's comments following this statement indicate that he is aware of the dangers in what he suggests, but he proceeds on that basis. Childs is interested in "the reality constitutive of these biblical witnesses."[41] That "reality" is not only "testified to in the Bible." It is "that living reality known and experienced as the exalted Christ through the Holy Spirit within the present community of faith."[42] In a Christological formulation of the kind that Childs makes central to his perspective, the text as such is subordinated to other claims. A consequence is that the "unsettling texts" exercise almost no influence on Childs's interpretation and argument.

A sharp contrast to the approach of Childs occurs in the powerful work of David Blumenthal, who takes his beginning points from the brutality of the Holocaust.[43] In contrast to the "canonical reading" of Childs, Blumenthal reads texts "*seriatim* . . . one after another, one by one in succession, which matches the way we live. We live *seriatim*."[44] This approach yields an accent upon "caesura, fragmentedness, irruption"—of course, the very matters that Childs wants to exclude.[45]

With relentless determination, Blumenthal insists on attending to all of the texts: "By contrast, I choose to engage seriously the texts as we have received them . . . There is, thus, for me, a certain sacredness to the tradition, prima facie, and I try to work within it. For this reason, I reject attempts to 'clean up' the Psalms, to interpret away the rage, to make them more 'pious.'"[46] Blumenthal mentions, as I have also, that his-

---

39. Childs, *Biblical Theology of the Old Testament and New Testament*, 665.

40. Ibid., 80.

41. Ibid., 83.

42. Ibid., 86.

43. Blumenthal, *Facing the Abusing God*.

44. Ibid., 47–48. See Jack Miles, *God: A Biography*, on a seriatim reading throught the whole Old Testament canon.

45. Ibid., 9.

46. Ibid., 239.

toricism and an assumption of moral evolution are two ways to dispose of parts of the text with which one does not agree.[47] Of course, he rejects any such maneuver. By attending seriatim to all of the texts, Blumenthal comes to the interpretive conclusion that the God of the Bible "is abusive, but not always."[48] In any case, he makes much room for unsettling texts that Childs drops from purview.

It is important that both Blumenthal and Childs allow for plurivocity in the text. Blumenthal judges, "In the end, the text has more than one meaning, the reader reads on more than one level, and the teacher teaches more than one meaning. Text and life itself are multifaceted; interpretation is multidimensional. piurivocity is normal; not hierarchy, not the single authoritative teaching . . . Plurivocity is, thus, not only normal; it is normative, it is what the norm should be."[49] Childs agrees, "There is a 'reader response' required by any responsible theological reflection."[50] But Childs of course qualifies such an allowance. "Yet it is crucial to theological reflection that canonical restraints be used and that reader response be critically tested in the light of different witnesses of the whole Bible . . . There is a biblical rule of faith which sets the standard for family resemblance . . . Once the task of discerning the kerygmatic content of the witnesses has been pursued, it is fully in order to offer an analogical extension of this kerygmatic message by means of a modern reader response."[51] This qualification of course causes Childs to part decisively from Blumenthal, in the end, concerning unsettling texts.

A Näively Realistic View

This still leaves us with the question, what to do with these texts that are there, as Blumenthal insists, but texts that are enormously problematic, as Childs insists. My suggestion is that we take a "näively realistic" view of the text as a "script" of Yahweh's past. Such näiveté, for this purpose, overrides our critical judgments. Without a hypothesis of moral evolution, it is clear that Yahweh "moves on" as a character in the text, as any character

47. Ibid.

48. Ibid., 247.-48.

49. Ibid., 239.

50. Childs, *Biblical Theology of the Old Testament and New Testament*, 335.

51. Ibid., 335–36.

surely will move on in the drama.[52] Thus these texts are in Yahweh's past, but they are at the same time assuredly in Yahweh's past. I propose, with an analogue from "the enduring power of the past" in therapeutic categories, that these "past texts" are enduringly painful memories still available to the character of Yahweh, mostly not operative, but continuing to work even in the present. They must therefore be taken seriously even in the canonical, "final form" of the text.

This means that a "truer" picture of Yahweh cast in canonical or theological form has moved beyond these texts but has not superseded these texts, just as no human person understood in depth ever supersedes or scuttles or outgrows such ancient and powerful memories. There lingers in the character of Yahweh ancient memories (texts) that belong to the density of Yahweh and that form a crucial residue of Yahweh's character. Yahweh may not be, in a "truer" "canonical" understanding, a God who abandons. But this past marking of Yahweh is still potentially available in the current life of Yahweh (for the text lingers) and must in any case be taken as a crucial part of the career of Yahweh. Yahweh cannot simply will away this past, nor can the interpreters of Yahweh.

For the interpreting community (especially for the religious communities of interpretation but also for the academic community) that intends to face the fullness of the text, the witness to Yahweh and the interpreters of the witness must take into full account that past and those memories that are in important ways still present, available, and potentially operative. This in turn suggests that it is faithful to the text and healthy for the reading community that there is in this shared, read past an unsettling dimension that has wounded, troubled, and betrayed those with whom Yahweh has to do. This past of wound, trouble, and betrayal, moreover, still tells in the present. I suggest that such a recovery of the past is not like "critical excavation," for it is not a past that is over or finished but a past that persists like any such held script.[53] Full embrace of these texts permits the interpretive community to embrace fully its theological past, which is marked by abandonment (and other dimensions). It is not necessary to claim that such an unsettling dimension is normative or presently operative but only that it has been there in the past and continues to be present in the present. Thus the God of "steadfast love and mercy" is at the same time also the God who has abandoned, and all

52. See Patrick, *The Rendering of God in the Old Testament*, 28–60.

53. See the comment of Alter, *The World of Biblical Literature*, 133, on "excavative" reading.

current steadfastness bears the wounding mark of that ancient, undenied reality.

Such an interpretive strategy affirms that the canonical text is indeed the full telling of the tale of Yahweh, a tale that has odd and unpleasant dimensions to it.

1. As an interpretive perspective, such a procedure permits some thematic closure in the direction that Childs wants to go but not such closure that it eliminates the candor of the text itself, which has generated the candor of Blumenthal. It occurs to me that while many historical critics insistently resist Childs's closure, they finally make common cause with Childs, though for very different reasons. Childs tends to shave the text to fit "the creed," whereas historical critics have tended to shave the text to fit Enlightenment reasonableness that wants to eliminate disruption and incongruity in the text. Neither "canonical" nor "critical" readers entertain the näiveté to permit a rendering of the text as the dramatic reality of this God with this people.

2. But my main concern is not interpretive theory. Rather my concern is pastoral responsibility, the kind of pastoral responsibility that belongs to any "classic" read in a theologically serious interpretive community.[54] First, I propose that seeing these texts as a past pertinent to the present, even if now suppressed or denied, permits the interpretive community to see fully who Yahweh has been and potentially is. There is no cover-up of who this God is, no notion that this character can be made to conform to our preferred Enlightenment or orthodox categories of reading. A "second näiveté" permits the reading community to take this God with theological seriousness in all of Yahweh's consternating Jewishness, in all of Yahweh's refusal of domestication.[55]

Second, if this character be understood as a real live agent who concerns the life of the reader or the reading community, the reader is thereby authorized and permitted to entertain unsettling dimensions of one's own life (or one's community) as palpable theological dimensions of reality. Both canonical and critical reading that fend off the unsettling texts encourage denial and cover-up of the intimate savageness of life. But when the reading community can see that brutality, abusiveness, and abandonment are live and present in the past of this God, it is credible to

54. Tracy, *The Analogical Imagination*, has explored a notion of "classic" as a category for religious texts.

55. The term "second näiveté" is Ricoeur's. See Wallace, *The Second Näiveté*.

take the same dimension in one's own life as past realities that continue to have potential power in the present.

It is not at all my intention to take a therapeutic or instrumental approach to the character of Yahweh. Nonetheless, theological, interpretive, textual candor does have important pastoral consequences. The only way beyond such woundedness is through such woundedness. This ancient woundedness perdures in text and in life. But when voiced and accepted, as the text invites us to do, the ancient woundedness is robbed of its present authority. As long as one pretends that these texts are not "back there," a terrible denial is required, which denies movement into a healing present and a healed future.

It is a delight to honor James Crenshaw, who has thought and written most persistently and most honestly about this unsettling side of the text and its God. Crenshaw has indeed shown us that critical analysis and pastoral realism can live close together. Together they can make a pact to engage in denial and cover-up. But they need not. This text, when read without too many protections (canonical or critical), does not protect in such ways. A refusal to deny or censure invites the movement of this Character and the reading community into new dimensions of peaceableness.

Bibliography

Albrektson, Bertil. *Studies in the Text and Theology of the Book of Lamentations*. Studia Theologica Lundensia 21. Lund: Gleerup, 1963.

Alter, Robert. *The World of Biblical Literature*. New York: Basic Books, 1992.

Balthasar, Hans Urs von. *Theo-drama: Theological Dramatic Theory I, Prolegomena*. San Francisco: Ignatius, 1988.

———. *Theo-drama: Theological Dramatic Theory II, The Dramatis Personae*. San Francisco: Ignatius, 1990.

Blumenthal, David R. *Facing the Abusing God: A Theology of Protest*. Louisville: Westminster John Knox, 1993.

Brueggemann, Walter. *Israel's Praise: Doxology against Idolatry and Ideology*. Philadelphia: Fortress, 1988.

———. "James L. Crenshaw: Faith Lingering at the Edges." *Religious Studies Review* 20.2 (1994) 103–10.

———. "Shattered Transcendence? Exile and Restoration." In *Biblical Theology: Problems and Prospects*, edited by Steven J. Kraftchick et al., 169–82. Nashville: Abingdon, 1995.

———. *Texts under Negotiation: The Bible and Postmodern Imagination*. Minneapolis: Fortress, 1993.

Calvin, John. *Commentary on the Book of the Prophet Isaiah*. Translated by William Pringle. Calvin's Commentaries 8. Grand Rapids: Baker, 1979.

Campbell, Charles L. *Preaching Jesus: Hans Frei's Theology and the Contours of a Post-liberal Homiletic*. Grand Rapids: Eerdmans, 1997.

Childs, Brevard S. *Biblical Theology in Crisis*. Philadelphia: Westminster, 1970.

———. *Biblical Theology of the Old and New Testaments: Theological Reflection on the Christian Bible*. Minneapolis: Fortress, 1992.

———. *The Book of Exodus: A Critical Theological Commentary*. OTL. Philadelphia: Westminster, 1974.

———. "The *Sensus Literalis* of Scripture: An Ancient and Modern Problem." In *Beiträge zur alttestamentlichen Theologie: Festschrift für Walther Zimmerli zum 70. Geburtstag*, edited by Herbert Donner et al., 80–93. Göttingen: Vandenhoeck & Ruprecht, 1977.

Crenshaw, James L. "Wisdom and Authority: Sapiential Rhetoric and Its Warrants." In *Congress Volume: Vienna 1980*, edited by J. A. Emerton, 10–29. VTSup 32. Leiden: Brill, 1981.

Davis, Ellen F. "Exploding the Limits: Form and Function in Psalm 22." *JSOT* 53 (1992) 93–105.

Desmond, Adrian, and James Moore. *Darwin*. New York: Viking Penguin, 1991.

Fish, Stanley. "Rhetoric." In *Critical Terms for Literary Study*, edited by Frank Lentricchia and Thomas McLaughlin, 203–22. Chicago: University of Chicago Press, 1990.

Frei, Hans W. *The Eclipse of the Biblical Narrative: A Study in Eighteenth and Nineteenth Century Hermeneutics*. New Haven: Yale University Press, 1974.

———. "The 'Literal Reading' of Biblical Narrative in the Christian Tradition: Does It Stretch or Will It Break?" In *The Bible and the Narrative Tradition*, edited by Frank McConnell, 36–77. New York: Oxford University Press, 1986.

Gerstenberger, Erhard S. *Der bittende Mensch: Bittritual und Klagelied des Einzelnen im Alten Testament*. WMANT 51. 1980. Reprinted, Eugene, OR: Wipf & Stock, 2010.

Hall, Douglas John. *Toward an Indigenous Theology of the Cross*. Philadelphia: Westminster, 1976.

Handelman, Susan A. *The Slayers of Moses: The Emergence of Rabbinic Interpretation in Modern Literary Theory*. SUNY Series on Modern Jewish Literature and Culture. Albany: SUNY Press, 1982.

Hillers, Delbert R. *Lamentations*. Anchor Bible 7A. Garden City, NY: Doubleday, 1972.

Jarratt, Susan C. *Rereading the Sophists: Classical Rhetoric Refigured*. Carbondale: Southern Illinois University Press, 1991.

Knight, Douglas A., ed. *Semeia* 25: *Julius Wellhausen and His Prolegomena to the History of Israel*. 1983.

Koch, Klaus. "Gibt es ein Vergeltungsdogma im Alten Testament?" *ZTK* 52 (1955) 1–42. Reprinted in *Um das Prinzip der Vergeltung in Religion und Recht des Alten Testaments*, edited by Klaus Koch, 130–80. Wege der Forschung 125. Darmstadt: Wissenschaftliche Buchgesellschaft, 1972.

———. "Is There a Doctrine of Retirbution in the Old Testament?" In *Theodicy in the Old Testament*, edited by James L. Crenshaw, 57–87. IRT 4. Philadelphia: Fortress, 1983.

Kselman, John S. "'Why Have You Abandoned Me?' A Rhetorical Study of Psalm 22." In *Art and Meaning: Rhetoric in Biblical Literature*, edited by David J. A. Clines et al., 172–98. JSOTSup 19. Sheffield: JSOT Press, 1982.

Lanham, Richard A. *The Motives of Eloquence: Literary Rhetoric in the Renaissance*. New Haven: Yale University Press, 1976.

Levenson, Jon D. *Creation and the Persistence of Evil: The Jewish Drama of Divine Omnipotence*. San Francisco: Harper & Row, 1988.

Linafelt, Tod. *Surviving Lamentations: Catastrophe, Lament, and Protest in the Afterlife of a Biblical Book*. Chicago: University of Chicago Press, 2000.

Miles, Jack. *God: A Biography*. New York: Knopf, 1995.

Miller, Patrick D. *Sin and Judgment in the Prophets: A Stylistic and Theological Analysis*. SBLMS 27. Chico, CA: Scholars, 1982.

Mintz, Alan. *Hurban: Responses to Catastrophe in Hebrew Literature*. New York: Columbia University Press, 1984.

Moltmann, Jürgen. *The Crucified God: The Cross of Christ as the Foundation and Criticism of Christian Theology*. Translated by R. A. Wilson and John Bowden. Minneapolis: Fortress, 1993.

Patrick, Dale. *The Rendering of God in the Old Testament*. OBT. Philadelphia: Fortress, 1981.

Ricoeur, Paul. "Biblical Hermeneutics." *Semeia* 4 (1975) 107–45.

Rorty, Richard. *Consequences of Pragmatism: Essays 1972–80*. Minneapolis: University of Minnesota Press, 1982.

Sheppard, Gerald T. *The Future of the Bible: Beyond Liberalism and Literalism*. Toronto: United Church Publishing House, 1990.

Tracy, David. *The Analogical Imagination: Christian Theology and the Culture of Pluralism*. New York: Crossroad, 1981.

Wallace, M. I. *The Second Naiveté: Barth, Ricoeur, and the New Yale Theology*. Studies in American Biblical Hermeneutics 6. Macon, GA: Mercer University Press, 1990.

5

A Characteristic Reflection
on What Comes Next

(Jer 32:16–44)

It is a delight to offer an essay in acknowledgment of Gene Tucker's major contribution to our common life of teaching and scholarship. For me, as for many others, he has been a reliable and generous source of support and encouragement.

In his Yale dissertation and in derivative studies, Tucker paid attention to "contracts," including the contractual arrangement of Jeremiah in his purchase of his family's patrimony (Jer 32:1–15).[1] Tucker's investigation concerned the form of the contract itself and therefore he did not venture into 32:16–44, which I now propose to take up. Whereas his interest was primarily form-critical, my own study is concerned with this "supplement" to the narrative of contract as a piece of characteristic theological reflection in the faith of ancient Israel.

A possible way to organize a theology of the Old Testament/Hebrew Bible is to pay attention to the most "characteristic" speech of Israel about God.[2] By such rhetoric, I refer to frequently recurring phrases, words, and themes which Israel regularly employed in what appear to be

---

1. Tucker, "The Legal Background of Genesis 23"; and Tucker, "Covenant Forms and Contract Forms." In the latter article Tucker mentions the narrative of Jer 32:1–15.

2. Brueggemann, "Crisis-Evoked." For such characteristic speech, Fisch (*Poetry with a Purpose*, 188) uses the happy term "covenantal discourse." In such characteristic speech, we may identify the modes of the "grammar" of Israel's faith.

situations of urgency, when Israel is forced back to its most reliable rhetorical resources.[3] To be sure, a judgment about what is "characteristic" is to some extent subjective. I believe, nonetheless, that such a procedure would have served von Rad well in his credo hypothesis.[4] Instead of arguing, as he unsuccessfully did, that the credo recitals are very early, he might have argued only that they are "characteristic," thus avoiding the insoluble problems of historicity. Here I focus on Jer 32:16–44 in order to examine the ways in which it articulates what is characteristic in the faith-rhetoric of Israel.

Authenticity and Allusion

The literature upon these verses is not very extensive nor very helpful.[5] It is largely preoccupied with two questions: (1) a determination of what is "authentic" and what is "expansion" from the words of the prophet, and (2) what allusions to preceding literature can be identified as the "sources" of the present phrasing.[6]

On the first question, scholars are largely predictable in their conclusions. William Holladay seeks to match text to occasion with some precision, and Robert Carroll regards the text as an exercise in late scribal activity.[7] Christopher Seitz is surely in broader sweep correct that the whole is a "concluding supplement," whereby a specific reference to the land has been transposed into a general statement about Israel's fu-

---

3. I have recently explored the ways in which rhetoric is decisive for the faith and theological work of Israel, that is, a speech practice not dependent upon any "essentialism"; Brueggemann, "Texts that Linger, Not Yet Overcome."

4. Von Rad, *The Problem of the Hexateuch and Other Essays*, 1–78. There are now many well-established critiques of von Rad's program. Among the earliest of these was Hyatt, "Were There an Ancient Historical Credo in Israel and an Independent Sinai Tradition?" Miller, *The Divine Warrior*, 166–70, facing von Rad's problem on the credo, has alternatively suggested Exodus 15 as a candidate for model credo; but he still seeks "early" and not "characteristic" speech.

5. In addition to the influential commentaries of Holladay (*Jeremiah*) and Carroll (*Jeremiah*), studies pertinent to our text include Diepold, *Israel's Land*; Nicholson, *Preaching to the Exiles*; Seitz, *Theology in Conflict*; Wanke, *Untersuchungen zur sogenannten Baruchschrift*; and Weippert, *Die Prosareden des Jeremiabuches*. None of these studies, however, deals with this text in any extensive way at all.

6. These issues are carefully and thoroughly reviewed by Holladay, *Jeremiah 2*, 202–20.

7. Carroll, *Jeremiah*, 625 and passim.

ture.[8] For our purposes, the delegitimation of what is not "authentic" is inappropriate and unhelpful, for we are concerned with the rhetorical-theological shape and intention of the whole.

A like answer to the second question, identification of allusions to extant sources, may be given.[9] It is beyond doubt that these verses are a veritable collage of antecedent usages. It is, however, their present configuration and function that interest us. Thus on neither question need issues of "excavative" criticism long detain us.[10]

Prayer and Response

It is of course recognized that these verses, which no doubt had a complex literary history, are divided into two forms, a prayer of Jeremiah (32:16–25) and an oracular response by Yahweh (vv. 26–44). Scholars have of course recognized that the opening verse of the prayer (v. 17) and the opening verse of the oracle (v. 27) are paralleled in their common use of the term *pela'*, which in the NRSV is rendered "too hard."[11] It is curious, and perhaps worth noting, that the use of *pela'* in the prayer is an indicative assertion, and in the response it is a question. These two uses are perhaps inverted from what we might expect. The form of prayer and oracular response might have led us to expect a question in the prayer and an assertion in the oracle, but the text has it otherwise. It will be my plan to take up in turn the prayer and the oracle, and then to consider the function of the whole, after the narrative of contract in vv. 9–14 and after the remarkable oracle of promise in v. 15.

Theodicy as Pastoral Crisis

The first part of our text is cast as a prayer of Jeremiah (32:16–25). While the casting of the prayer is not unimportant, it is important to recognize,

8. Seitz, *Theology in Conflict*, 212 n. 13.

9. On these allusions, which may take a variety of forms, see Hays, *Echoes of Scripture in the Letters of Paul*, 18–20 and passim. Hays takes over the notion of literary "echoes" from J. Hollander.

10. Alter (*The World of Biblical Literature*, 133; *The Art of Biblical Narrative*, 13–14) uses the term "excavative" to refer to reading methods that approach the biblical text by way of philology, archaeology, and comparative ancient religions.

11. Holladay (*Jeremiah 2*, 206) suggests that Gen 18:14 is the source for both vv. 17 and 27. On the Genesis text, see Brueggemann, "'Impossibility' and Epistemology."

with Samuel Balentine, that prayers in prose texts of the Old Testament/Hebrew Bible can serve "as a means of conveying ideological and theological perspectives."[12] At that level this prayer, in the mouth of the prophet, is an exercise of Israel's recurring issue of theodicy. The issue of theodicy, in the world of ancient Israel, is not, as it has become in the modem world, a speculative problem. It is rather a concrete pastoral theological crisis, because Israel, with Job-like determination, clings passionately and relentlessly to the conviction that coherent moral sense can be made of its lived experience by reference to the will, purpose and commands of Yahweh. Were Israel to give up that conviction, the practical problem of theodicy would evaporate: but of course Israel cannot and will not give it up.

Following Greenberg, Balentine rightly insists that such prayers must be understood in their narrative context.[13] Thus, even if vv. 16–25 are "late" and "expansionist" in context they are evoked by the preceding narrative which jarringly articulates Israel's sense of incongruity between lived reality and Yahweh's voiced purpose. The incongruity concerns the lived experience of destruction and displacement and the voiced purpose of rehabilitation and resettlement. Israel, moreover, has no way to process this incongruity except to reuse its classic modes of rhetoric in daring and venturesome ways.

The intention of the prayer is to enter faithfully and unflinchingly into that profound incongruity, and to see what sense can be made. One can characterize the mood of the prayer as one of trustful incredulity, that is, the praying voice takes the command and promise of v. 15 as "absurd,"[14] but at the same time obeys and does not doubt. In coping with this deep incongruity, which is context-specific to 32:1–15 but which is also paradigmatic for Israel's faith, the prayer must mobilize Israel's rich resources of rhetoric that here are brought together in a remarkable theological statement.[15] Thus it may be that there is "literary growth" here, but in the final form of the text, one must ask how these several rhetorical

---

12. Balentine, *Prayer in the Hebrew Bible*, 12.

13. Ibid., 27. See Greenberg, *Biblical Prose Prayer*, 8.

14. See Carroll, *Jeremiah*, 625.

15. Carroll (ibid., 621) regards the entire narrative about the purchase of the land as a "paradigmatic account." Because of that, Carroll regards the historical character of the event as being undermined. For my purpose, I am content to disregard the question of historicity and work with what is the ostensive history of the text.

strategies together serve Israel's faith in the face of Yahweh's staggering reversal of intention.

We may identify five rhetorical strategies, that is, characteristic modes of speech, which together constitute the prayer.[16]

1. After the narrative introduction of v. 16, the prayer is set in the context of *doxology* (vv. 17, 18b–19a). The opening ejaculation, 'ahah, is a cry which characteristically responds to an unexpected divine announcement, most often negative.[17] The doxology focuses upon Yahweh's strength and power, as evidenced in the creation of heaven and earth. (As we shall see, there is a dimension of creation theology here, used to enhance Yahweh's splendor. That accent is not nearly as prominent in the oracle which follows.) It is the doxology about the wonder of creation that leads to the affirmation that Yahweh is *pela'!* Creation itself is confirming evidence that Yahweh is capable of anything (*kol-dabar*), anything regarded by humankind as "impossible."[18] The doxology continues in vv. 18b–19a with the assertion:

> O great and mighty God whose name is Yahweh of hosts, great
> in counsel and mighty in deed; whose eyes are open to all the
> ways of mortals . . .

Yahweh is extolled for power and for watchful monitoring of the whole of creation. The language here appears to be influenced by sapiential traditions, for Yahweh is thus the guarantor and orderer of all of creation.[19]

2. The doxology of vv. 17, 18b–19a is intertwined in vv. 18a, 19b with a different, though not unrelated, pattern of rhetoric. In these two

16. I choose here to speak of "rhetorical strategies." In a paper honoring Gene Tucker, it is important to recognize that what have come to be called rhetorical strategies are in fact closely related to literary forms, on which see Tucker, *Form Criticism of the Old Testament*. I prefer the much more dynamic nomenclature of "strategy," because we are inquiring about what the text intends to accomplish.

17. See the other texts in BDB, 13.

18. The phrase "Yahweh of Hosts" is missing from the LXX. Here and in a number of places the MT of our chapter is longer. None of these differences, however, distract from my argument. On the comparison of texts, see Janzen, *Studies in the Text of Jeremiah*.

19. It is not unproblematic to identify something as "sapiential," as Crenshaw has made clear. I refer to the theological claim that Yahweh is the upholder and guarantor of an order that is both cosmic and moral, and not one who intrudes with concrete acts. The contrast has been well articulated by Westermann, *Elements of Old Testament Theology*, Part III. It is not clear that this is necessarily "sapiential." See Schmid, *Gerechtigtkeit als Weltordnung*.

half verses, reference is made to the ancient formula of Exod 34:6–7, which articulates *a structure of "deed–consequence"* concerning God's commands.[20] This formulation, deeply rooted in the tradition of Moses, voices a two-sidedness if not contradiction in Israel's faith. God does *ḥesed* (cf. Exod 34:6a). This text, however, does not linger over that positive affirmation. Its intent, rather, is in the two verbs, *šlm* and *pqd*, which seem to pick up themes from Exod 34:7b, concerning tight moral accountability.[21] Thus right into the next generation, just deserts are assured, especially negative ones. The provision for *ḥesed* is not negated, but *ḥesed* is clearly marked by a requirement of reciprocity. The prayer thus far has set in close juxtaposition a doxology and a statement of *rigorous covenantal accountability*. It has, however, exhibited no interest in the relation between the two statements.

3. In the long middle section of this passage (32:20–23a), the prayer makes use of the elements of a *well-established credo*.[22] The key elements in the recital, of course are deliverance from Egypt and entry into the land. The latter point is grounded in the promise to the ancestors.[23] It is worth noting here the language of "sign and wonder," terms not unrelated to *pela'* in v. 17. In this usage, the rhetoric is completely confined to Israel's communal experience. It includes nothing of a more comprehensive (creation) horizon, as is found both in the doxology and in the derivative use of the deeds–consequence formulation of Exod 34:6–7, which in this text speaks of "all the ways of the sons of *'adam*" (v. 19). Here the rhetoric is drawn much closer to the specific content of Israel's glorious past, which concretely attests to Yahweh's capacity to do "hard things."

4. As might be expected in the tradition of Jeremiah–Deuteronomy, the unreservedly positive recital of 32:20–23a is quickly broken off.[24] It

20. The classic presentation of this construct is that of Koch, "Gibt es ein Vergeltungsdogma im Alten Testament?" See also an abridged version in English "Is There a Doctrine of Retribution in the Old Testament?"

21. Koch ("Is There a Doctrine of Retribution in the Old Testament?" 60–61, 75–78) pays attention to both of these verbs. In n. 40, Koch acknowledges his debt to Fahlgren, *Ṣedaka.*

22. See n. 4 above. Von Rad's credo hypothesis has been reiterated in many places, and has now been critiqued as well in many places.

23. On the crucial nature of the ancestral narratives for the "Mosaic events" of the credo, see Moberly, *The Old Testament of the Old Testament.*

24. I have chosen simply to speak of the tradition of "Jeremiah–Deuteronorny." The complexity of the relation between Jeremiah and the Deuteronomic tradition is yet to be sorted out. Here I simply refer to that entire complex tradition without

is followed in vv. 23b–24 with an abrupt adversative waw, which introduces a *lawsuit form*. The indictment is filled out with three negatives,
"not listen," "not walk in," "not do." Israel is completely recalcitrant and
unresponsive to Yahweh's actions.

The indictment is matched by a sentence, also introduced with an
abrupt *waw* (v. 23b), rendered in NRSV by "therefore." Oddly enough,
the sentence stays in the voice of the prayer and addresses the punishing
God in the third person, "you summoned." After the general announcement of "evils" (disasters) (v. 23b), the sentence consists in the specificity of the siege-ramps of the Babylonians, and then is generalized by the
stylized formulary, "sword, famine, pestilence." In a quite brief statement,
the covenant curses have been voiced in three distinct ways: disasters,
siege-ramps, and sword/famine/pestilence.

We have seen that the prayer does not trouble over the tension between doxology and the assertion of tight moral accountability as deeds–
consequence. Now, in parallel fashion, the prayer does not linger over the
devastating juxtaposition of positive recital (vv. 20–23a) and the harsh lawsuit (vv. 23b–24) which seems to negate the recital.[25] Such a juxtaposition
compels the reader to conclude that Jerusalem has come to its final ending
in sword, famine and pestilence, without any sustaining power from those
old remembered deeds. Such a sequence of recital/lawsuit presents a complete and coherent theodicy. "Evil" comes from doing "evil." Evil evokes
God's response in kind.[26] Such a way of reasoning provides a demonstrable
vindication of the tight moral reasoning of vv. 18b–19a, which allude back
to Exod 34:7b. Yahweh "will by no means clear the guilty, but visiting the
iniquity of the parents." The two terms "iniquity" (*'wn*) and "visit" (*pqd*) in
these verses are the same as in Exod 34:7b. Yahweh is serious and cannot
be mocked. Jerusalem has come to its rightful termination, as already fore-
warned in the oldest Mosaic tradition. The entire tradition of Jeremiah–
Deuteronomy has been aimed at such a theodic conclusion.

5. Such a conclusion, however, does not yet reckon with the context in which the prayer is set. In v. 25, we encounter yet another abrupt

---

needing to probe those complexities.

25. On the negation and inversion of the credo, see the way in which the language
of Exodus is turned against Israel in Jer 21:5–6. See Moran, "The End of the Unholy
War and the Anti-Exodus."

26. Miller (*Sin and Judgment in the Prophets*) has explored this understanding of
covenantal curse and prophetic sentence. Miller has also included a close critique of
Koch's notion of "deed–consequence."

waw, which turns the cogent theodicy of vv. 18b, 19b–24 on its head by a reiteration of the earlier divine oracle of v. 15.[27] Verse 25 seems to jump over the carefully wrought theodic statement of the main body of the prayer, back to the initial doxology of v. 17. Here again is the foundational address, *"'adonai* YHWH," we heard in v. 17. And here again is the full pronoun *"attah,* addressed to Yahweh as in v. 17. And here again is a reference back to Yahweh's magisterial performance. In v. 17, it is "you made," here it is "you said." The two assertions form an envelope around the more conventional theodicy and appeal to the creating, asserting God who is capable of anything (*kol-dabar*), even an "impossibility." The primal impossibility of v. 17 is "the heavens and the earth."

Now the impossibility is "Buy the field . . . though" (v. 25).[28] In truth, Yahweh did not utter the imperative "buy" in this verse, as is here claimed. It was Jeremiah's cousin Hanamel who spoke the word as an imperative (vv. 7–8), but his utterance is taken as "the word of the Lord" (v. 8). The instruction to buy contradicts everything on the horizon, the current reality of Babylonian occupation as well as Israel's carefully reasoned theodicy which justifies a harsh ending wrought by Yahweh.

The carefully framed structure of the prayer in five elements is:

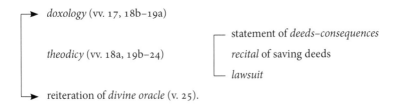

The completed prayer takes into full account Israel's normal covenantal reasoning which squares completely with the current situation of Jerusalem. The whole makes coherent sense of faith and experience, both of which now face an exhausted, drastic ending. The purpose of the prayer, however, is to confront both experience and tradition by a new disclosure that is rooted in doxology and eventuates in a coming possibility, authorizing a present human act of daring obedience. This divine oracle

27. It is worth noting that while v. 25 alludes back to the oracle of v. 15, in fact it is not strictly a reiteration. In v. 15, the key verb "buy" (*qnh*) is in the niph'al, but in v. 25 it has become a qal imperative. The form in v. 25 is consistent with the narrative use of the verb in vv. 7–8, in the mouth of Hanamel.

28. The term rendered "though" in the NRSV helps to make sense of the adversative force in the verse, but in fact the Hebrew is yet again a powerful *waw*.

of command and promise is not rooted either in the old tradition of covenant or in the present circumstance of defeat, but is a new utterance.

The prayer thus makes use of Israel's most trusted, characteristic theological rhetoric in order to utter a newness that violates all trusted rhetoric. The arrangement of the theodicy in the main body of the prayer (vv. 18a, 19b–24) had permitted the lawsuit to veto the recital. The lawsuit had won. Except for the God of *pela*'! The wonder of all creation in v. 17 comes down to a specific transaction that the context defines as nonsensical. In the end, this explosive rhetoric pushed Israel out of its perceived context into a world grounded only in the speech of the God for whom nothing is too hard.

Four Yahweh Words

The oracle of Yahweh (vv. 26–44) is positioned to be a response to the prayer of vv. 16–25.[29] No indication is given in the text, however, that the oracle is a response. But if my reading is correct, that the affirmation of Yahweh's *pela*' in v. 17 leads to the command of v. 25 which overrides the conventional rhetoric of vv. 19b–24, then a response from Yahweh is not inappropriate. Verse 25 converts the promise of v. 15 into an imperative. But the prayer appears to end in v. 25 with a puzzlement. The speaker cannot fathom that in the face of the theodicy of vv. 19b–24, the command of v. 25 is uttered. What can it mean? How shall it be understood? Is it serious? Is it possible? Shall it be acted upon? In the present arrangement of the text, we may take the two large units as prayer and response, even if the oracle was originally independent, or added only later to this expanded text.

As prayer and response, we may notice, the structural arrangement is not unlike that of the book of Job. In the book of Job, there are three primary voices, the explanatory friends, the unaccepting Job, and the lordly resolution.[30] Here the explanatory element of faith is voiced in vv.

29. For purposes of convenience, I shall refer to all of vv. 26–44 as "an oracle." While all its parts belong to that form of speech, the several "messenger formulae" indicate that it is no single speech. Treatment of it in the singular is convenient for contrasting it with the preceding prayer, but my analysis will consider each element separately.

30. On these voices, see Brueggemann, "The Third World of Evangelical Imagination." Wharton ("The Unanswerable Answer") has seen that even though the response of Yahweh in Job 38:1ff. is severe and uncompromising, it is a response, which is what

19b–24, and the voice beyond convention is in vv. 17, 25. And now comes the lordly resolution.

The oracle is marked by four messenger formulae in vv. 26, 28, 36, and 42, perhaps signs of ongoing supplementation and expansion. I will consider each of these units separately, even though they are not proportionate in length to each other.

1. The first messenger formula in v. 26 introduces only the brief, freighted statement of v. 27. This initial and abrupt statement of Yahweh consists in three parts. First, there is the ejaculatory particle, *hinneh*. Secondly, there is the self-assertion of Yahweh as "the God of all flesh." And thirdly, there is a rhetorical question (in the same form as Gen 18:14), enquiries about Yahweh's capacity to do *pela'*. The three elements function in the present setting in ways that correspond to the three elements of v. 17 in the prayer: (1) the ejaculatory particle is matched in v. 17 by *'ahah*, (2) there is a doxology about creation, and (3) an assertion of *pela'*. Thus the oracle, like the prayer, begins with a sweeping assertion, rooted in the wonder of creation, here signified by "all flesh." This doxological claim is then extended to any and all *pela'*. The God who governs "all flesh" can indeed do "all things" (*kol-dabar* in v. 17). The sentence in v. 27 concerning *pela'*, unlike the parallel statement in v. 17, is not an assertion but a question. It may be that this is simply a rhetorical question. Or it may be a serious probing question which intends to evoke an answer and a commitment from the one who prays.[31] In either case, the subject is again surfaced, but with much less of a conclusive statement.

2. The much longer speech, introduced by the second messenger formula of v. 28, concerns a lawsuit speech (vv. 28–35). As one might expect, the sentence concerning the fate of the city at the hands of the Babylonians is interwoven with a series of massive indictments. The sentence is confined to vv. 28–29a and 31b and concerns the sure destruction of the city. The indictment is much more extensive (vv. 29b–31a, 32–35). The indictment remains general through v. 33, even though there is specificity about the list of perpetrators in v. 32. The governing language of the Deuteronomic tradition concerns "evil, provoke, arouses, evil, provoke." The only specificity is found in vv. 34–35 concerning the abomination and high places, offering to Molech, but even that statement

---

Job most wanted and sought.

31. On the possibility of this intention for rhetorical questions on the lips of Yahweh, see Janzen, "Metaphor and Reality in Hosea 11." Holladay (*Jeremiah 2*, 212) suggests that the question is ironic.

is stylized.[32] The only other element is the characteristic exceptionalism that Yahweh did make special efforts concerning Judah but these also were resisted (cf. 2 Kgs 17:18–20).

The outcome and intent of this second "message" is that Judah is locked with Yahweh into a hopeless process of disobedience and commensurate punishment. The oracle does not indicate that the destruction of Jerusalem is itself a *pela'* but we may infer that this event is an unthinkable wonder which was judged to be "impossible." It is unthinkable, but surely credible in Yahweh's world of *šlm* and *pqd*, given us in the prayer (vv. 18–19). Thus again, we have a self-contained, all-encompassing theodicy which leaves no element unaccounted for.

3. The third messenger formula (v. 36) is clearly the decisive one in this long oracle. Unlike the other three formulae, it is introduced with *we'attah* and marks a decisive discontinuity from the preceding utterances.[33] The MT has *laken* (lacking in LXX) which is a curious use given the non sequitur which follows. What comes now is not "therefore." It comes from nowhere, except out of the unfettered mouth of Yahweh.

The subject of this third message is again the city, the one just under massive nullification in vv. 28–31. The city is the one under the formulaic abuse of "sword, famine, pestilence" (cf. v. 24). Verse 36, however, treats all of this negativity only as a dependent clause. The main clause begins in v. 37 with a marker, *hinni* (cf. v. 27). The utterance now introduces three new and powerful verbs:

> I will gather,
>> I will return,
>>> I will settle.

These verses do not deny what has previously been said (and experienced), for they are voiced in an immediate context of "anger, wrath, and indignation."[34] But now, the culminating point is *lbth* ("in safety").

32. For a possible historical-theological understanding of the offering of children to Molech, see Levenson, *The Death and Resurrection of the Beloved Son*, 3–52. We can see in these indictments a move from the general and stylized to the concrete, just as we have seen in the sentences in vv. 23b–24.

33. Muilenburg ("The Form and Structure of the Covenantal Formulation") has, in passing, pertinent observations on the particle *we'attah*.

34. In speaking of what Jerusalem "experienced," I refer to the ostensible experience reflected in the text. Such an "experience" may indeed be fictive, and it may be that the notion of "exile" is primarily an ideological concept. I do not claim more than what is in the text itself for "experience," which may indeed be ideology-generated.

Because of these three verbs, all will be well. There is no explanation given, no linkage to the rightful punishment just announced, but a new announcement, preceded only by a magisterial messenger formula.

This startling assertion, surely a *pela'* as wondrous as anything in the old recital, is reinforced by a series of assertions in vv. 38–41 which bespeak the making of new covenant. In v. 38, the standard "covenant formula" is uttered which figures so prominently in the exilic hope of the books of Jeremiah and Ezekiel.[35] This formula is followed by the promise of "one heart" and "one way," whereby Israel (Judah, Jerusalem) will be gladly committed to obedience, with a positive inclination and without any resentful grudge or resistance.[36] That new obedience, moreover, will yield "good," that is, covenant blessings.[37]

The rhetoric of new covenant and its blessing is intensified in vv. 40–41, so that the "new heart" and "new way" and the covenant formula are now heightened with the adjective *'olam*—"everlasting covenant"—in which Yahweh will never turn from doing "good" and Israel will never depart from "fear of me." Both parties are revived to a new and glad mutual fidelity that will not again be disrupted. This remarkable promise, surely apela', is reinforced in two ways. First, the term *b'emth* (v. 41) corresponds to *lbth* in v. 37. Israel will rest *in security*, Yahweh will plant *in fidelity*. Secondly, the final phrase of v. 41 is typically the phrasing of the tradition of Deuteronomy, "with all my heart and all my soul." Except that here the terms pertain to Yahweh's own intense and unreserved resolve for fidelity toward Israel. This is a most extreme and singular commitment on the part of Yahweh. It is not clear that the "everlasting covenant"[38] is "unconditional."[39] Perhaps, in good Deuteronomic fashion, it is conditional upon obedience to torah. But Israel's "one bean" and "one way" affirm that Israel will never depart from the torah, and therefore the

35. On the formula, see Smend, *Die Bundesformel* [ET = "The Covenant Formula."]

36. The modifier "one" for heart and way is rendered variously in the versions. It is possible that instead of *'hd* a Hebrew text had *'hr* or *hdš*, thus to read "other" or "new." Clearly such variants give the phrase a very different nuance, though the intent in any case is clear.

37. On the term "good" as "covenant blessing," see Hillers, "A Note on Some Treaty Terminology in the Old Testament"; Moran, "A Note on the Treaty Terminology of the Sefire Stelas."

38. See n. 36 for this possible rendering.

39. On the problem of the "unconditional," see Post, "Conditional and Unconditional Love"; and Wrong, *The Problem of Order*, 42–54.

conditions are assuredly met and the covenant will not and need not be disrupted. That is, the conditions are not abrogated, but guaranteed.

4. The fourth messenger formula (v. 42) introduces one more assurance which becomes fully concrete after the more relational, covenantal language of vv. 36–41. In v. 24, Yahweh's resolve for "good" will overcome the "evil" asserted in vv. 28–35.[40] The term "good" is continued from vv. 39–41 where it is used three times. The term in the foregoing is undifferentiated, but now "good" is made quite specific. The reference to "field" in v. 43 refers back to the promise of v. 15 and the imperative of v. 25.[41] That singular promise in the niph'al of v. 15 (unlike the qal imperative in v. 25) is then fully expanded in v. 44, so that "field" becomes the several geographic regions of Judah and Benjamin, that is, David's patrimony. Finally the whole is tied to ch. 31 (v. 23) and to ch. 33 (vv. 7, 11, 26) by the key phrase "restore their fortunes."[42]

In light of my more detailed comments on vv. 16–25, we may now summarize the rhetorical strategies employed in this complex and multifaceted oracle:

1. Verse 27 is a self-announcement of Yahweh which we may take as self-praise, that is, doxology in Yahweh's own mouth. The tone is not unlike the whirlwind speeches of the book of Job.

2. The long second message is a lawsuit speech, an intermingling of indictment and sentence, with primary emphasis upon the former (vv. 28–35).

3. The decisive turn in the passage, with a series of strong verbs, is an anticipatory recital of God's transformative, rescuing action which is to come.

4. The tight covenant formulation of vv. 38–41 is not easy to categorize, because the rhetoric is quite complex. For our purposes, I suggest it is a revisitation of the old deed–consequence construct of covenantal obedience. This time, however, it is altogether positive. thus the old assumptions about Israel's recalcitrance which caused the construct to be

---

40. On the displacement of "evil" by "good" in the tradition of Jeremiah, see 29:11; 42:6.

41. The term "field" is singular as it is in v. 25, whereas it is plural in v. 15. The singular seems to stay much closer to the initial command in vv. 7–8 which did refer to a particular field. The plural moves beyond this particular reference in a paradigmatic direction. The versions make adjustment in the term.

42. On this formula and its intention for Israel's hope, see Bracke, "The Coherence and Theology of Jeremiah 30–31," 148–55.

used primarily for threat and open-ended uncertainty are now overcome by an assurance, in which both parties are sure to do the right deeds and yield the best consequences.

     5. The final message of vv. 42–44 is a promissory oracle of impossibility.

Intention and Construction

The analysis of rhetorical strategies I have presented makes it clear in some detail that the intention and construction of the prayer and the oracle are closely paralleled. Scholars have of course noted the parallelism concerning *pela'* in vv. 17 and 27. We may observe the following, fuller parallelism which is reasonably comprehensive of both passages:

Prayer	Oracle
doxology (vv. 11, 18b–19a)	self-praise as doxology (v. 27)
formula of "deeds–consequence" (vv. 18a, 19b)	formula of "deeds–consequence" is now made positive (vv. 38–41)
a recital of memory (vv. 20–23a)	a recital of anticipation (vv. 36–37)
lawsuit speech (vv. 23b–24)	lawsuit speech (vv. 28–35)
oracle of impossibility (v. 25)	oracle of impossibility (vv. 42–44)

It is not my intention to suggest that these two texts are completely parallel in either form or substance, nor to force parallels in an excessively rigorous way. Two qualifying comments are especially important First, the second element which I have entitled "formula of deed–consequence" may be the least compelling parallel. In the prayer this element is governed by the verbs *šlm* and *pqd*, which together make a clear case. Such language is absent in vv. 38–41. I suggest a parallel because vv. 38–41 clearly envision complete obedience and its contingent, unmitigated "good." These verses do not suggest that torah obedience is any less urgent now or in time to come than it was under the aegis of Moses, but only that such obedience is now assured. The important difference between the old economy of obedience and the new is that vv. 38–41 leave no uncertainty or option, as is reflected in v. 18a, 19b and in the formula more generally. But that difference makes all the difference in the envisioned time of well-being which is to come.

Secondly, the recital in vv. 20–23a is conventional and standard. I am not sure that it is correct to teriil vv. 36–37 a recital, but it does depend upon Yahweh's active verbs, as does the old recital. The difference of course is that what is there stated is all promised and anticipated, not yet in band and therefore not remembered. This recital anticipates that Yahweh's verbs will create bth, well-being not unlike the circumstance of "milk and honey" wrought in the events of Moses and Joshua.

Rhetorical Strategies

It is not my purpose to do a form-critical analysis, but to observe complex rhetorical strategies which permit theological reflection and affirmation in ancient Israel.[43] This rich array of quite distinct forms and rhetorical maneuvers may suggest a process of expansion in this extended text. My impression, however, is that the use of such rhetorical strategies is necessary, not merely to extend the statement, but in order to express exactly the delicate point to be made among exiles concerning the present state of Judah and its future potential intended by Yahweh.

The text does not want to depart from the heavy claims of Israel's old convictions concerning the moral shape and moral accountability of the historical process. This is evident in the prayer, in the formula of deeds and consequences, in the nullification of the old recital and in the lawsuit speech, that is, in all those elements I have termed "theodicy." In the oracle, the lawsuit of vv. 28–35 makes the same point at great length.

This extended reassertion of an insistence upon the moral shape and accountability of Israel's public life, however, does not say everything that here wants to be said. There is in ancient Israel a deep sense of the tension between Yahweh's free capability and Yahweh's steady system of sanctions. The theological intention of both prayer and oracle is to affirm that system of sanctions, but then to give voice to the odd ("impossible") capacity of Yahweh to break out beyond Yahweh's own system

43. The volume of Forms of the Old Testament Literature (Eerdmans) for Jeremiah has not yet appeared, so we await that detailed analysis. In the meantime I am in fundamental agreement with Collins ("Is a Critical Biblical Theology Possible?") that biblical theology must begin with and pay close attention to genre analysis. That is what I have sought to do in this essay.

of sanctions. The categories for that "breaking beyond" are, in terms of rhetoric, doxology, promise, oracle, and substantively, *pela'*.

By juxtaposing this rich arrangement of available rhetorical strategies, the text evidences how much depends upon utterance, and how diverse and dense are Israel's rhetorical possibilities, in order to bear witness to Yahweh's fragile order (creation, moral coherence) in which Israel lives and to the delicate possibilities that constitute Israel's world of faith. The abrupt shifts of rhetoric, for example in vv. 25, 36, leave Israel staggered, perhaps breathless (but not speechless). We subsequent readers are left to ponder: what if some scribe (or whoever) had not hosted such profound rhetorical incongruity . . . what then? But, of course, someone did.

Conclusion

In its final form, Jeremiah 32, ostensibly a comment on land purchase, is in truth a mediation upon Yahweh's *pela'*. This peculiar chapter of narrative and prose speech is odd amidst a series of poetic promises in chapters 30–31 and 33. Chapter 32 is odd because it is partly narrative and all prose, and because it concerns such a specific act as the purchase of land. Its purpose is to move Israel to the edge of "covenantal nomism," and then to plunge beyond it into newness, as Israel had to do in exile.[44] Such breaks beyond the conventional system of covenantal sanctions are not easy or assured. They are hard fought and hard won, partly growing out of Yahweh's resolve and partly out of Israel's daring speech. The chapter moves exiled Israel along to a possibility as wondrous as the creation of "heaven and earth," "for all flesh," as concrete as a field signed, sealed and witnessed.

This carefully shaped theological mediation takes on larger canonical power, as subsequent readers are not concerned with Jeremiah's specific patrimony. In adjudicating the odd interface between wondrous creator and beloved creation, this theological reflection asserts the inexplicable chance for newness. That odd interface concerns system and sanction, and perhaps more. The "more" so readily mocked, yet so greatly treasured by synagogue and church, is the "more" which Israel still bespeaks to a fated, shut-down world.

---

44. The term "covenantal nomism" is taken from Sanders, *Paul and Palestinian Judaism*, 511–15 and passim. The term is of course an anachronism with reference to Jeremiah 32, but I believe it accurately connotes what must be affirmed about the requirement of the commandments in emerging Judaism.

It is my impression and urging that in this text we encounter much of Israel's "characteristic speech." Of course the old recital, the formulation of deeds and consequences, and the lawsuit speech are characteristic. That characteristic speech is broken by a more deeply required speech about *pela'*. This speech, because of the Utterer, also becomes characteristic in Israel. In speech about *pela'*, however, it is Israel's rhetorical work to insist that what seems to be characteristic, *pela'*, is in fact every time inscrutable, inexplicable and uncharacteristic. Israel's rhetorical imagination serves to employ its characteristic ways of speech about this Holy Uncharacteristic Possibility.

Professor Tucker knows all this. I hope he will find my move from form to faith a credible one, for the legitimacy of our discipline as a public enterprise depends upon some such maneuver.

Bibliography

Alter, Robert. *The Art of Biblical Narrative*. New York: Basic Books, 1981.

———. *The World of Biblical Literature*. New York: Basic Books, 1992.

Balentine, Samuel. *Prayer in the Hebrew Bible: The Drama of Divine-Human Dialogue*. OBT. Minneapolis: Fortress, 1993.

Bracke, John Martin. "The Coherence and Theology of Jeremiah 30–31." PhD diss., Union Theological Seminary, Richmond, 1983.

Brueggemann, Walter. "Crisis-Evoked, Crisis-Resolving Speech." *BTB* 24 (1994) 95–105. Reprinted in Brueggemann, *Deep Memory, Exuberant Hope: Contested Truth in a Post-Christian World*, edited by Patrick D. Miller, 91–109 + 135–38. Minneapolis: Fortress, 2000.

———. "'Impossibility' and Epistemology in the Faith Traditions of Abraham and Sarah (Genesis 18.1–15)." *ZAW* 94 (1982) 615–34.

———. "Texts that Linger, Not Yet Overcome." In Brueggemann, *Deep Memory, Exuberant Hope: Contested Truth in a Post-Christian World*, edited by Patrick D. Miller, 77–90. Minneapolis: Fortress, 2000. (Chap. 4 in this volume.)

———. "The Third World of Evangelical Imagination." *HBT* 8/2 (1986) 61–84.

Carroll, Robert P. *Jeremiah: A Commentary*. OTL. Philadelphia: Westminster, 1986.

Collins, John J. "Is a Critical Biblical Theology Possible?" In *The Hebrew Bible and Its Interpreters*, edited by William Henry Propp et al., 1–17. Biblical and Judaic Studies 1. Winona Lake, IN: Eisenbrauns, 1990.

Diepold, Peter. *Israel's Land*. BWANT 5/15. Stuttgart: Kohlhammer, 1972.

Fahlgren, K. Hj. *Ṣedaḳa: Nahestehende und entgegengesetzte Begriffe im Alten Testament*. Uppsala: Almquist & Wiksell, 1932.

Fisch, Harold. *Poetry with a Purpose: Biblical Poetics and Interpretation*. ISBL. Bloomington: Indiana University Press, 1988.

Greenberg, Moshe. *Biblical Prose Prayer as a Window to the Popular Religion of Ancient Israel*. Berkeley: University of California Press, 1983.

Hays, Richard B. *Echoes of Scripture in the Letters of Paul*. New Haven: Yale University Press, 1989.

Hillers, Delbert R. "A Note on Some Treaty Terminology in the Old Testament." *Bulletin of the American Society of Oriental Research* 116 (1964) 46–47.

Holladay, William L. *Jeremiah: A Commentary on the Book of the Prophet Jeremiah*. 2 vols. Hermeneia. Philadelphia: Fortress, 1986, 1989.

Hyatt, J. Philip. "Were There an Ancient Historical Credo in Israel and an Independent Sinai Tradition?" In *Translating and Understanding the Old Testament: Essays in Honor of Herbert Gordon May*, edited by Harry Thomas Frank and William L. Reed, 152–70. Nashville: Abingdon, 1970.

Janzen, J. Gerald. "Metaphor and Reality in Hosea 11." *Semeia* 24 (1982) 7–44.

———. *Studies in the Text of Jeremiah*. HSM 6. Cambridge: Harvard University Press, 1973.

Koch, Klaus. "Gibt es ein Vergeltungsdogma im Alten Testament?" *ZTK* 52 (1955) 1–42. Reprinted in *Um das Prinzip der Vergeltung in Religion und Recht des Alten Testaments*, edited by Klaus Koch, 130–80. Wege der Forschung 125. Darmstadt: Wissenschaftliche Buchgesellschaft, 1972.

———. "Is There a Doctrine of Retribution in the Old Testament?" In *Theodicy in the Old Testament*, edited by J. L. Crenshaw, 57–87. IRT 4. Philadelphia: Fortress, 1983. (Abbreviated version of the German article.)

Levenson, Jon D. *The Death and Resurrection of the Beloved Son: The Transformation of Child Sacrifice in Judaism and Christianity*. New Haven: Yale University Press, 1993.

Miller, Patrick D. Jr. *The Divine Warrior in Early Israel*. HSM 5. Cambridge: Harvard University Press, 1973.

———. *Sin and Judgment in the Prophets: A Stylistic and Theological Analysis*. SBLMS 27. Chico, CA: Scholars, 1982.

Moberly, R. W. L. *The Old Testament of the Old Testament: Patriarchal Narratives and Mosaic Yahwism*. OBT. Minneapolis: Fortress, 1992.

Moran, William L. "The End of the Unholy War and the Anti-Exodus." *Bib* 44 (1963) 333–42.

———. "A Note on the Treaty Terminology of the Sefire Stelas." *JNES* 22 (1963) 173–76.

Muilenburg, James. "The Form and Structure of the Covenantal Formulation." *VT* 9 (1959) 347–65.

Nicholson, E. W. *Preaching to the Exiles: A Study of the Prose Tradition in the Book of Jeremiah*. Oxford: Blackwell, 1970.

Post, Stephen G. "Conditional and Unconditional Love." *Modern Theology* 1 (1991) 435–46.

Rad, Gerhard von. *The Problem of the Hexateuch and Other Essays*. Translated by E. W. T. Dicken. Edinburgh: Oliver & Boyd, 1966. Republished as *From Genesis to Chronicles: Explorations in Old Testament Theology*. Edited by K. C. Hanson. FCBS. Minneapolis: Fortress, 2005.

Sanders, E. P. *Paul and Palestinian Judaism*. Philadelphia: Fortress, 1977.

Schmid, H. H. *Gerechtigkeit als Weltordnung*. BHT 40. Tübingen: Mohr/Siebeck, 1968.

Seitz, Christopher R. *Theology in Conflict: Reactions to the Exile in the Book of Jeremiah*. BZAW 176. Berlin: de Gruyter, 1989.

Smend, Rudolf. *Die Bundesformel*. Theologische Studien 68. Zurich: EVA-Verlag, 1963. ET = "The Covenant Formula." In Smend, *'The Unconquered Land' and*

Other Essays: Selected Studies, edited by Edward Ball and Margaret Barker, 41–72. Translated by Margaret Kohl. Society for Old Testament Study. Burlington, VT: Ashgate, 2013.

Tucker, Gene M. "Covenant Forms and Contract Forms." *VT* 15 (1965) 487–503.

———. "The Legal Background of Genesis 23." *JBL* 85 (1966) 77–84.

———. *Form Criticism of the Old Testament.* Guides to Biblical Scholarship. Philadelphia: Fortress, 1971.

Wanke, Gunther. *Untersuchungen zur sogenannten Baruchschrift.* BZAW 122. Berlin: de Gruyter, 1971.

Weippert, Helga. *Die Prosareden des Jeremiabuches.* BZAW 132. Berlin: de Gruyter, 1973.

Westermann, Claus. *Elements of Old Testament Theology.* Translated by Douglas W. Stott. Atlanta: John Knox, 1978.

Wharton, James A. "The Unanswerable Answer: An Interpretation of Job." In *Texts and Testaments: Critical Essays on the Bible and Early Church Fathers: A Volume in Honor of Stuart Dickson Currie*, edited by W. Eugene March, 37–70. San Antonio, TX: Trinity University Press, 1980.

Wrong, Dennis H. *The Problem of Order: What Unites and Divides Society.* New York: Free Press, 1994.

6

A Shattered Transcendence?
Exile and Restoration

THE EXILE—AS EVENT, EXPERIENCE, memory, and paradigm—looms large over the literature and faith of the Old Testament. Together with the restoration, the Bxile emerged as the decisive shaping reference point for the self-understanding of Judaism.[1] Moreover, the power of exile and restoration as an imaginative construct exercised enormous impact on subsequent Christian understandings of faith and life as they were recast in terms of crucifixion and resurrection.

Three Propositions on the Exile

We may take as foundational for our theological reflection three propositions that are beyond dispute:

1. The Exile was indeed *a real historical experience* that can be located and understood in terms.of public history.[2] It is clear that a considerable

---

1. Miller and Hayes (*A History of Ancient Israel and Judah*, 416) write: "The fall of the city and the exile of its citizens marked a watershed in Judean history and have left fissure marks radiating throughout the Hebrew Scriptures. The 'day of judgment' heralded in prophetic announcements had notjustdavmed, it had burst on Judah with immense ferocity."

2. See the data summarized by Miller and Hayes, ibid., 416–36; and Bright, *A History of Israel*, 343–72.

number of persons were deported by the Babylonians, though different accounts yield different results. In any case, much of the leadership of the community was deported. It is conventional to conclude that the socio-political situation of the exiles was not terribly difficult, though Smith has made a strong case for the notion that, in fact, the deported Jews in exile faced enormous hardship.[3]

2. While the actual number of persons exiled must have been relatively modest, the Exile as a theological datum became a governing paradigm for all successive Jewish faith.[4] That is, the experience, articulation, and memory of the Exile came to exercise influence upon the faith, imagination, and self perception of judaism quite disproportionate to its factual actuality. As a result, the Exile became definitional for all Jews, many of whom were never deported. Part of the reason that a modest historical fact became a dominant paradigm for self-understanding, no doubt can be understood in terms of the exercise of social imagination and social power by the Jews who were in exile, who insisted upon and imposed their experience on Judaism as normative for all Jewishness.

The community of the deported established ideological, interpretive hegemony in Judaism, insisting that its experience counted the most Such a sociopolitical explanation, however, does not fully account for this interpretive turn in Judaism.

In addition to the interpretive authority of the exilic community in the political process, the intrinsic power and significance of the Exile must be acknowledged. Since the Mosaic articulation of covenantal faith, built as it is around stipulation and blessing and curse—an articulation appropriated in the prophetic tradition-Israel has been subject to the moral seriousness of its own covenantal-ethical enterprise. Thus the Exile required, power politics notwithstanding, construal in Israel in terms of those covenantal categories. As a result, the Exile is an event not only of historical displacement, but of profound moral, theological fracture.

That moral, theological fracture generated two primary responses. On the one hand, the paradigm of exile/ restoration is concerned with the *moral failure* of Israel, so that exile is punishment and judgment from God. This is a dominant stream of *"golah* theology," voiced especially in the tradition of Deuteronomy. On the other hand, however, it is clear that the crisis of exile cannot be contained in the categories of covenantal sanctions. Thus

3. Smith, *The Religion of the Landless.*

4. See Neusner, *Understanding Seeking Faith*, 137–41 and passim; and Joyce, *Divine Initiative and Human Response in Ezekiel*, 12–17.

there was also the posing of urgent questions concerning *the fidelity of God* that are more profound than a simple moral calculus of blessing and curse. These questions are voiced, for example, in the prophets, in the priestly tradition, and perhaps in Job. Thus the immediate questions of moral symmetry and the more subtle question of theological fidelity created a large arena for Israel's venturesome theological reflection.[5]

3. The experience and paradigmatic power of the Exile evoked in Israel a surge of theological reflection and a *remarkable production of fresh theological literature.*[6] The Exile decisively shattered the old, settled categories of Israel's faith. It did not, however, lead either to abandonment or despair.[7] Israel was driven to reflect on the moral, theological significance of exile. The characteristic tension between acknowledgment of shattering on the one hand, and the refusal of despair and abandonment on the other hand, required, permitted, and authorized in Israel daring theological energy which began to probe faith in wholly new categories which are daring and venturesome. Indeed, it is not an overstatement to say that exile became the matrix in which the canonical shape of Old Testament faith is formed and evoked.[8] In that context, the old traditions are radically revamped and recharacterized,[9] and the theological process strikes out in quite fresh and inventive ways.

5. See the analysis of Friedman, *The Exile and Biblical Narrative* on the two great narrative responses to the crisis of exile.

6. See Ackroyd, *Exile and Restoration*; Klein, *Israel in Exile*; Janssen, *Juda in der Exilszeit*; and Joyce, *Divine Initiative and Human Response in Ezekiel*.

7. The reality of exile may have led some to despair, but not in the community that generated the text Scarry, *The Body in Pain*, has shown how speech counters the dismantling of personhood. In parallel fashion I submit that text counters despair, both as text-making and text¥reading. The exilic community was intensely engaged in text-making and text-reading as a counter to despair.

8. I take this to be a widely accepted judgment. Sanders, *Torah and Canon* has argued this case effectively. Canon criticism, he writes, "begins with questions concerning the function of those ancient traditions which were viable in the crucifixion–resurrection experience of the sixth and fifth centuries B.C. and which provided the vehicle for Judaism's birth out of the ashes of what had been . . . But if one's interest is rather in the actual history of how the Bible came to be, what events gave rise to the collecting of the materials actually inherited, and why these traditions were chosen and not others, then two main historical watersheds impose themselves. The Bible comes to us out of the ashes of two Temples, the First or Solomonic Temple, destroyed in 586 B.C., and the Second or Herodian Temple, destroyed in A.D. 70" (xix, 6). See the discerning statement by Morgan, *Between Text and Community*, on the canonical power of the exilic experience.

9. This is the essential dynamic of von Rad's two-volume Old Testament theology.

These three factors, historical experience, paradigmatic power, and inventive literary imagination, are crucial for recognizing the context of the Exile as decisive for shaping Old Testament faith. These three factors, however, in and of themselves, do not constitute a theological probe. They are the context for such a probe. Our intention here is to push beyond historical-literary issues to theology proper.

What Happened to God?

The literary-historical-cultural aspects of the Exile have posed the general, overarching question of *continuity and discontinuity*. This rubric permits us to consider a number of subpoints in relation to the general problematic. The dominant Wellhausen paradigm for Old Testament history and interpretation revolves around the question of continuity and discontinuity.[10] Wellhausen's powerful model insisted upon a significant discontinuity between the earlier faith of Israel and the later development of Judaism. It is not clear to what extent Wellhausen 's model was designed to critique and even depreciate later Judaism, which he found inferior to earlier prophetic faith, nor is it clear to what extent that depreciation was either motivated by or served (unwittingly) a kind of anti-Semitism. In any case, very much critical Christian scholarship has regarded the emergent faith of the Jewish postexilic community as inferior, so that a clear line has been drawn from the earlier prophetic faith to the New Testament.[11]

Distinct from Wellhausen's powerful paradigm, none has thought more carefully and perceptively about the question of continuity and discontinuity than has Peter Ackroyd. In a series of four articles, Ackroyd has carefully and judiciously reflected on the crises of history and culture, and the powerful drive for continuity in the midst of the cultural, historical

---

See von Rad, *Old Testament Theology*, 2:263–77 and passim; and P. D. Hanson, "Israelite Religion in the Early Postexilic Period."

10. For a careful review and assessment of the contribution of Wellhausen and his dominant paradigm, see the essays in Knight, ed., *Julius Wellhausen and His Prolegomena to the History of Israel*.

11. It should be possible to acknowledge some crucial discontinuity between ancient Israel and emergent Judaism without a judgment of inferiority. But to assert discontinuity without "bootlegging" inferiority requires an important break with the assumptions of the Wellhausen paradigm. P. D. Hanson, "Israelite Religion in the Early Postexilic Period," has enunciated the discontinuity without suggesting inferiority.

break.[12] Ackroyd has considered the ways in which cult objects (temple vessels), theological constructs, and reutilization of textual formulations have served the concern for continuity.[13] It does not surprise us that in the end Ackroyd concludes that continuity is the overriding reality for Judaism: "The restoration and the destruction are all of a piece; discontinuity is resolved in the discovery of a continuity within it."[14]

There are two very different reasons why Ackroyd comes down on the side of continuity. First, there was in and through the Exile, a surviving continuity of vibrant Judaism as a community. As a historical fact, the Jews did indeed have continuity, and they claimed that continuity for themselves. Second, Ackroyd poses questions of social history; he is concerned with the community over time and through time. Moreover, Ackroyd is interested in institutional sociology, and therefore is attentive to the gestures, textual and otherwise, which sustain continuity. A historical critic could hardly entertain the notion of deep discontinuity, so that there is an inevitable bias toward continuity in our common work of criticism.

I do not at all suggest that Ackroyd has misconstrued the data, for his historical methods serve well to understand the community that lives in and through an ongoing tradition. I suggest, however, that Ackroyd's analysis has not, in fact, penetrated beyond cultural, institutional, community-generated continuities to the more difficult theological question, namely, what happened to God in the process of the Exile? Or to put the question more critically, what does the text say happened to God?

In putting the question in this way, a methodological acknowledgment as required. To do biblical theology, I suggest, requires us to leave off the kind of critical observation that stands outside the text, and to enter into the dynamic that operates inside the text and its claims. Or to put it differently, biblical theology, unlike historical criticism, requires us to approach the text more "realistically," as though this were indeed a word about God and about God's life, very often a word from God about God's life.[15] Such an approach may appear critically to be na-

---

12. Ackroyd, "Continuity: A Contribution,"; Ackroyd, "Continuity and Discontinuity"; Ackroyd, "The Temple Vessels"; and Ackroyd, "The Theology of Tradition."

13. Intertextuality, as reflected in the work of Michael Fishbane, provides a powerful way to maintain a flexible continuity in contexts of discontinuity.

14. Ackroyd, "Continuity: A Contribution," 15.

15. Such a statement makes no assumptions about inspiration, revelation, or authority. I refer to such "theological realism" in terms of the claims made by the text itself. The ground for such a claim is of course theological, but in the first instance, it can

ive, but it is the only way we have to penetrate the difficulty of God's own life in the Exile.[16]

When we ask a theological question of the text, as distinct from a literary, historical, or sociological question, the issue of continuity and discontinuity takes on a different configuration. Whereas concerning literary, historical, and sociological questions, one can point to evident continuities that overide discontinuities (as Ackroyd has done so well), a theologrcal focus on the rendering of God's own person as a character in Israel's large drama of faith is not so unambiguously on the side of continuiry. The texts attest that the Exile constituted a significant crisis in God~s own life. As a character rendered in Israel's "covenantal discourse," as a character central to the plot of Israel's self-presentation, God is deeply impinged upon by the crisis of the Exile.[17] The theme of continuity asks whether the character of Yahweh connnues to be the same character in, through, and beyond the Exile. The theme of discontinuity asks whether (and to what extent) the character of God is decisively changed by the crisis of exile, for example, if God ceases to be in some crucial way who this God was heretofore.

The evidence is not clear and consistent. The articulation of the text, nonetheless, makes clear that the displacement and suffering of exile breaks something of God's own self, both permitting and requiring Yahweh to be presented in a different way. It is clear that such a substantive theological argument depends upon a) the texts being taken as "realistic" speech about God, and b) the metaphor of personhood as the governing image, so that a rendering of the person of God in this drama is what is available to Israel (and derivatively, available to us), Clearly, there are in the Exile literary continuities through reused speech formulae, historical continuities through genealogy, and sociological continuities through cultic acts and gestures. These continuities, however, all appear to be organized to cope with the peculiar reality of discontinuity with which God struggles.

---

be heeded on the grounds of the text as a "classic" that requires our attendance.

16. On such an understanding of the text, see Patrick, *The Rendering of God in the Old Testament*. This approach understands theology as dramatic rendering and proceeds by bracketing out metaphysical questions.

17. On the notion of "covenantal discourse," see Fisch, *Poetry with a Purpose*, 118–31. The gain of Fisch's assertion is that it takes seriously the claim of the text itself without excessive historical-critical reservation. See Fisch's "theological realism" concerning the Psalms (108–14).

In putting the theological question in this way, I note two implications that more directly relate to Professor Beker's own work and writing. First the continuity/discontinuity of Israel's God in exile is a theological counterpart to the christological problematic in the NT concerning the relation of the "Jesus of history" to "the risen Christ."[18] The New Testament Church struggles to assert continuity in the person of Jesus through the events of Good Friday and Easter, but also must assert that in those events there is a decisive, transformative discontinuity in the person of Jesus. So it is as well concerning the God of Israel in the Exile.

Second, Beker's own poignant and remarkable discussion of suffering and hope is a reflection on the power of hope in the midst of suffering.[19] Beker's mode of expression asserts that hope confronts and overrides suffering. An alternative model might be that hope arises precisely in and through suffering. In either case, the life of the God of Israel in the midst of exile, a life of suffering in solidarity, and of powerful resolve against displacement, is a life which struggles for continuity in the brokenness. I mention this connection to Beker's work in order to suggest that the question I pose is an intensely practical issue, for Israel sees through this crisis of God how real suffering is, how seriously suffering is taken, and how suffering impinges even upon the life of God, both to shatter something old in God's own life, and to evoke something utterly new in God's life.[20]

I have selected three texts from different exilic sources which explore different dimensions of the way in which God is voiced.[21] To be sure, one can understand the different voices in these texts critically, such as, to explain their different theological claims by referring to the literary, historical sources. But if one is theologically "realistic," the diverse voicings evidence the struggle in God's life over the way God will be God in the face of such a crisis.

---

18. On the question of continuity and discontinuity, see Käsemann, "Blind Alleys in the 'Jesus of History' Controversy"; Fuchs, *Studies of the Historical Jesus*, 11–31; and Dunn, *Unity and Diversity in the New Testament*. See Professor Beker's theological discussion of the question, *Paul the Apostle*, 192–208.

19. Beker, *Suffering and Hope*.

20. For the purposes of my argument, it cannot be insisted upon too strongly that the mode of God's self-presentation is dramatic, and that we are witnessing the character of God through a drama. The warrant for such a mode of discourse is that the text itself proceeds in this way.

21. On the several theological resources from the Exile which give different voice to God, see the works of Ackroyd and Klein cited in n. 6, and Friedman in n. 5.

A God of Compassion—Deuteronomy 4:23–31

The critical problems concerning the history and unity of the first text, Deut 4:23–31, are considerable.[22] They are made more complex by the dominant judgment of two redactions by the Deuteronomistic tradition.[23] Specifically vv. 29–31 are widely judged to be a secondary redaction.[24] Thus the text may be composite. In any case, the entire passage as it stands reflects a concern about the Exile. Verse 26 speaks of "utterly perish from the land," and v. 27 of "scatter." The phrase "from there" (v. 29) no doubt refers to exile, so that the text as we have it advances from a warning about exile (vv. 23–28) to a situation in exile and an anticipation after exile (vv. 29–31). And if vv. 29–31 are indeed an intrusion, as critical study has concluded, then they are an intrusion reflective of God's new exilic situation.

In this sustained and extended speech, Moses traces a remarkable move in the character of Yahweh. Put concisely, Moses voices Yahweh *before* exile and *after* exile around the geographical/temporal reference to "from there" (v. 29). Prior to "from there," Israel is not yet "there," not yet in exile, nor is Yahweh yet addressed "from there." Prior to exile, Mosaic Israel is defined by the demands, sanctions, and warnings of Sinai. The burden of the speech of Moses is that attentiveness to the Torah is the condition for remaining in the land (vv. 25–26). The theological dimension of this preexilic warning is that Yahweh is "a devouring fire, a jealous God" (v. 24), a God who will brook no rival and tolerate no disobedience. The entire warning and urgency of Moses grows out of the character of Yahweh, a God who is uncompromising about demand. Thus the ominous warning of Moses is appropriate to preexilic Israel and grows from the jealousy of Yahweh.

Were the character of Yahweh sustained into exile in continuity, we would expect Israel, in exile and beyond exile, to continue to deal with a jealous, uncompromising God. The God who is available "from there," however, is not the devouring God from preexile. In the middle

---

22. Mayes, "Deuteronomy 4 and the Literary Criticism of Deuteronomy," supported by the argument of Braulik, has made a strong case for the literary unity and coherence of the passage. See Lohfink, *Höre Israel!*, 87–120; and Braulik, *Die Mittel deuteronomischer Rhetorik*.

23. See Cross, *Canaanite Myth and Hebrew Epic*, 274–89; and Nelson, *The Double Redadion of the Deuteronomistic History*.

24. See Wolff, "The Kerygma of the Deuteronomic Historical Work," 96–97.

of the text, in the middle ofIsrael's experience, and we may believe, in the middle of God's life With Israel, there is a new "there"—exile. When Moses continues his testimony about the God with whom Israel has to deal, everything is changed. Of course one may say that this change reflects layers in the redactional process, and therefore different theological perspectives. Or the change may only reflect the pastoral emergency of the Exile when the producers of theological literature said something different to meet new needs. If, however, we are to do theology, what emerges in the text is a real break in God's way with Israel, such as a real break in God's way of being God. Now there is no more talk of devouring fire and jealous God. Now Moses speaks of a "merciful God" (v. 31). The *'el qanna'* (v. 24) has become the *'el rahum* (v. 31); the one who scattered in anger is the one who will not forget covenant.

There is, of course, continuity in this God to whom Moses bears witness. If one follows the rhetorical pattern of the text, however, there is also a discernible discontinuity in the move from *'el qanna'* to *'el rahum*. This God who keeps the same name has ceased to be, so far as the text is concerned, a jealous, devouring God and has now become a God of compassion. Of course one may conclude simply that one need not say everything about God in every sentence, and that the God of Israel has all along been *'el qanna'* and *'el rahum*. That, however, is not the way the text works. I submit, rather, that in this one text, the voice of Moses expresses a profound break in the character of God, and that break makes visible the emergence of a God of compassion whom Yahweh has not been before in this text, an emergence evoked by the Exile.

Thus we may provisionally suggest that as hope arises in the midst of suffering, hope that did not heretofore exist, so the mercy of God is evoked, formed, and articulated just here. The formal reality of discontinuity permits a substantive assertion of compassion. And if one follows Trible's notion of compassion as "womb-like mother love,"[25] then the Exile becomes the place where the character of God turns in a quite fresh direction.

Real Abandonment—Isaiah 54:7–10

Perhaps the most remarkable text for our theme is Isa 54:7–10. Having just utilized the metaphor of a wife (Israel) deserted by her husband (Yahweh; vv. 4–6), the poem asserts the restoration of the relationship

25. Trible, *God and the Rhetoric of Sexuality*, 31–59.

when the husband takes a fresh initiative to restore the relation. Within this metaphor, the husband makes wo quite distinct assertions, each re-iterated in a parallelism. First, "I forsook you" (*'azabtik*), "I hid my face" (*histarti*).[26] Second, "I will gather you" (*qabbesek*), "I will have compassion" (*rihamtik*).[27] The contrast of the husband's two moves are: abandon/gather; hide/have compassion.

Three interpretive questions may be posed about these assertions: Was the abandonment a real abandonment. Was the absence a real absence? Did God in truth abandon covenant partner Israel? The wording of the poem is candid and unambiguous. The abandonment is real and complete, without qualification.

Such an assertion is difficult when there is a felt need to claim that God's resolve is unbreakable, for example, when continuity is stressed in every circumstance.[28] Thus John Calvin seeks to find a way around the clear statement of the text in the interest of continuity:

> When he says that he forsook his people, it is a sort of admission of the fact . . . What the prophet says in this passage must there-fore refer to our feelings and to outward appearance, because we seem to be rejected by God when we do not perceive his pres-ence and protection. And it is necessary that we should thus feel God's wrath, even as a wife divorced by her husband deplores her condition, that we may know that we are justly chastised. But we must also perceive his mercy; and because it is infinite and eternal, we shall find that all afflictions in comparison are light and momentary.[29]

Such a reading, however, clearly goes against the wording of the text itself. Serious theology is placed in jeopardy when texts are, in this way, explained away. Calvin's comment is an example of the way in which a

26. On the double movement, see Zech 1:15–17 and Isa 60:10–14. The former text has important parallels to our text. On the "hidden face" of God, see Balentine, *The Hidden God*, esp. 148; and Perlitt, "Die Verborgenheit Gottes."

27. On the double theme in Jeremiah, see Lust, "'Gathering and Return' in Jer-emiah and Ezekiel"; and Raitt, *A Theology of Exile*.

28. Frei (*The Identity of Jesus Christ*) holds a magisterial view of the single story of God focused on Jesus Christ. That single and magisterial story necessarily asserts the profound and universal continuity. Against such a claim of any "great story," see the protest of Lyotard, *The Postmodern Condition*. See the judicious comments of Placher, *Unapologetic Theology*, 156 and passim, concerning a "universal" story and the Chris-tian narrative.

29. Calvin, *Commentary on the Book of the Prophet Isaiah*, 140.

concern for theological continuity (transcendence) wants to outflank and override the text.

In the face of postwar tragedy in Europe, Kornelis Miskotte voices a much more sober reading of the text, directed against an interpretative posture like that of Calvin:

> The very first thing that is said here makes it clear that this situation actually cannot be understood on the two-dimensional level of experience and its interpretation [so Calvin]. It is a real abandonment. And those who did not recognize and understand it as an actual abandonment by God are now compelled to hear it proclaimed as God's own word. It was an actual abandonment by God. Without this proclamation of the (partially recognized and partially unrecognized) abandonment by God, the prophetic word is not in the full sense the word of God. He scattered the people, he hid his face from them. The fact is that we have actually lived under the condition of this act; but it is only the Word that reveals to us that it is an act of God.[30]

Miskotte's reading poses much more difficult theological questions than does the reading of Calvin, but it surely is more faithful to the text. The poem asserts a profound discontinuity without qualifications, as Israel's condition vis-à-vis God. All transcendental guarantees about God are shattered; God's goodness in Israel is decisively broken. It is instructive that it is Miskotte's European experience of discontinuity that both permitted and required a radical rereading of the text.

The break in abandonment and anger is "for a brief moment" (*rega'*; vv. 7–8). We may ask, as Israel must have asked, how long is a *rega'*? The word suggests that while the abandonment by God was total and without qualification, it was only for an instant. Or we may reverse the proposition: the abandonment was only for an instant, but long enough for it to be massive, total, and decisive. The other uses of *rega'* do not illuminate us very much because they are the same appeal to brevity, but to decisiveness.[31] That is "a moment" is long enough for a total inversion or transformation. I suggest that in this word as it is used here, we are at the crux of the issue of discontinuity and continuity for Israel in exile. The time span of the break interests us because we wonder if it was so brief that the carryover of God's commitment still prevails.

---

30. Miskotte, *When the Gods Are Silent*, 405. See also Karl Barth, *Church Dogmatics* II/1, 372–73.

31. Cf., for example, Exod 33:5; Isa 26:20; 47:9; Ps 30:6; Lam 4:6.

In considering "for a moment," perhaps an analogy will aid us. The moment of God's abandonment is like the effect the breaking of an electrical circuit has on a digital clock. The breaking of the circuit may be only for an instant. To my unscientific observation, it appears that sometimes the circuit breaks briefly when the power goes off, but not so long as to disrupt the time reporting of the clock. The clock continues to function through the brief break in power. At other times, or with other clocks, the seemingly same disruption of current does break the functioning of the clock, and it must be reset. In both cases the break is "for a moment," but in one case continuity persists, and in the other it does not. Thus the "instant" of circuit breaking is a delicate one, and one does not know when a clock (or one clock rather than another) will be disconnected and cease to function accurately.

In like manner, this poem, I suggest, intends us to focus our theological attention on the instant of the breaking of God's loyal love. We are left by the poem to ponder whether the "breaking of the circuit" of God's faithfulness precludes the continued function of the covenantal commitment of God. It is for Israel a close call; whether or not the current leaps the break for Yahweh determines continuity or discontinuity for Israel. This poem deliberately lodges the entire issue of continuity and discontinuity on the freight of one word, a word so delicate we cannot decide precisely. Thus the hard verb "abandon" is set next to the adverb "for a moment," and there the matter rests. The verb in the end is more decisive than the adverb. The husband did indeed abandon the wife in wrath; but it was only for an instant, "a twinkling of an eye."[32] It was enough of a circuit break to cut the connection, briefly, but decisively. This double statement of the acknowledgment of real abandonment by God is followed with a counter theme introduced by an adversative conjunction:

> but with great compassion I will gather you . . .
> but with everlasting love I will have compassion on you,
> > says Yahweh, your Redeemer. (vv. 7–8)

Miskotte comments on the "reverse" of the rejection:

> This at the same time reveals that this word is a saving word—by reason of the fact that the event [for example, the Exile] is now past and is no longer the ultimate truth about our condition . . . Therefore the church must be all the more aware of the reverse

32. Cf. 1 Cor 15:52.

side of this truth, namely, that grace, which is the annulment of judgment, confirms and corroborates the judgment as God's judgment. In the multidimensional realm of his freedom, God does not arbitrarily pass from one to the other, from yes to no, from rejection to acceptance. He resists the resistance. He breaks the rebellion by breaking his own heart.[33]

Abandonment, wrath, and *hiddenness* are countered by *steadfast love, compassion,* and *redeemer.*

Because of the adverb *'olam,* we may inquire about the relation of the negative and affirmative triads. When *'olam* is rendered "everlasting," we might conclude that God's *ḥesed* was at all times operative, for example, before, during, and after the abandonment. On that reading, the abandonment by the husband does not cut deeply, and an underlying continuity is affirmed in spite of the hiddenness of God's face (so Calvin). An alternative reading, however, does not regard the qualifying *'olam* as mercy before and during, but only after the abandonment. Thus the relation of rejection and embrace is not an ongoing parallelism whereby *ḥesed* denies ultimate seriousness to abandonment, but the two are sequential. *Ḥesed* arises out of, after, and in response to the rejections, so that *ḥesed* stands on the other side of :the discontinuity, and not in powerful opposition to the discontinuity. Thus the "everlastingness" of *'olam* is into the future, but not through the past of Israel's exile.

Thus we may answer our three interpretive questions:

1. The abandonment is real and not only "seems" so;

2. The abandonment is for an instant, but long enough to matter decisively; and

3. The promised *ḥesed* is *after and in response to* the abandonment, and not in its midst as an antidote.

The upshot of this reading is that there is discontinuity in God's own resolve for Israel, a discontinuity that evokes, permits, and requires a new response by the compassionate God who is redeemer.

---

33. Miskotte, *When the Gods Are Silent,* 405. Miskotte understands that the move from abandonment to compassion happens only through God's deep pathos, that is, through "the breaking of his own heart." Westermann, *Isaiah 40–66,* is not as explicit, but alludes to the same reality: "A change has come over God. He ceases from wrath, and again shows Israel mercy" (274). In his comment, however, Westermann speaks of the way Israel's "heart throbbed," but does not draw God's heart into the trouble in the same way.

This reading of discontinuity is sustained by the following lines in vv. 9–10. "This [the Exile] is like the days of Noah" (RSV).[34] God swears "from wrath" (*miqṣop*) and from "rebuking" (*migar*), as Yahweh "swore that waters would not again pass over the earth" (cf. Gen 8:21–22; 9:11). In the analogue of the flood, it is clear that the promise in Genesis is a promise that it will not happen "again"; it is a promise after the Flood which precludes its replication.[35] There was a real flood, a real release of chaos, a real abandonment of the earth which left creation bereft of God's protective care. Thus in the flood story, the promise and assurance do not persist through the Flood, but come in sequence after the discontinuity of the Flood.[36] The analogue supports our reading vv. 7–8 as a statement of deep discontinuity, with the same "again" implied; that is, the exile of abandonment will not happen again, as it manifestly has happened this time.

The sequencing of abandonment and compassion in v. 10 is not a denial of recently experienced discontinuity, but an assurance against future discontinuity. Mountains and hills are juxtaposed to God's *ḥesed* and *berit šalom*.[37] Now in light of the promise, God's compasSionate resolve is more reliable than the ordering of creation. That assurance is given and received post-Flood, post-Exile, post-abandonment. Thus out of the massive discontinuity of chaos (flood, exile), God arrives at a new, overriding resolve for fidelity and compassion which wells up out of the discontinuity. The husband who has abandoned now embraces. The God who has been wrathful acts in compassion. The relation that has been breached is now solidified. Out of discontinuity comes a profound decree of continuity, after the discontinuity. The text exhibits no interest in and makes no comment on how it is that the newness arises out of, from, and in the midst of the break. The movement of this sequence is not unlike the sequence we have found in Deut 4:23–31. In Isa 54:7–10, it is from

---

34. Much of the Noah-flood story is from P, and therefore from the Exile. Thus it is not unexpected that that flood narrative should be on the horizon of this exilic poet.

35. For example, the "again" (*'od*) of Isa 54:9 is clearly reminiscent of the same word in Gen 9:11, with the same intention.

36. Anderson, "From Analysis to Synthesis," 23–29, has shown that Gen 8:1 is the pivot of the Flood narrative, for instance, when God, remembers Noah. In the structure of the narrative, that decisive *remembering* is preceded by God's *forgetting* of Noah. In the same way, in Isaiah 54, God s act of compassion is preceded by a real act of abandonment. Thus the analogy of our text to that of the Flood narrative applies to the enure dramatic structure of the narrative.

37. On "covenant of peace" see Batto, "The Covenant of Peace."

wrath to compassion; in Deut 4:23–31, it is from jealousy to compassion. The situation of exile features a profound recharacterization of God.

A Counter Assertion—Jeremiah 31:35–37

The cosmic reference of Isa 54:10 which contrasts "mountains and hills" with "steadfast love and covenant of peace" leads us to our third text, Jer 31:35–37. These verses immediately follow the new covenant passage (vv. 31–34). The announcement of "new covenant" appears to accent the discontinuity between the new covenant and the old covenant which it is not like (v. 32). Indeed, the dominant tendency of the Jeremiah tradition is to accent the discontinuity of exile. Oddly, vv. 35–37, immediately following, are a stunning statement of continuity. These verses counter the main tendency of Jeremiah and make a high claim of continuity. Whereas Isa 54:10 acknowledges that the structures of creation may indeed "depart" (*mos*) and "be removed" (*mot*) in this text it is assumed that the "fixed order" of creation will not "depart" (*mos*).[38] In Isa 54:10, God's *hesed* to Israel is more reliable than creation; in this text, God's guarantee of Israel "all the days" is as assured as the fixed order of creation which is utterly assured. Thus the argument on the same subject, to make the same claim, is stated very differently. Whereas Isa 54:10 moves beyond the experience of discontinuity to make its claim,[39] our verses appeal to the experience of continuity to make a similarly large claim.

This assertion of utter continuity is not one we expect in Jeremiah. It is as though the tradition cannot finally settle the matter of continuity and discontinuity. Each time it makes an assertion, it must follow with a counter assertion. As a result, even in the Jeremiah tradition, preoccupied as it is with discontinuity, there is added this counter voice that insists that God's guarantee of Israel is not and cannot be disrupted.[40] The ostensive protasis-apodosis structure of the passage, twice voiced, appears to be governed by a conditional "if"; the rhetoric, in fact, denies any conditionality (against the

---

38. For that reason, this text does not need an *'od* of reassurance. That is, this text entertains no discontinuity, and therefore there is no need for reassertion and new promise.

39. In Isa 54:9–10, the claim for the future is based on *'od*.

40. On the late dating of vv. 35–37, see Carroll, *Jeremiah*, 115–16; and Holladay, *Jeremiah 2*, 199. Holladay dates the text to the time of Nehemiah, My argument, however, is that in doing theology, one must move beyond such critical judgment to take the realistic assertion of the text. Such a posture, I suppose, is one of "second naiveté."

grain of Jeremiah), and assumes an unconditional relation between God and Israel. In this text, even the Exile allows no disruption in Israel's life with God because of God's steadfast love and fidelity. Unlike Isa 54:7–8, Israel's partner does not abandon and does not actin wrath.

Four Observations

We may take these three texts—Deut 4:21–23; Isa 54:7–10; and Jer 31:35–37—as representative of the theological reflection evoked by the Exile. These three disclosures together suggest that the issue of continuity and discontinuity was for Israel an urgent issue, one that admitted of no simple or settled solution.

Four observations arise from this analysis:

1. While the historical, sociopolitical dimension of the Exile is hardly in doubt, the Exile cannot be treated simply as a historical problem concerning the continuity of the community. The Exile is a deep problem for the character of Yahweh, as well as the community of Israel. Thus exile constitutes a profound theological problem and must be treated theologically as a crisis for God. The texts we have considered are all decrees in the mouth of God, for example, disclosures of a moment in God's own life which cannot be explained simply as a historical or sociological issue.

2. The theological crisis that these texts enunciate and with which they struggle is that *the transcendence of God is placed in deep jeopardy* by the Exile. From this it follows that even God's abiding commitment to Israel is at risk, impinged upon by the reality of the Exile. It is our common theological propensity, as indicated by Calvin, to exempt God from such jeopardy, to imagine that at bottom, Israel's God is not subject to the terms of the historical process. Such transcendentalism, of course, offers assurance, but must necessarily refuse to take either the text or Israel's experience of exile with real seriousness. These texts entertain the thought that God is radically vulnerable to the realities of Israel's life.

In making this affirmation, Israel breaks with magisterial "common theology" that reduces God to a part of a fixed, predictable retribution system.[41] Such a "common theology" cannot countenance the Exile as a crisis

---

41. Such "common theology" necessarily interprets exile simply as punishment in a sharper system of retribution. On "common theology," see Gottwald, *The Tribes of Yahweh*, 667–91; and Brueggemann, "A Shape for Old Testament Theology, 1: Structure Legitimation."

for God, and cannot entertain the stunning affirmation concerning God's own life which emerges in the midst of such jeopardized transcendence.

3. The texts assert the jeopardy of transcendence but cannot finally adjudicate the extent or depth of that jeopardy. That is, the texts refuse to come down cleanly either for continuity or discontinuity. In each case the text tends to counter the tradition in which it is embedded. Deuteronomy 4, which ends in compassion "from there," counters the familiar "theology of command" featured in Deuteronomy. Isaiah 54 is embedded in the vibrant affirmation of exilic Israel, but pauses over God's radical abandonment in the Exile (cf. 40:2). The affirmation of continuity in Jer 31:35-37 lives in tension with the Jeremianic inclination to discontinuity. In this way, the texts keep the question of the jeopardy of God's life with Israel delicately open. Every tilted statement is promptly corrected by a counterstatement, thus permitting no-statement to be a final one. Israel's way of doing theology, or more fundamentally, God's act of self-disclosure, bespeaks a profound and ambiguous lack of closure that resists every systematic closure.

4. The texts *move toward God's compassion*. This is true more directly of Deuteronomy 4 and Isaiah 54 than of Jeremiah 31, but see Jer 30:18; 31:20; and 33:26. Indeed, God's compassion seems to be the primary and powerful theological emergent of the Exile. The exile evokes new measures and fresh depths of compassion in the character of God. Taken pastorally, the articulation of God's compassion is a humanly needed assurance. Taken theologically, the Exile evokes in God a new resolve for fidelity, a resolve that was not operative prior to the hurt and dread of the Exile.[42] That resolve on God's part is, to be sure, seeded in old texts (cf. Exod 34:6-7); the Exile, however, provides a rich array of texts voicing this newly central and newly appreciated theological datum. The Exile permits God to become toward Israel whom God was not.[43] The fresh characterization of God seems to atise, inexplicably, but freely in, through, and out of exile. The tone of God's speech toward Israel is dramatically transformed through this terrible jeopardy, a jeopardy that God shares with Israel.

42. The new resolve of God in our texts is not unlike the new resolve of God in the Flood narrative (Gen 8:20-22; 9:8-17). In the Flood narrative no reason is given for that new resolve, as none is given here.

43. Critically, the changes can be explained by the identification of distinct literary sources. Such distinctions, however, often violate the intention of the final form of the text, which is the proper material for doing biblical theology.

The Theological Reality of Exile

The Exile is the moment in the history of Israel and in the life of God when an irreversibly new theological datum is introduced in the horizon of faith. In conclusion, I suggest three dimensions of our interpretive work which are impinged upon by this theological reality emerging in exile:

1. The paradigm of "exile and restoration," which has as its theological counterpart God's abandonment and God's new compassion, provides crucial and decisive categories for understanding the crucifixion and resurrection of Jesus and the New Testament *"dialectic of reconciliation."*[44] While trinitarian theology has opened a variety of ways of getting from Friday to Sunday,[45] the typology of exile suggests:

44. Moltmann, *The Crucified God*, has most powerfully insisted upon this dialectic of crucifixion and resurrection, refusing to let the Resurrection overcome or nullify the centrality of the Crucifixion in the story of God's life.

45. On getting from Friday to Sunday, Steiner, *Real Presences*, 231–32, concludes with a pathos-filled statement: "There is one particular day in Western history about which neither historical record nor myth nor Scripture make report. It is a Saturday. And it has become the longest of days. We know of that Good Friday which Christianity holds to have been that of the Cross. But the non-Christian, the atheist, knows of it as well. That is to say that he knows of the injustice, of the interminable suffering, of the waste, of the brute enigma of ending . . . We know also about Sunday. To the Christian, that day signifies an intimation, both assured and precarious, both evident and beyond comprehension, of resurrection, of a justice and a love that have conquered death. If we are non-Christians or non-believers, we know of that Sunday in precisely analogous terms . . . The lineaments of that Sunday carry the name of hope (there is no word less deconstructible).

"But ours is the long day's journey of the Saturday. Between suffering, aloneness, unutterable waste on the one hand and the dream ofliberation, of rebirth on the other. In the face of the torture of a child, of the death of love which is Friday, even the greatest art and poetry are almost helpless. In the Utopia of the Sunday, the aesthetic will, presumably, no longer have logic or necessity. The apprehensions and figurations . . . which tell of pain and of hope, of the flesh which is said to taste of ash and of the spirit. which is said to have the savour of fire, are always Sabbatarian. They have risen out of an immensity of waiting which is that of man. Without them, how could we be patient?"

Steiner's poignant statement from outside the Christian faith (as a Jew) is paralleled from inside the Christian community by Nicholas Lash. Lash, *Easter in Ordinary*, writes: "In a fascinating section of *What Is Man?*, Buber distinguishes between "epochs of habitation and epochs of homelessness." Whether we like it or not, ours is an epoch of homelessness . . . But homelessness is the truth of our condition, and the "gifts of the spirit," gifts of community and relationships, forgiveness and life-giving, are at least as much a matter of promise, of prospect, and of the task that is laid upon us, as they are a matter of past achievement or present reality" (216, 268).

Both Steiner and Lash voice the discontinuity and affirm that our current habitation is in the homelessness between. The Old Testament moment of exile is indeed one

a. that the abandonment of God is real and decisive, albeit brief, and

b. that the God who is evidenced in Easter is decisively different from the God who abandons and is abandoned on Friday.

The theological reality of the Exile warns against any protective transcendentalism in the midst of the failure of God's life with Israel and Israel's life with God.[46] Thus NT theology might take more seriously this paradigm which comes to govern the imagination of Judaism, as a way of reflecting upon the abandonment of Jesus and the rule of the risen Christ.

2. The new theological datum of exile impinges upon the crisis of modernity and postmodernity in theology. There is in the Exile a decisive disclosure of God that should warn us against certain theological temptations. Three aspects of our crisis occur to me in this connection.

a. Much theological work has been a search for universals, an attempt to articulate "truth" that lies outside the concrete experience and testimony of the confessing community.[47] Against every such universal, the claims of the biblical God come down to particular moments of embrace and abandonment, to particular verses of texts, and to particular moments (*rega'*) of crisis. More than anywhere else in the OT, in the Exile Israel faces "the scandal of particularity" in all its pathos. Such an exilic voicing of God stands powerfully against any would-be universals.

b. Much of theology, particularly as voiced in conventional confessional traditions, has sought to voice God in transcendental categories which leave God freed from, and untouched by, the vagaries of historical discontinuity. The disclosure of God in these exilic texts refuses such a posture and allows no certitudes about God out beyond the jeopardy of discontinuity.

c. The moral propensity of modernity is ragingly enacted in the brutality expressed in technological categories, most dramatically (but not exclusively) in the Holocaust. It may indeed be that the Exile is no adequate paradigm for the technological brutality quintessentially expressed

---

long Saturday, which afterward may seem to have been "a moment."

46. Moltmann, *The Crucified God*, underscores the abandonment which overrides every claim of transcendence. Thus "The Fatherlessness of the Son is matched by the Sonlessness of the Father" (243).

47. Lyotard, *The Post-Modern Condition*, insists that there are only concrete narratives and claims in communitles of testimony. The reality of Israel's struggle with God requires the giving up of every universal. See his appeal on 40 to a figure from Wittgenstein, that a town consists of many little houses, squares, and streets. See the remarkable argument by Toulmin, *Cosmopolis*, 31–32 and passim.

in the Holocaust;[48] nonetheless we are the generation that has witnessed massive hurt generated through technological strategies that bespeak the power of death and the absence of God. The technological production of massive pain makes all our conventional theology open to questions, and drives us to the more elemental categories of God's presence and absence, God's abandonment and reemergence.[49] In the exilic texts, human failure evokes God's absence and abandonment; *mutatis mutandis*, our shameless linkage of brutality and technology may evoke a moral calculus that requires God's absence. It may, however, be that same shameless linkage of brutality and absence that evokes God's reemergence in a fresh posture. In, with, and under the brutality and pain, God emerges anew as the generator of human possibility.[50] The new theological data of exile has much to teach us about our current theological situation, much that we should already have learned but did not.

3. The importance of the new theological data of the Exile not only offers decisive material for the shaping of New Testament theology and crucial illumination of a substantive kind for our current theological task. Its major offer to us is the suggestion of new ways of doing theology in poetic, narrative forms that eschew conventional modes of discourse, that offer God as a speaker in the poetry, a character in the narrative plot, a God who moves in and through terrible disjunctions to newness. Thus the rhetoric of these texts shapes God's own life with Israel

a. "From there" (Deut 4:29),

b. "but . . . but," (Isa 54:7–8), and

c. "if . . . then, if . . . then" (Jer 31:35–37).

Such a way of theology is concrete, particular, and inherently subversive of every settlement, spilling over from daring rhetoric into public reality, where exiles must live and trust.

---

48. See Rubenstein, "Job and Auschwitz."

49. Fackenheim, *To Mend the World*, has most eloquently characterized our new, post-Holocaust theological situation which requires theology to lower its voice back to more concrete claims which are brought to speech only in communities of hurt and risk.

50. Beker (*Suffering and Hope*, 91) concludes: "Finally, a biblical theology of hope allows us to be realistic and honest about the poisonous reality of death and dying in our world . . . And so the biblical vision still offers a promissory word in the face of suffering due to the power of death." Beker's final affirmation is rooted exactly in the testimony of exiles who discern God making promises to exiles, in exile, beyond exile.

It is a delight to join in congratulations to Chris Beker and in expressing gratitude for his work. His own study, marked by pain, candor, and hope, is a model for doing exilic theology which mediates new possibility. Our common work in Old Testament, New Testament, and systematic theology now is gathered around new questions, new modes of discourse, and new public possibilities. If we are able to get beyond ourselves, we may discern clues in our own "break point," that God's old transcendence is at risk, and that God may make new compassion-shaped resolves. Both God's risk and God's new compassion-shaped resolve refuse and resist domestication, either through our certitude or through our despair.

Bibliography

Ackroyd, Peter R. *Continuity: A Contribution to the Study of the Old Testament Religious Tradition*. Oxford: Blackwell, 1962. Reprinted in *Studies in the Religious Tradition of the Old Testament*, 3–16. London: SCM, 1987.

———. "Continuity and Discontinuity: Rehabilitation and Authentication." In *Tradition and Theology in the Old Testament*, edited by Douglas A. Knight, 215–34. Philadelphia: Fortress, 1977. Reprinted in *Studies in the Religious Traditions*, 31–45.

———. *Exile and Restoration*. OTL. Philadelphia: Westminster, 1968.

———. *Studies in the Religious Tradition of the Old Testament*. London: SCM, 1987.

———. "The Temple Vessels: A Continuity Theme." In *Studies in the Religion of Ancient Israel*, 166–81. VTSup 23. Leiden: Brill, 1972. Reprinted in *Studies in the Religious Tradition of the Old Testament*, 46–60.

———. "The Theology of Tradition: An Approach to Old Testament Theological Problems." *Bangalore Theological Forum* 3 (1971) 49–64. Reprinted in *Studies in the Religious Traditions of the Old Testament*, 17–30.

Anderson, Bernhard W. "From Analysis to Synthesis: The Interpretation of Genesis 1–11." *JBL* 97 (1978) 23–39.

Balentine, Samuel E. *The Hidden God: The Hiding of the Face of God in the Old Testament*. New York: Oxford University Press, 1983.

Barth, Karl. *Church Dogmatics*, II/1, *The Doctrine of God, Part 1*. Edinburgh: T & T Clark, 1957.

Batto, Bernard F. "The Covenant of Peace: A Neglected Ancient Near Eastern Motif." *CBQ* 49 (1987) 187–211.

Beker, Christiaan. *Suffering and Hope: The Biblical Vision and the Human Predicament*. Philadelphia: Fortress, 1987.

———. *Paul the Apostle: The Triumph of God in Life and Thought*. Philadelphia: Fortress, 1980.

Braulik, Georg. *Die Mittel deuteronomischer Rhetorik*. AnBib 68. Rome: Biblical Institute Press, 1978.

Bright, John. *A History of Israel*. 3rd ed. Philadelphia: Westminster, 1981.

Brueggemann, Walter. "A Shape for Old Testament Theology, 1: Structure Legitimation." *CBQ* 47 (1985) 156–68. [Reprinted in Brueggemann, *Old Testament Theology:*

Essays on Structure, Theme, and Text, edited by Patrick D. Miller, 1–21. Minneapolis: Fortress, 1992.]

Calvin, John. *Commentary on the Book of the Prophet Isaiah*. Translated and edited by John King. Grand Rapids: Baker, 1979.

Carroll, Robert Carroll. *Jeremiah: A Commentary*. OTL. Philadelphia: Westminster, 1986.

Cross, Frank Moore. *Canaanite Myth and Hebrew Epic: Essays in the History of the Religion of Israel*. Cambridge: Harvard University Press, 1973.

Dunn, James D. G. *Unity and Diversity in the New Testament: An Inquiry into the Character of Earliest Christianity*. Philadelphia: Westminster, 1977.

Fackenheim, Emil. *To Mend the World: Foundations of Future Jewish Thought*. New York: Schocken, 1982.

Fisch, Harold. *Poetry with a Purpose: Biblical Poetics and Interpretation*. ISBL. Bloomington: Indiana University Press, 1988.

Frei, Hans W. *The Identity of Jesus Christ: The Hermeneutical Bases of Dogmatic Theology*. Philadelphia: Fortress, 1975.

Friedman, Richard Elliott. *The Exile and Biblical Narrative: The Formation of the Deuteronomistic and Priestly Works*. HSM 22. Chico, CA: Scholars, 1981.

Fuchs, Ernst. *Studies of the Historical Jesus*. Translated by Andrew Scobie. SBT 1/42. Naperville: Allenson, 1964.

Gottwald, Norman K. *The Tribes of Yahweh: A Sociology of the Religion of Liberated Israel, 1250–1050 B.C.E.* Maryknoll, NY: Orbis, 1979.

Hanson, Paul D. "Israelite Religion in the Early Postexilic Period." In *Ancient Israelite Religion: Essays in Honor of Frank Moore Cross*, edited by Patrick D. Miller Jr. et al., 485–508. Philadelphia: Fortress, 1987.

Holladay, William L. *Jeremiah 2*. Hermeneia. Minneapolis: Fortress, 1989.

Janssen, Enno. *Juda in der Exilszeit: Ein Beitrag zur Frage der Entehung des Judentums*. Forschungen zur Religion und Literatur des Alten und Neuen Testaments 51. Göttingen: Vandenhoeck & Ruprecht, 1956.

Joyce, Paul. *Divine Initiative and Human Response in Ezekiel*. JSOTSup 51. Sheffield: JSOT Press, 1989.

Käsemann, Ernst. "Blind Alleys in the 'Jesus of History' Controversy." In *New Testament Questions of Today*, 23–65. Translated by W. J. Montague. London: SCM, 1969.

Klein, Ralph W. *Israel in Exile: A Theological Interpretation*. OBT. Philadelphia: Fortress, 1979.

Knight, Douglas A., ed. *Semeia 25: Julius Wellhausen and His Prolegomena to the History of Israel*, 1983.

Lash, Nicholas. *Easter in Ordinary: Reflections on Human Experience and the Knowledge of God*. Charlottesville: University Press of Virginia, 1988.

Lohfink, Norbert. *Höre Israel! Auslegung von Texten aus dem Buch Deuteronomium*. Die Welt der Bibel 18. Dusseldorf: Patmos, 1965.

Lust, J. "'Gathering and Return' in Jeremiah and Ezekiel." In *Le Livre de Jérémie: le prophète et son milieu, les oracles et leur transmission*, edited by P.-M. Bogaert, 119–42. Bibliotheca Ephemerides theologique Lovaniensium 54. Leuven: Leuven University Press, 1981.

Lyotard, Jean Francois. *The Postmodern Condition: A Report on Knowledge*. Minneapolis: University of Minnesota Press, 1984.

Mayes, A. D. H. "Deuteronomy 4 and the Literary Criticism of Deuteronomy." *JBL* 100 (1981) 23–51.

Miller, J. Maxwell, and John H. Hayes. *A History of Ancient Israel and Judah.* Philadelphia: Westminster, 1986. [2nd ed., 2006.]

Miskotte, Kornelis H. *When the Gods Are Silent.* New York: Harper & Row, 1967.

Moltmann, Jürgen. *The Crucified God: The Cross of Christ as the Foundation and Criticism of Christian Theology.* Translated by R. A. Wilson and John Bowden. New York: Harper & Row, 1974.

Morgan, Donn F. *Between Text and Community: The "Writings" on Canonical Interpretation.* Minneapolis: Fortress, 1990.

Nelson, Richard D. *The Double Redaction of the Deuteronomistic History.* JSOTSup 18. Sheffield: JSOT Press, 1981.

Neusner, Jacob. *Understanding Seeking Faith: Essays on the Case of Judaism.* Brown Judaic Studies 73. Atlanta: Scholars, 1986.

Patrick, Dale. *The Rendering of God in the Old Testament.* OBT. Philadelphia: Fortress, 1981.

Perlitt, Lothar. "Die Verborgenheit Gottes." In *Probleme biblischer Theologie: Gerhard von Rad zum 70. Geburtstag,* edited by Hans Walter Wolff, 367–82. Munich: Kaiser, 1971.

Placher, William C. *Unapologetic Theology: A Christian Voice in a Pluralistic Conversation.* Louisville: Westminster John Knox, 1989.

Rad, Gerhard von. *Old Testament Theology.* Vol. 2, *The Theology of Israel's Prophetic Traditions.* Translated by D. M. G. Stalker. New York: Harper & Row, 1965.

Raitt, Thomas M. *A Theology of Exile: Judgment and Deliverance in Jeremiah and Ezekiel.* Philadelphia: Fortress, 1977.

Rubenstein, Richard L. "Job and Auschwitz." *USQR* 25 (1970) 421–37.

Scarry, Elaine. *The Body in Pain: The Making and Unmaking of the World.* New York: Oxford University Press, 1985.

Sanders, James A. *Torah and Canon.* Philadelphia: Fortress Press, 1972. [2nd ed., Eugene, OR: Cascade Books, 2005.]

Smith, Daniel L. *The Religion of the Landless: The Social Context of the Babylonian Exile.* Bloomington: Meyer-Stone, 1989.

Steiner, George. *Real Presences: Is There Anything in What We Say?* London: Faber & Faber, 1989.

Toulmin, Stephen. *Cosmopolis: The Hidden Agenda of Modernity.* New York: Free Press, 1990.

Trible, Phyllis. *God and the Rhetoric of Sexuality.* OBT. Philadelphia; Fortress, 1978.

Westermann, Claus. *Isaiah 40–66: A Commentary.* Translated by David M. G. Stalker. OTL. Philadelphia: Westminster, 1969

Wolff, Hans Walter. "The Kerygma of the Deuteronomic Historical Work." In *The Vitality of Old Testament Traditions* by Walter Brueggemann and Hans Walter Wolff, 83–100. 2nd ed. Atlanta: John Knox, 1982.

7

The Epistemological Crisis
of Israel's Two Histories

(Jer 9:22–23)

Prophecy and Wisdom

Two DEVELOPMENTS IN RECENT Old Testament scholarship, when brought together, may illuminate the words and ministry of Jeremiah. First, recent emphasis on wisdom studies has shown that the sapiential tradition is not at all peripheral to the reflective life of Israel.[1] Wisdom studies are vexed by difficult questions, largely definitional in character. Depending on definitions, we may broadly locate wisdom influence at many points in the Old Testament with Crenshaw,[2] we may take a narrow view and resist the notion that sapiential influences can be identified outside conventional wisdom literature.

This paper does not intend to engage those sticky debates in relation to Jeremiah. While attention has been given to the possibility of wisdom influences in Amos and Isaiah,[3] only the most surface attention has thus

---

1. The literature is extensive and well known. See the bibliography by Crenshaw, "Selected Bibliography." Special note should be taken of the work of Crenshaw, Murphy, von Rad, and Zimmerli, and of the phrase of Whybray, "The Intellectual Tradition of Israel."

2. Crenshaw, "Method in Determining Wisdom Influence upon 'Historical' Literature."

3. See Terrien, "Amos and Wisdom"; Wolff, *Amos, the Prophet*; and Whedbee,

far been given to Jeremiah.[4] It seems likely that Jeremiah himself utilized the and/or imagery of the wisdom teachers.[5] But lacking definitions, that will not be insisted upon here.

More important is the awareness that the appearance of wisdom influences (wherever they appear) of necessity raises important epistemological issues. When the conventions of a society seem to function, when life is coherent and manageable, when all the definers of reality agree on perception, epistemological questions are screened out and need not ever be raised, much less agreed upon.[6] It is likely that most of the wisdom teachers, at least the ones usually stereotyped by that label, function with such an epistemological consensus. And predictably, their teaching need not be risky nor very profound. They could work from "assured results."

It is when the conventions of society collapse, the consensus disappears and life is experienced as incoherent, that the community is pressed to re-examine its epistemological presuppositions and deal with the fundamental issues of how the known is known and what is known.[7] It is the suggestion of this study that Jeremiah lived precisely in a time of

---

Isaiah and Wisdom.

4. See the sparse suggestions of Lindblom, "Wisdom in the Old Testament Prophets."

5. See McKane, "Jeremiah 13:12–14: A Problematic Proverb." Several matters will require a quite new perspective on the question: (a) Muilenburg ("Baruch the Scribe") has opened new possibilities in understanding those parts of Jeremiah which may be tilted toward sapiential influences. More radically, Wanke (*Untersuchungen zur sogenannren Baruchschrift*) has called into question our usual presuppositions about Baruch; (b) the matter of Jeremiah's relation to Deuteronomic circles of tradition must be rethought in light of the work of Weinfeld (*Deuteronomy and the Deuteronomic School*) with the prospect of wisdom influences; (c) it is now clear that the rigid distinction of categories among various traditions cannot be sustained in the neat manner of Mowinckel. For all these reasons, new categories of interpretation will need to be found for Jeremiah studies which, among other things, take wisdom influences into account.

6. In the following references to epistemological issues, I am working with the constructs especially articulated by Berger, *The Sacred Canopy*; Luckmann, *The Invisible Religion*; and Berger and Luckmann, *The Social Construction of Reality*. Pertinent also is the notion of "life-world" from Schutz and Luckmann, *The Structures of the Life-World*. The wisdom teachers reflected in the positive teaching of proverbs presumed a life-world in which there was a major consensus which needed to be neither challenged nor defended.

7. See the discussion of anomie by Merton, *Social Theory and Social Structure*, chapters 4 and 5, Jeremiah clearly spoke in a context of anomie which was derived from Israel's ineffective ways of knowing. Crenshaw has been especially sensitive to these matters in his concern for wisdom and theodicy.

collapse of the consensus when the epistemological issues were most raw. The wisdom tradition that he apparently criticizes likely belonged to the royal definers of reality. They continued to operate by a now discredited consensus. And conv Jeremiah (perhaps characteristically for a prophet) insists that epistemological questions must be raised which will seriously challenge the illusionary regnant consensus and the royal definition of reality.[8] Thus, I suggest, we may circumvent the problem of an adequate definition of wisdom if we discern the clash between those who presume an epistemological consensus (wisdom teachers, perhaps, but surely royal ideologues) and those who press the hard, unanswered epistemological issues (Jeremiah and, in my view, the prophets generally).[9]

If wisdom is characterized in some way as the deposit of the best observations coming from a long history of reflection on experience, then it is likely that this epistemology will settle for things which enhance continuity.[10] The substance of such a deposit will inevitably be conservative in its support of things as they are.[11] It is the task of the prophet, in such a context, not simply to protest such a deposit, but to raise fresh

---

8. Underwood, *The Church, the University and Social Policy*, has shown how the crucial task of ministry is the raising of epistemological issues. It means to be concerned with "systems of knowledge and power" (1:126). It is clear that this was the crucial task in the time of Jeremiah as in the present time, when the old consensus has collapsed. It may well be that Hosea and Jeremiah, both of whom stress "knowing," are the very ones who have in Israel discerned the depth of the crisis and are aware that any lesser question is futile.

9. I do not intend to utilize any narrow, precise definition of "wisdom" nor do I presume any necessarily close relation between royal court and an identifiable wisdom school. Rather I am concerned more broadly with the whole way in which an established community of opinion preserves, discerns, knows and decides. Wisdom both affirms and presents a critique of this unexamined intellectualclimate. It is my impression that scholarship may miss these urgent issues if it focuses on narrow and precise definitions and misses the epistemological crisis. My approach here addresses what Crenshaw calls "wisdom thinking." This approach enables us to take seriously the stress on falseness, so well underscored by Overholt, *The Threat of Falsehood*. Šqr does not refer to concrete acts, but to a wrong discernment of all of life.

10. Whybray, *The Intellectual Tradition in the Old Testament*, has advanced the discussion by speaking more inclusively of an "intellectual tradition" rather than a wisdom movement. This paper urges that wisdom be recognized as the consensus by which established order sustains and legitimates itself. Dennis J. McCarthy, SJ, has suggested the phrase, "intellectual patrimony" (oral communication).

11. See Gordis, "The Social Background of Wisdom Literature"; and Kovacs, "Is There a Class-Ethic in Proverbs?"

epistemological questions which may have been screened out by the not disinterested tradition of perception.[12]

Israel's Two Histories

Second, in addition to the widespread attention to wisdom in the Old Testament, it is also clear from recent study that we may identify two histories in the community of Israel, each powered by a different memory, each providing a different lens through which life may be experienced. One such history we may characterize as *Mosaic–covenantal*. It focused upon the radical intrusion of Yahweh through saving events on behalf of the historically powerless. That history is of course borne by the great succession of Moses, Joshua, and Samuel, and continued to inform the prophets. That history experienced and presented the God of Israel as an intruder who was continually calling establishment reality into question. The tradition referred consistently to his intention for freedom and justice which characterized his coming to Israel. George Mendenhall has articulated this in sociological categories to suggest that this history powered a people's revolt against tyrannical urban government.[13] It represented a radical critique that prevented the absolutizing of the present arrangement. It also yielded a promise that an alternative social arrangement is yet to be given.

The other history we may characterize as *Davidic–royal*. It was shaped by the conviction of Yahweh's abiding, sustaining presence in behalf of legitimated political-cultural institutions, especially the royal house and derivatively the royal temple. Whereas the first history is radically concerned for *justice*, this royal history is more concerned for order ("peace and prosperity") and it relies on the institutions which are designed to create and maintain that order.

This Davidic–royal history can be assessed in more than one way. Read positively from a political perspective, the development of enduring social institutions enabled Israel to survive and develop as a responsible historical entity. Theologically, it permitted an institution to be a vehicle for a vision of a messianic reality expressed, e.g., in Psalm 72. This

12. On the discussion of the relation of interest and perception in heremeneutics, see Herzog, "Liberation Hermeneutic as Ideology Critique?"; Miranda, *Marx and the Bible*; and Sano, "Neo-Orthodoxy and Ethnic Liberation Theology."

13. His programmatic statement is in *The Tenth Generation*, but he had indicated the major line of his argument already in "The Hebrew Conquest of Palestine."

monarchial reality provided a guarantee of a humane order in a social world of hostility and threat. Such an institutionally self-conscious order of course needed a management mentality to sustain itself and to preside over its resources. It also needed protection (might), resources (riches), and technical skill (wisdom) to accomplish its goals.[14]

This same history can also be assessed negatively. Mendenhall most critically has characterized this history as "the paganization of Israel."[15] The development of bureaucracy, harem, standing army, tax districts and temple are not only institutions which concretize a social vision. They are also ways by which pagan, i.e., non-covenantal, patterns of life were adapted from Israel's neighbors.[16] This radical adaptation caused the abandonment of a certain vision of history, the loss of a covenantal notion of God and humanity and a forgetting of the messianic vision the monarchy was intended to guarantee. In short, all the epistemological questions were settled in terms of self-serving continuity. Proper protection became a way of authoritarian management. Necessary skill in governance became a way of preventing change. The consensus of the new institution created a context in which human questions could no longer be raised.[17]

Now it may be that Mendenhall has overstated the case. It is likely that this Jerusalem version of history and reality also has a more positive value as the only possibility of cultural continuity and creativity in Israel. But we may not miss the high cost in terms of human freedom and justice.[18]

These two histories, Mosaic–covenantal and Davidic–royal, continue in tension with each other all through Israel's story. During the period of the United Monarchy, it is likely that the rival priestly orders carry these rival traditions. Frank Cross[19] has indicated that the Aaronite order,

14. That list is not so different from the conclusion of Mendenhall, "The Monarchy," 156, "in any given culture, ideology, social organization and technology" are both essential and interrelated. The triad of Jer 9:22 must be understood not in terms of moral virtues, but in terms of sociological realities.

15. Cf. Mendenhall, "The Monarchy," 160; and Mendenhall, "Samuel's Broken Rib," 67.

16. See the primary evidence and example of Mendelsohn, "Samuel's Denunciation of Kingship in Light of the Akkadian Documents from Ugarit."

17. See the statement of Gottwald, "Biblical Theology or Biblical Sociology?" showing the political implications of some forms of religious consensus.

18. The royal consciousness is never primarily concerned about such matters. In that context one might observe the "interest" served in the program of Skinner, *Beyond Freedom and Dignity*.

19. Cross, *Canaanite Myth and Hebrew Epic*, 195–215.

perhaps linked to Hebron and Bethel, was in conflict with the Mushite order, associated perhaps with Nob and Shiloh.[20]

In the period of the divided monarchy, it seems likely that the same two consciousnesses are in tension, borne by the dynasty and the prophets.[21] The enduring conflict between them surfaces in the unresolved epistemological question of what is known and how it is known. The royal (sapiential) tradition,[22] inevitably conservative, fashions a life-world which is essentially settled. What is valued, i.e. true and life-giving, consists in the resources managed by the king and his retinue. Alternatively, the Mosaic–covenantal tradition is. characteristically in tension, as it finds the core of a legitimate epistemology in the Exodus–Sojourn–Sinai memories, stories of intervention by Yahweh on behalf of the politically, historically disenfranchised against the Egyptian royal reality. The royal consciousness developed a consensus which screened out such an unbearable concern. It was unbearable because, on the one hand, it kept raising to consciousness those very elements in society which had been declared non-existent.[23] On the other hand, it was unbearable because it articulated a freedom and sovereignty for God which would not be domesticated by the royal apparatus.

This sustained tension between the two histories, as Paul Hanson has now shown,[24] continues into Israel's later history. Hanson has labeled the two opinions as "pragmatic" and "visionary." As he characterizes the two, they are radically distinguished by their epistemology. The pragmatists are those who benefit from the way things currently are. They give religious legitimacy to the present arrangement of realized eschatology. The visionaries are the "world-weary" who have been treated unfairly and so dare to risk and hope. They hold together the tragedy of human

20. See the development from Cross's suggestion by Halpern, "Levitic Participation in the Reform Cult of Jereboam I."

21. See Rendtorff, "Reflections on the Early History of Prophecy in Israel," who explores the dialectical relation of king and prophet.

22. It is my judgment and presupposition in this paper that sapiential tendencies, broadly identified, can best be understood in relation to the royal consciousness. For the purposes of this paper, I do not regard the more precise and technical issues of definition to be pertinent. Nor do I wish to deny the force of the "clan hypothesis." But it seems clear that as far as Jeremiah is concerned, he deals with a royal phenomenon.

23. On the royal attitude to peasant, see the unpublished paper by Halligan, "The Role of the Peasant in the Amarna Period." The power of the throne is enormous in denying history to the powerless.

24. Hanson, *The Dawn of Apocalyptic.*

denial with a conviction of God's sovereign freedom which will lead to a new future, calling the present into question.

Not in any of these instances—not in the United Monarchy with Zadok and Abiathar, not in the Divided Monarchy with kings and prophets, not in the later period with the accommodators and hopers—is the issue resolved. It is always a question of *singular reliance* on Yahweh or a more *prudent*[25] embrace of the gifts of culture that seem more secure and that are not always obviously incompatible with Yahweh. The question of *prudence* and *singular reliance* focuses the epistemological issue. It is that issue that is addressed in this discussion of Jeremiah and wisdom in Jer 9:22–23.

Jeremiah and the Alternative Covenantal Vision

Jeremiah is placed at a critical juncture in the on-going tension between these two histories. The international history of the time suggested radical changes and disappearance of the old certainties. The internal political history of Judah is characterized by vacillation in foreign policy, with unrelieved fascination with Egypt, by an extraordinary sequence of kings who could not develop a sustained policy, and by a peculiar reform movement which impacted at least the king and no doubt his very particular constituency.

Jeremiah's perception of his people and his leaders is that things had gone utterly sour. Or in our terms, the Davidic–royal history had reached a point of irredeemable failure. The very consciousness which appeared dominant and seemed to have coopted the Mosaic tradition had failed. The prophet is repelled by what he sees. For him, it is a question whether the royal consciousness can be penetrated at all. The royal consciousness, secure in its own illusionary perceptual consensus, continued its risky game of self-deception (cf. Jer 6:14; 8:11), engaging in the traditional royal ploys of purchased justice, denied humanness, double-tongued diplomacy. In that make-believe world, the royal apparatus could finally overcome or outlast every threat and question. While the royal arrangement potentially may have been the vehicle for a peculiar social vision, it had by this time become concerned only for self-securing and self-justification, and indeed, for survival.

25. There can be little doubt that "prudence" is crucial to a sapiential approach to life. What is apparent in the sociological studies cited is that such prudence is never politically or socially disinterested. Prudence is concerned not to disturb the present ordering. (Amos 5:13 is characteristic in that regard.)

Jeremiah's sense of the history of his people with Yahweh was so different that he could hardly communicate. He raised questions that lay outside the grasp of his royal contemporaries. Informed by a tradition of the freedom and sovereignty of God who could create and destroy, who could begin things and end things,[26] he took as his program that Yahweh will "build/plant," "tear down/pluck up."[27] Kings in Israel seldom recognized that there had been beginnings when God would plant and build—because the royal reality appeared to be ordained forever. The royal perception was that there was no history before it, because it is the source of history. And surely there could be no ending, never plucking up and tearing down, because royal reality will endure. The royal arrangement fully contains history and things will continue to be as they have been. Jeremiah insists that there are radical turns, pasts to move from and futures to embrace. Kings know no past or future, but only "now" is to be defended and celebrated.

Jeremiah translated his alternative covenantal vision into an alternative political reality. Babylon is called and ordained by Yahweh to cause an end to a royal history which ·presumed it would go on forever:

> Behold, I will send for all the tribes of the north, says the Lord, and for Nebuchadnezzar, the King of Babylon, my servant, and I will bring them against this land and its inhabitants, and against all these nations round about. (Jer 25:9)[28]

That of course is more than kings can take and more than the royal consciousness can ever receive. It must be dismissed as a "weakening of the hands" of the king (38:4).

So the issue is joined between the two histories. It is joined visibly, for Jeremiah is in deathly conflict and great danger from those who cannot bear his word (11:21–23).[29] It is also joined internally, for Jeremiah

---

26. There can be little doubt that Jeremiah belongs to the circle of northern tradition fed by Mosaic memories and expressed in the traditions of Hosea and Deuteronomy.

27. Variations on the theme occur in 1:10; 12:14–17; 18:7–9; 24:6; 31:28; 32:10; 42:10; 45:4. Cf. Bach, "Bauen und Pflanzen."

28. See also Jer 27:6 and 43:10. While it may be that textual problems can lessen the claim of these particular texts as Lemke ("Nebuchadnezzar, My Servant") has argued, there is little question that this expectation from Babylon is central to Jeremiah's discernment of Yahweh's will for Judah, Cf. Overholt, "King Nebuchadnezzar in the Jeremiah Tradition."

29. In an unpublished paper, "Jeremiah and the 'Men of Anatot,'" McBride has suggested that the men of Anathoth are not among the villagers of his home community

knows in his person the wrenching of the two histories in conflict.[30] In his person there is anguish over valuing what is, deeper anguish over abandoning it for the sake of Yahweh's freedom and sovereignty. Jeremiah anguishes because he himself is not sure which history is true history. He cannot easily walk away from royal reality which must at times appear to be the only real history.[31] And yet he is deeply sure that that epistemology is based on an unreality. That wisdom is based on a consensus which has no correspondence to reality.

The Collision of Epistemologies

It is the suggestion of this essay that in 9:22–23 these two issues, (a) the problem of wisdom and the epistemological crisis, and (b) the two alternative histories in Israel, come together and provide in this text a focal point[32] from which the work of Jeremiah can be discerned. In these verses Jeremiah voices in sharpest form the hard epistemological questions facing Judah, the royal consciousness notwithstanding. In these verses, the two histories collide and are sorted out, in a way characteristic for the prophets and in a way quite unacceptable to the royal consciousness.[33]

---

but must be located "within the Jerusalem establishment of the prophet's day, particularly among prominent Temple personnel." Such a judgment would strengthen the intensity of the conflict between the two perceptions of reality.

30. It is not necessary to pursue the question of the meaning of Jeremiah's "laments" here. Even if Reventlow (*Liturgie und prophetisches Ich bei Jeremia*, 205–57) is not correct in their being public liturgical pieces, he is surely correct in seeing that the struggle concerns not a private problem but anguish over the course and end of Israel's public life. On that anguish as it reflects an alternative consciousness, cf. Heschel, *The Prophets*, esp. 108–27.

31. That issue is clearest in the encounter with Hananiah, Jeremiah 27–28. Cf. Kraus, *Prophetie in der Krisis*, 82–104.

32. Duhm, *Das Buch Jeremia*, 97, had dismissed the text as "ein harmlos unbedeutender Spruch." On the contrary, this paper suggests that it may provide a decisive point of entry to understand the tensions and intent of the tradition of Jeremiah.

33. The verses contain no textual problems which need detain us. Perhaps the last negative of v. 22 might have an added conjunction to parallel the second, but it is not necessary. In v. 23, the LXX has a conjunction before the second object of the participle, but that also is unnecessary. The authenticity of the saying has been challenged by Duhm and recently by Holladay, *Jeremiah: Spokesman Out of Time*, 59. The following, however, retain it: Giesebrecht, *Das Buch Jeremia*, 61–63; Rudolph, *Jeremia*, 63; Bright, *Jeremiah*, 75–80. There seems no compelling reason to regard the words as other than those of Jeremiah.

Only in a most general way can anything be determined about the present placement of the verses in the text. It is possible that the unit is displaced here.[34] In the general movement of Jer 8:4—10:25, we may note the recurrent reference to themes of "know" and "wisdom":

- My people do not know the ordinance of Yahweh. (8:7b)

- How can you say "we are wise" . . .
  Behold the *false* pen of the scribes have made it a *lie*.[35]
  The *wise* men shall be put to shame . . .
      and what *wisdom* is in them? (8:8–9)

- They did not *know* how to blush. (8:12b)[36]

- They do not *know* me, says Yahweh. (9:2b [ET: 3b])

- They refuse to *know* me, says Yahweh. (9:5b [ET: 6b])

- Who is the man so *wise* that he can *understand* this? (9:11 [ET: 12])

- Send for the *wise* women to come . . . (9:16b [ET: 17b])[37]

- I *know*, O Yahweh, that the way of man is not in himself,
  that it is not in man who walks to direct his steps,
  Correct me, O Yahweh . . . (10:23–24a)[38]

- Pour out thy wrath upon the nations that *know* you not. (10:25a)

Two problems must be acknowledged in such a listing. First, it is likely that this is a collection of various fragments that have no original coherence. Nonetheless, they have been brought together, and it may well be that our themes of *knowing* and *wisdom* have been the guide for

---

34. So Peake, *Jeremiah and Lamentations*, 1:169; Streane, *Jeremiah*, 68.

35. On *šqr* here and characteristically, see Overholt, *The Threat of Falsehood*, 74–82. The lie refers to a fundamental misconception of covenantal reality.

36. On forgetting how to blush, see the remarkable words of Heschel, *Who is Man?*, 112–14. He quotes our verse in making the contrast between self-glorification and "a sense of ultimate embarrassment."

37. Clearly the term refers to skill and so is not theologically important. Cf. 4:22 for a similar use. Nonetheless, it adds to the semantic field being explored by the prophet.

38. This saying clearly echoes sayings in the book of Proverbs. Cf. von Rad, *Old Testament Theology*, 1:439, and his comment on Prov 16:9; 19:21; 21:2; 16:2; 20:24; 21:30–31. Each raises the issue both of this passage and of our primary text. The plea for correction with the word yiisar suggests a sapiential-educational tradition. Cf. Kraus, "Geschichte als Erziehung," 267–71. Note the importance of the word to Hosea. Whybray (*Intellectual Tradition in the Old Testament*, 128), while suggesting the term belongs to the sphere of education, denies it specifically to wisdom.

bringing them together.[39] Second, it is obvious that the words italicized have a variety of different nuances, exploring a whole field of meanings. But perhaps even with this recognition, it is not too much to conclude that in all of them the poetry means to pose the central epistemological question that Jeremiah discerned at the end of royal history. The ones who claim to know do not know. There is no knowledge of the Torah (8:7), nor of how to blush (8:12), nor of Yahweh (9:2, 5; 10:25). The only positive knowing (10:23–24) is done by Jeremiah himself in a statement suggesting that he knows what the others do not know. Thus, even the positive statement is another way of asserting that the others do not know. Most of all, what they do not know is that man (= king) is not self-reliant. Jeremiah's knowledge is contrasted with the non-covenantal foolishness of the royal consciousness.[40] This climactic statement recognizes that human well-being is not derived from human capacity.

Thus 10:23–24 speak of true wisdom. But the wisdom of Judah, presumably held by members of the other history in the royal circle, is a joke (cf. 8:8–9), because in all their pretension, they cannot do what must be done. The wise men have failed (9:11[12]), and the only wisdom now valued is that which knows how to weep (9:16[17]), i.e. those who do not pursue their self-deception continuously but who have the sensitivity to respond appropriately to death.[41] That is, the real wisdom appropriate to the moment is to recognize the end that surely has come upon this people. There is no other wisdom in Judah that now can make any difference.

The entire "unit" uses images which are at least reminiscent of wisdom teaching. It employs analogy (8:6–7), rhetorical questions (8:4–5, 8–9, 12, 19, 23; 9:11[12])[42] as well as admonition (9:3–4[4–5]). Thus the style of the unit, if it may be regarded now as a unit, raises the question

---

39. Westermann, *Jeremia*, 36, suggests the principle of *Stichwort*.

40. See Gowan (*When Man Becomes God*) on the problem of hybris as it shapes royal consciousness. See McKane (*Prophets and Wise Men*, 89–90), who speaks of "self-contained . . . sagacity," and helpfully relates our passage to a trajectory of related passages.

41. Cf. Amos 5:16. Perhaps the same motif is present in Matt 5:4, surely a sapiential form. The blessed are the ones who are wise enough to know the appropriate response to the proper time. Royal consciousness is likely not attentive to the times, because the establishment believes only in managed time. Cf. Jer 8:7 on not knowing the times, surely not the time for repentance and death, and von Rad, *Wisdom in Israel*, 138–43.

42. In Brueggemann, "Jeremiah's Use of Rhetorical Questions," I have shown that Jeremiah's use of the form serves to call into question conventional presuppositions and conclusions, a very different function from the usual wisdom teaching.

of knowing and wisdom in a context of painful ending and death. True knowing consists in facing Yahweh's remarkable freedom. Real wisdom consists in acknowledging death and responding appropriately (9:20[21]). The foolishness of the so-called wise is to have business as usual. The lie they speak (8:8; 9:2, 4 [3, 5]), the deception they practice (9:4–5[5–6]) is that they continue in the illusion of the royal history that knows no end or beginning but only cherishes *shalom* (8:11, 15) and anticipates healing (8:22)[43] but cannot recognize that this history is finished. It is the other history, of planting and building, of plucking up and tearing down, in which Judah must now participate. Kings cannot do that.

So the epistemological issue is joined. It is not a theoretical issue of experience and authority. It is a question of having defined reality in ways that keep what is real from ever surfacing. And Jeremiah must now use his best imagination to show that it is history with a covenant-making God that is the only history. Every other history is an illusion and a deception.

Two Contrasting Triads

Thus 9:22–23 is not inappropriate to its present context, which concerns wisdom/foolishness on the way to death. Jeremiah had discerned that while the royal consciousness presumed its own continued well-being, that history was already destined for death. The form of this saying is likely sapiential,[44] but that is difficult to sustain in light of our fuzzy definitions. The messenger formula at the beginning seems inappropriate to its style, but it may be imposed on this saying in order to claim authority in the harsh conflicts of epistemologies. (In chapters 8–10, the messenger formula occurs elsewhere only in 9:6, 16 [7, 17].) The concluding formula,

43. See Muilenburg, "The Terminology of Adversity in Jeremiah," 46, 50, 57 and passim.

44. So Weiser, *Das Buch Jeremiah*, 89; von Rad, *Wisdom*, 102–3; and Scott, *Proverbs and Ecclesiastes*, xxxv. This saying apparently meets the requirements of Crenshaw as well. Dürr (*Erziehungswesen*, 182) has not only linked our passage to wisdom but has explicitly related it to Prov 3:7. Gerstenberger in turn has found Prov 3:7 to be a summary and motto for wisdom instruction generally; cf. Gerstenberger, *Wesen und Herkunft des "Apodiktischen Rechts,"* 49. If both Dürr and Gerstenberger are correct, as seems likely, then our passage may indeed express a central wisdom teaching. However, the teaching is much more concrete than is Prov 3:7. The warning is not only against "evil," but wisdom, riches and power. The urging is not only toward fear of Yahweh but also toward very specific covenantal factors.

ne'um yahweh, also occurs in 8:17; 9:2, 5, 8, 21, 24 [3, 6, 9, 22, 25], but seems to recur in various settings without impacting the rhetoric.[45]

Thus both formulae seem to be extraneous and may be discounted. Without them the saying appears to be a didactic statement, consisting in two parts, first three negative admonitions, then a contrasting positive with three members together with a motivational clause:

> Let not (*'al*)[46] the wise one glory in his wisdom, and
>
> Let not (*'al*) the mighty one glory in his might
>
> Let not (*'al*) the rich one glory in his riches
>
> But (*ki' 'im*) let him who glories, glory in this,
>
> that he understands and knows me.
>
> Surely (*ki*) I am Yahweh who does kindness,
>
> justice, and righteousness in the land.
>
> Surely (*ki*) in them I delight.

The three negatives, all modifying *yithallel*,[47] introduce a triad. The reflexive verb serves here to turn the subject back on himself.[48] What is prohibited by the negative plus the reflexive is preoccupation with self and self's resources.[49] The alternative is sharply presented by the abrupt *ki' 'im*. The same verb is used, but the object now is not self-resources. The boast now concerns Yahweh.

45. Cf. Rendtorff, "Zum Gebrauch der Formel '*ne'um Jahwe*' im Jeremiabuch"; and North, "The Expression The Oracle of Yahweh as an Aid to Critical Analysis," x. The form is apparently not integral to this unit, as is also the case in a number of passages in Jeremiah.

46. It is worth noting that the negative is not *lo'* as might be expected, but *'al*, which might also stress the sapiential connection, as Gerstenberger would argue.

47. The hithpael form of *hll* is not used often. In Proverbs it is used three times negatively (25:14; 27:1; 30:14) and once positively (31:30). Elsewhere, it is used for praise to Yahweh (Pss 34:3; 63:12; 64:11; 105:3; 106:5; 1 Chr 16:10; Isa 41:16; 45:25; and especially to be noted Jer 4:2). It is used negatively in Pss 49:7; 52:3; 97:7. Outside of these poetic passages, it is used only in 1 Kgs 20:11, on which comment will be made below.

48. Too much should not be made of the grammatical form in claiming this. Its usage simply shows two primary functions, (a) in praise of Yahweh; and (b) inordinate celebration of something else, often implying pride and self-preoccupation. Mendenhall suggests the form means "saying *hallelu* to self" (oral communication).

49. In such uses it is the very opposite of the affirmation of Jer 10:23–24, also a wisdom saying.

The two motivational clauses, both introduced by *ki*, serve to delineate further this recommended choice so sharply contrasted with the previous objects of wisdom, might, and riches. Yahweh is not to be confused with or associated with wisdom, might or riches, He is differently characterized, again by a triad: *ḥesed*, *mišpaṭ*, and *ṣedaqah*. That triad is surely deliberately cast in parallel form but radically contrasted in substance. The second *ki* clause further identifies what is legitimate for approval and celebration.

The form is clearly didactic, but not strenuously hortatory.[50] The *ki' 'im* is too common a form to be identified as sapiential. But we may note a peculiarly close parallel in Prov 23:17–18a:

> Let not (*'al*) your heart envy sinners,
>> But (*ki 'im*) continue in the fear of Yahweh all the day.
> Surely (*ki 'im*) there is a future,
>> and your hope is not cut off.[51]

The parallel in form is close, but not total in the three parts: *'al, ki 'im, ki 'im*. But the second *ki 'im* in the proverb does not function as a disjunctive as does the first but in fact serves as a motivational clause. With that provision, the form is a striking parallel to the passage under consideration which has *'al, ki 'im, ki*. The rhetorical stress of our unit falls on *ki 'im* which serves to contrast the two triads. The *ki 'im* is used broadly and is not the monopoly of any circle of tradition. While it serves to contrast, it may also serve to introduce a radical call to a certain kind of behavior:

> And now, Israel what does Yahweh your God require of you,
>> but (*ki 'im*) to fear . . . to walk . . . to love,
>>> to serve . . . to keep . . . ? (Deut 10:12–13)
>
> And what does Yahweh require of you
>> but (*ki 'im*) to do justice,
>> to love kindness, and
>> to walk humbly with your God? (Mic 6:8)[52]

50. The tone is not unlike the "summary-appraisal form" identified by Childs, *Isaiah and the Assyrian Crisis*, 128–36. Our form contains a number of conclusions not dissimilar to the climactic conclusion of Childs's form. Similarly, these conclusions do not urge a specific action but simply make a non-discussable judgment about conduct and consequences.

51. The form with this particle serves to make a sharp, unqualified distinction between sinners and fearers of the Lord. Characteristically in such parallelisms, it serves to contrast.

52. While this teaching is now set in a prophetic context, it also echoes a sapiential

It may be used to introduce a new teaching which replaces the old:

> In those days they shall no longer say:
>> "The fathers have eaten sour grapes,
>> and the children's teeth are set on edge."
>
> But (*ki 'im*) every one shall die for his own sin;
>> each man who eats sour grapes,
>> his teeth shall set on edge. (Jer 31:29–30)[53]

It may be used to contrast what is in quantity but of indifferent value and what is rare but precious:

> But (*ki 'im*) the poor man had nothing but one little ewe lamb which he had bought. (2 Sam 12:3)[54]

It serves to create an opening for new behavior:

> Yahweh made a covenant with them, and commanded them,
> "You shall not fear other gods or bow yourselves to them
>> or serve them or sacrifice to them;
> but (ki 'im) you shall fear Yahweh . . .
>> You shall not serve other gods
> But (*ki 'im*) you shall fear Yahweh your God . . ." (2 Kgs 17:35–36, 38–39)[55]

These parallel uses make clear the radical contrast Jeremiah draws between the two triads, which are not simply lists of virtues and vices but which embody the core of the two histories and which provide the parameters of contrasting epistemologies. The form itself would suggest that there is a deathly way and a life-giving way for Israel, Jeremiah's context

---

concern. Note the address to "man," in contrast to Deut 10:12, where the same address is to Israel. Note also that the items urged are similar to those urged in our verses.

53. In a way similar to the rhetorical question, the particle challenges conventional wisdom expressed in the proverb and sets out an alternative.

54. It is not necessary to insist that this parabolic form is sapiential, but its structure and intent do make a contrast in what is to be valued in a way that is surely congenial to wisdom teaching.

55. The contrast set forth by the Dtr is surely didactic. Given the suggestions of Weinfeld, we may suggest that the contrast here between service to Yahweh and to the other gods is not unlike the sharp sapiential contrast of Prov 8:32–36, which presents ways to life and death.

is one in which the death-choosers think their way will lead to life. His anguish is that he has discerned its sure end in death.

Critique of the Royal Consciousness

The first triad—*wisdom, might, riches*—characterizes one history in Israel, the royal history. These three terms occur nowhere else together. The prophet has constructed a new triad that intends to summarize the whole royal history which has continually reassured and deceived its key actors, but which has now brought Judah to the point of death. One could not imagine a more radical critique of the royal consciousness, for Jeremiah disposes in one stroke of all the sources of security and well-being upon which the royal establishment is built.

His critique is of course more radical than the older proverbial wisdom. That reflective tradition had been aware of the temptation of riches (Prov 11:28; 23:4; 28:20). It saw the positive good of riches but believed they are gifts that will be given and are not to be pursued for themselves (Prov 3:16; 8:18; 10:4, 22; 22:4; 28:25).

Even that tradition is radical enough to see that riches deceive and are finally linked to foolishness which will destroy:

> A rich man is wise in his own eyes
>
>> but a poor man who has understanding (*bin*) will find him out. (Prov 28:11)[56]

But we are still in the area of relatively simple virtue in a quid-pro-quo world. In that world there is little reflection at all upon the problem of might. It is not particularly celebrated and other things are better (Prov 16:32), but it is scarcely an item of interest. And certainly wisdom receives no critique, except as noted, when one is "wise in his own eyes." In that world, *might* is of little concern, *wisdom* is to be valued, and only *riches* are seen as a danger.

Thus Jeremiah's polemic does not grow out of that tradition in any direct sense. It is only when these matters are discerned in royal history

---

56. McKane, *Proverbs*, 621, has observed that this saying equates wealth and impiety, poverty and piety. The fool is one who will not submit to Yahweh and to Torah. McKane observes that the question of theodicy has surfaced, surely an issue that came to full expression in the pathos of Jeremiah. This saying on wisdom is more radical than most in Proverbs and reflects the tradition to which Jeremiah appeals.

that they are a threat. That history, beginning with Solomon,[57] has turned these three matters into a way of life which is self-securing and finally numbing, both toward human need as well as divine purpose. While Jeremiah may draw upon wisdom teaching, he fashions this negative summary out of a direct response to royal history which seemed utterly secure and yet which now had led to death. That he adds wisdom and might to the sapiential warning on riches indicates how he has deepened the critique to an epistemological level:

(1) Riches are of course a royal prerogative. They are the gift to the king(1 Kgs 3:11, 13; 2 Chr 1:12, Dan 11:2; Esth 1:41; 5:11). They are an identifying mark of a good king (of David, 1 Chr 29:12, 28; of Solomon, 1 Kgs 10:23; 2 Chr 9:22; of Jehoshaphat, 2 Chr 17:5; 18:1; of Hezekiah, 2 Chr 32:27). They are the king's to give (1 Sam 17:25). Riches belong precisely to royal awareness.

(2) Might does not refer here simply to the fullness of manhood as it sometimes does. Here it refers to the capacity of the royal establishment to work its will by human power before which none may issue a challenge. *Gbr* is the peculiar claim of the king (2 Sam 10:7; 16:6; 20:7; 23:9–22). The regime managed to order its own universe and combine the mythic power of virility together with the hardware of a war machine.[58]

(3) And wisdom in such a context is no longer the power to discern, but the capacity to manage and control, to reduce everything to royal proportions. By placing wisdom in the context of this triad, Jeremiah has defined and nuanced it in a harshly critical way. Wisdom is presented as self-serving. The form itself makes wisdom negative.

The triad as a whole speaks of placing trust in places from which can come no health, but the king never knows it. The critique of Jeremiah thus may be related to several other passages. (1) Psalm 49, often associated with the sapiential tradition of Israel,[59] reflects on men who trust in their wealth and who boast of the abundance of their riches.

---

57. Mendenhall, *The Tenth Generation*, 121, refers to our saying in identifying the meaning of Solomon. There can be little doubt that in his regime, this alien ideology that Jeremiah resists became legitimated in Israel.

58. Mumford, *The Myth of the Machine*, has in a general way shown the dialectical development of technology and mythic claims. More specifically related to Israel, see Mendenhall and Gottwald in the works cited.

59. There can be little doubt that this psalm is informed by wisdom traditions. Cf. Mowinckel, "Psalms and Wisdom," 213–15; and Murphy, "A Consideration of the Classification 'Wisdom Psalms,'" 161–63.

> Yes, he shall see even the wise die . . .
>
>> and leave their wealth to another
>
> Man cannot abide in his pomp (*yqr*) . . .
>
>> This is the fate of those who have foolish confidence . . .
>
>> (vss. 11, 13, 14a; cf. 17–18, 21 [ET 10, 12, 13a; cf. 16–17, 20])

The psalm discerns the boundary of self-securing. These apparent sources of long life and well-being can promise nothing.[60] (2) Psalm 52, not inappropriately assigned in the superscription against royal power, begins with an attack on a mighty man who boasts (*tithallel*) (v. 3[1]) and who trusts in the abundance of his riches and who seeks refuge in his wealth (v. 9[7]). The psalm concludes with a contrast of the well-being of the one who eschews might and riches and trusts the goodness of God. Thus David and Saul are presented as models of the two histories, David being the one who trusts and Saul the one who secures his own way and must surely come to ruin. (3) Isa 5:21–23 in turn presents a radical critique of those who are,

- wise in their own eyes (cf. Prov 28:11)

- mighty in drinking and

- takers of bribes.

While the third member of the triad is not quite "riches, "the triad is very close to that of our verse in Jeremiah.[61] The criticism ofIsaiah turns each element so that it must be negative: not wise, but wise in their own eyes, not mighty, but mighty in drinking, not rich, but only in bribes.

None of these texts—Psalms 49; 52; or Isa 5:21–23—contains our triad. But the various configurations suggest a pattern of critique against the most elemental values of the royal-urban consciousness which by the time of Josiah was bringing Judah to death. Each of these texts has affinities with what is commonly thought to be a wisdom teaching. Jeremiah challenges the foundations of the establishment credo.[62] In Jer 5:27–28

---

60. These verses have much in common with the general tenor of Ecclesiastes. Cf. Williams, "What Does it Profit a Man?" Jeremiah seems to refer to such a tradition. The difference is that he has, as they do not, a positive alternative to urge. On the triad, see esp. Qoh 9:11. Ecclesiastes asserts that neither might, nor riches, nor wisdom—the very items named in our passage—finally have any significance.

61. See Whedbee, *Isaiah and Wisdom*, 82–110, for a full discussion.

62. His radical critique is apparent in many places, but note especially 5:27–28. The prophet describes: (a) their self-deluding prosperity, (b) the disregard of order and boundary, and (c) the social consequences. In the political implications of the

he appears to appeal to a tradition of such criticism that likely is rooted in and derived from sapiential circles. But he has recast it in more radical ways. His critique characteristically is not interested in either inner attitudes or in conduct per se, but in the inevitable price paid in terms of human injustice. Thus he links deceit and oppression to refusal to know Yahweh (9:5[6]).[63] The practice of self-deception expresses itself in terms of oppression. That brings death, and Jeremiah had seen it clearly even though the royal mentality continued to deny it.

On Knowing Yahweh and Practicing Justice

The alternative history is expressed in two ways. First, to "know Yahweh." We have already noted the references in Jeremiah 8–10 on this theme. See also 2:8; 4:22; 5:4, 28–29; 7:5–6; 22:3, 16; 24:7; 31:34. The theme of knowing Yahweh has been well explored and requires no additional comment here. Wolff has established that it means knowledge of the mighty deeds and the torah claims.[64] Huffmon has shown that it refers to acknowledgment of covenantal sovereignty and required allegiance.[65] Thus the "refusal to know" is the fundamental critique against the royal consciousness because it could not embrace the serious impact of covenantal reality without giving up its claims and pretensions. Thus in contrast to the first triad, Jeremiah announces his primary theme which serves to discredit and dismantle the epistemology of the regime.

Jeremiah asserts that if Judah will have something of legitimate pride, she must terminate the royal history, which leads to death, and embrace the history of the covenant. That history, of course, is always precarious, never yields stately mansions, but in inscrutable ways brings life.[66]

---

epistemology, see Katsh, "The Religious Tradition or Traditions in a Traditionless Age," 213–17. Katsh shows how this tradition leads to democratic society and its absence to oppressive class society.

63. The text is difficult, but cf. Bright, *Jeremiah*, 66–72.

64. Wolff, "'Wissen um Gott' bei Hosea als Urform von Theologie," 533, 554.

65. Huffmon, "The Treaty Background of Hebrew *Yada'*"; Huffmon and Parker, "A Further Note on the Treaty Background of Hebrew *Yada'*."

66. On the inscrutable source of life as it relates to wisdom teaching, see Murphy, "The Kerygma of Proverbs," and Prov 8:32–36 on the gift of life from wisdom.

In terse fashion, the prophet inquires about national priorities in relation to national well-being. As in the more expansive statement of 22:13–17,[67] he lays out the life/death issues:

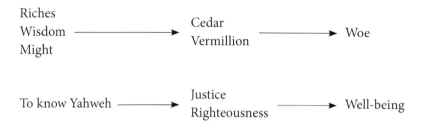

The anguish of the prophet is that he knows, cognitively and covenantally, what the royal community in its congenital stupidity could not learn.

Second, this alternative history is summarized in an equally powerful triad, *ḥesed, mišpat, ṣedaqah*. As in the first triad, the prophet has shrewdly expressed the central issue, namely, solidarity not only between person (king) and God, but in the community, the very solidarity against which wisdom/riches/might militate.[68]

This second triad occurs, to my knowledge, only in one other text, Hos 2:21–22, upon which Jeremiah is likely dependent.[69] It occurs only in these two prophets most deeply sensitive to the pathos of God[70] as articulated in covenant and most knowing about the deathly course of Israel. Only these two dare to entertain the alternative "knowing Yahweh," which will bring new life. Jeremiah has recited the entire history of death (riches, wisdom, might). Hosea has in parallel fashion reviewed the his-

67. On this text as a central one for our hypothesis of two histories, see Wolff, *Anthropology of the Old Testament*, 195–96.

68. Radical liberation theology is helping us discover that these phenomena are inherently against solidarity. This is the insight of the prophet, that riches, might and that kind of wisdom belong inevitably to the consciousness which practices domination and oppression and so destroys community.

69. On the relation of Hosea and Jeremiah, see Wildberger, *Jahwes Eigenstumsvolk*, 112; and Gross, "Hoseas Einfluss auf Jeremias Anschauungen." More recent tradition-critical study confirms this connection. More than any other they sensed the depth of the tragedy of Israel's royal consciousness. On "knowing" in Hosea, cf. 4:1, 6; 5:4; 6:4; 8:2.

70. On the pathos of God into which the prophets entered, see Heschel, *The Prophets*. On the ways in which the other consciousness leads to apathy, see Moltmann, *The Experiment Hope*, 69–84; and Sölle, *Suffering*.

tory of fickleness and betrayal. Incredibly, both of them can now use this triad to speak of an alternative history with the radically faithful one who can hring newness where death seemed final.[71] It is not very helpful to try to identify what in this comes from the traditions of wisdom or covenant or prophets. The epistemological crisis does not concern simply circles of tradition but the change made in all perceptions (of every tradition) by radical Yahwistic faith. Every epistemology is called into question when knowing begins in the faithfulness of Yahweh, which requires and evokes a responding faithfulness from Israel. Hosea and Jeremiah believed that a new history was possible, but on quite different grounds.

Trust and Desire

The two triads set the choice Israel must make. These triads, contrasted by the emphatic *ki 'im*, set in juxtaposition the two histories, the one of self-glorification, the other of vulnerable fidelity. By setting the two histories together as indeed they had finally collided in his time, Jeremiah sets the choice Israel must now make. We may learn more of the prophet's intent by noting the two envelope words, *hithallel* and *ḥapeṣ*. The crisis in Israel's history concerns a cause for glorification. Since Solomon, Israel had sought a cause for glory and since Solomon had been glorying in deathly things.

The act of boasting in and of itself is not bad. When it is addressed away from self toward God, it is of course approved and we may call it "praise" (Ps 34:3; cf. Jer 4:2; Ps 64:11). The problem for Jeremiah is not boasting, but it is boasting turned toward self, i.e., toward royal history as the generator of its own life, meaning, and security. Again we may note the affinities with the psalms already cited:

---

71. Yahweh is not only in favor of these things, but he does them. His doing them makes clear that he has freedom to act against and in spite of the royal management which attempted to circumscribe his action. The saying asserts that Yahweh will work his will in spite of all the ideological commitment to wisdom, riches and power which try to prevent it. This is in contrast to the mood of the time expressed in Zeph 1:12. On Yahweh as doer cf. Volz, *Der Prophet Jeremia*, 118, as well as Isa 9:6. On the participial form, see Job 9:9–12, with the double verb plus the concluding rhetorical question, and Amos 4:8. Thus the form is likely sapiential. The substance concerns his royal authority in the face of those who deny or circumscribe it. On the royal motif, see Jer 23:5; Pss 99:4; 103:7; and on wisdom formulation, Exod 34:7, with Dentan, "The Literary Affinities of Exodus XXXIV 6f."; see also Giesebrecht, *Das Buch Jeremia*, 62.

> Men who trust (*baṭaḥ*) in their wealth
> > and boast of the abundance of their riches. (Ps 49:7[6])

> Why do you boast, O mighty man . . .
> See the man who would not make God his refuge,
> > but trusted (*baṭaḥ*) in the abundance of his riches
> > and sought refuge in his wealth. (Ps 52:3, 9)

In both texts the term *tithallel* is parallel to *baṭaḥ*. Boasting thus is understood as misplaced trust. The word *baṭaḥ* occurs in various contexts, 5:17; 7:4; 8:13; 9:3[4]; 13:25; and Isa 31:1. See especially the harsh declaration of Jer 2:37: "Surely Yahweh has rejected those in whom you trust," and the contrast:

> Cursed is the man who *trusts* in man . . .
> Blessed is the man who *trusts* in Yahweh,
> > whose trust is in Yahweh. (17:5a, 7)

Again the two histories are clearly contrasted.

Concerning the formula used in our text, we may learn from the defiant statement of the king of Israel to the taunting Ben-Hadad: "Let not him that girds on his armor boast himself (*yithallel*)[72] as he that puts it off" (1 Kgs 20:11). Probably this was a sapiential saying that warned against claiming too much in prospect, in contrast to legitimate claims in retrospect.[73] Thus it is a warning against presuming too much for one's own powers in a situation likely to be beyond one's control. But it is now used in this narrative as a defiant affirmation of trust in Yahweh against enormous odds. On the basis of this parallel, Jeremiah may be understood as throwing down the gauntlet of radical faith against enormous odds, i.e., of trusting and obeying Yahweh's covenantal gifts and demands in the face of external threat and internal collapse. In the same defiant manner as 1 Kgs 20:11, Jeremiah asserts that the power of riches, wisdom, and might, the substance of royal history, is a poor match against *ḥesed*, *mišpaṭ*, and *ṣedaqah* in determining what will finally shape history.

---

72. This is the only text in the narrative traditions of the Old Testament in which the hithpael occurs. It is a remarkable passage that contrasts the boasting of Syria and the confidence in Yahweh expressed by Israel. On the formulae of the chapter as assertions of faith, see Zimmerli, "Das Wort des gottlichen Selbsterweises," 129.

73. Cf. Gray, *I & II Kings*, 376, and Hermisson, *Studien zur israelitischen Spruchweisheit*, 43.

Attention may also be called to David's defiance of Goliath.[74] While not a wisdom saying, it also makes a defiant contrast in the face of the enemy. The two-part assertion is not unlike that of our text:

> You come to me with a sword
>> with a spear and
>> with a javelin,[75]
>
> but I come to you in the name of Yahweh of hosts
>> the God of the armies of Israel
>> whom you have defied. (1 Sam 17:45)[76]

Again we are offered an assertion of the power of Yahweh against the apparent power of Goliath. The giant is mismatched because David's presuppositions lie outside Philistine awareness and call into question that entire understanding of reality.

In both 1 Kgs 20:11 and 1 Sam 17:45, sharply contrasting views of reality are presented in the context of war and in the face of a maJor threat. In both cases reliance on Yahweh calls into question the presuppositions of the other party. In a similar way Jeremiah uses what appears to be a sapiential form, perhaps honed by usage in a context of defiance against a stronger military power, to call Judah to a new history in covenant.[77] The Israelites whom Jeremiah addresses are as misinformed about reality as are Goliath and BenHadad. A wisdom teacher might declare what is proper for boasting and what is not. A war story might turn this against an arrogant enemy. But the form has been radicalized by Jeremiah to carry the fundamental challenge to royal presuppositions,

74. See the comment of Hermisson, ibid.

75. Note the triad. Too much should not be made of the triad, but perhaps it illuminates the pair of triads in our passage. The same historical consciousness is reflected in the triad sword/spear/javelin as in the triad riches/might/wisdom.

76. Attention might be drawn in this connection to 1 Sam 16:18 where David is presented as the one with the true wisdom and capacity to cope with the boaster. In that text he may well be a paradigm of the way in which wisdom and faith are held together. The critique of Jeremiah is that wisdom and its companion properties have displaced faith. Cf. Hermisson, *Studien zur israelitischen Spruchweisheit*, 125.

77. After this essay was completed, I became aware ofthe analysis of Jeremianic texts by Holladay, *The Architecture of Jeremiah 1–20*. In his analysis of Jeremiah 4–6, 8, Holladay suggests: "there is a steady movement in each of these sections from battle scenes to wisdom preoccupations . . . the battle is a lesson to the people" (67, 85). See ibid., 110–13, for a parallel comment on 8:14—9:8. What Holladay discerns in a larger structural analysis is indicated also concerning our verses.

and this against his own king. If that is a correct way of understanding the text, we may better understand the promise to Jeremiah (1:17–19) that he will be a safe man of war against the odds, for the risky proposition of Jeremiah against his contemporaries is at least as bold and risky as David against Goliath or Ahab against Ben-Hadad.[78]

The term of self-congratulations, *tithallel*, is balanced by the concluding term *ḥapeṣ* in our text.[79] Its climactic position gives its stress, so that the entire saying contrasts the self-congratulations of the royal managers and the unfailing desires of Yahweh. The prophet clearly means to assert that the history of Israel and her risky future will not be determined by self-securing but by his purposes. *Ḥapeṣ* cannot be assigned to any circle of tradition in particular. It is used for acceptance of cultic offerings, in wisdom instruction and in interpersonal relations.

Applied to Yahweh, several stresses are important: (1) The term is used to assert Yahweh's radical freedom to do what he wills (Pss 115:3; 135:6; Jonah 1:14). (2) In his radical freedom he may reject (Pss 65:12; 66:4; 5:5) and even will death (Judg 12:23; 1 Sam 2:24; Ezek 18:23). (3) His characteristic action is that he wills life and not death (Ezek 18:32; 33:11), but the gift of life requires radical turning. Thus the word bears the good news that Yahweh wills covenanted living. (In this regard as in so many, Jeremiah has affinities with Ezekiel and holds out the promise of life.) (4) The substance of his desiring of life is the triad of the alternative history of (*ḥesed, mišpaṭ, ṣedaqah*). When this is practiced, life comes. When it is not, death comes. This understanding of the will of Yahweh is twice articulated:

> Surely I DESIRE *ḥesed* and not sacrifice
> > *knowledge of God* rather than burnt offerings.
> > (Hos 6:6; cf. 1 Sam 15:22–23)[80]

> He does not retain his anger forever
> > because he DELIGHTS in *ḥesed*. (Mic 7:18)

---

78. On war themes in Jeremiah, see Bach, *Die Aufforderungen zur Flucht und zum Kampf im Alttestamentlichen Prophetenspruch*; and Miller, "The Divine Counsel and the Prophetic Call to War."

79. Holladay, *The Architecture of Jeremiah 1–20*, 123, comments on *ḥpṣ* in this text by observing the structural link to 6:10 which is the only previous occurrence.

80. Note that in 1 Sam 15:22–23, along with delight, there is also rejection, a point worth noting in the context of Jeremiah's crisis.

The dramatic teaching thus presents a good newstbad news pattern which surely will lead to life or death.

A Theology of the Cross

It is not too much to suggest that Jer 9:22–23 might provide a screen through which Jeremiah can be understood more generally. It is not at all, as Duhm suggested, "a harmless, meaningless text." Rather it articulates the basic issues that finally cannot be avoided in Judah, especially in the seventh to the sixth centuries. Our analysis suggests that Jeremiah spoke out of a complex relation with Israel's sapiential tradition. On the one hand he utilized a speech form and manner of instruction that is likely sapiential. On the other hand, he polemicizes against a self-contained wisdom that will bring death. The presumed wisdom of Israel has turned out to be a foolishness to death. Conversely, the foolishness of the fragile purposes of Yahweh,[81] which seems of little note, finally will bring life.

In categories of Christian faith, Jeremiah here presents a theology of the cross in protest against a theology of glory. In that way, the use of this saying by Paul in 1 Cor 1:26–31 is seen to be not casually or incidentally related. Rather in dealing with the scandal of the gospel, Paul has discerned that Jeremiah rightly presented the scandal which violates royal history.[82] The wisdom of kings is foolishness. The strength of kings is weakness. The riches of kings is poverty (cf. 2 Cor 8:9). What Paul discerned in Jesus of Nazareth[83] Jeremiah has seen about Judah's death gasp in his time. Things are not as they seem, especially to kings (cf. Prov 25:2). That is what wisdom always sought, to find out how things are. God's capacity to hide things outdistances the capacity of the kings to find out.

---

81. Cf. Isa 55:8–9. In what is likely a·sapiential motif, the poet insists God's purposes are different from those of his people. That contrast is fundamental to faithful wisdom, but never honored by kings who wish to monopolize wisdom and identify the regime with the purposes of God.

82. See the analysis of Bailey, "Poetic Structure of 1 Cor. 1:17—2:2."

83. Volz, *Der Prophet Jeremia*, 118–19, notes a derivative motif also in Jas 1:9–10; see also 2 Cor 10:27.

Bibliography

Bach, Robert. *Die Aufforderungen zur Flucht und zum Kampf im alttestamentlichen Prophetenspruch.* WMANT 9. Neukirchen: Neukirchener, 1962.

———. "Bauen und Pflanzen." In *Studien zur Theologie der alttestamentlichen Überlieferungen,* edited by Rolf Rendtorff and Klaus Koch, 7–32. Neukirchen: Neukirchener, 1961.

Bailey, Kenneth E. "Poetic Structure of 1 Cor. 1:17—2:2." *Novum Testamentum* 17 (1975) 268–96.

Berger, Peter. *The Sacred Canopy: Elements of a Sociological Theory of Religion.* Garden City, NY: Doubleday, 1969.

Berger, Peter, and Thomas Luckmann. *The Social Construction of Reality: A Treatise in the Sociology of Knowledge.* Garden City, NY: Doubleday, 1966.

Bright, John. *Jeremiah.* AB 21. Garden City, NY: Doubleday, 1965.

Brueggemann, Walter. "Jeremiah's Use of Rhetorical Questions." *JBL* 92 (1973) 358–74.

Childs, Brevard S. *Isaiah and the Assyrian Crisis.* SBT 2/3. Naperville. IL: Allenson, 1967.

Crenshaw, James L. "Bibliography." In *Studies in Ancient Israelite Wisdom,* edited by James L. Crenshaw, 46–60. Library of Biblical Studies. New York: Ktav, 1976.

———. "Method in Determining Wisdom Influence upon 'Historical' Literature." *JBL* 88 (1969) 129–42. Reprinted in *Studies in Ancient Israelite Wisdom,* 481–94.

———, ed. *Studies in Ancient Israelite Wisdom.* Library of Biblical Studies. New York: Ktav, 1976.

Cross, Frank Moore. *Canaanite Myth and Hebrew Epic: Essays in the History of the Religion of Israel.* Cambridge: Harvard University Press, 1973.

Dentan, R. C. "The Literary Affinities of Exodus XXXIV 6f." *VT* 18 (1963) 34–51.

Duhm, Bernhard. *Das Buch Jeremia.* Kurzer Hand-Commentar zum Alten Testament 11. Tübingen: Mohr/Siebeck, 1901.

Dürr, Lorenz. *Das Erziehungswesen im Alten Testament und im Antiken Orient.* Mitteilungen der Vorderasiatisch-Ägyptischen Gesellschaft 36/2. Leipzig: Hindrichs, 1932.

Gerstenberger, Erhard S. *Wesen und Herkunft des "Apodiktischen Rechts."* WMANT 20. 1965. Reprinted, Eugene, OR: Wipf & Stock, 2009.

Giesebrecht, F. *Das Buch Jeremia.* Göttingen Handkommentar zum Alten Testament. Göttingen: Vandenhoeck & Ruprecht, 1907.

Gordis, Robert. "The Social Background of Wisdom Literature." In *Poets, Prophets, and Sages,* 160–97. Bloomington: Indiana University Press, 1971.

Gottwald, Norman K. "Biblical Theology or Biblical Sociology?" *Radical Religion* 2 (1975) 42–57.

Gowan, Donald. *When Man Becomes God: Humanism and Hybris in the Old Testament.* Pittsburgh Theological Monograph Series 6. Pittsburgh: Pickwick, 1975.

Gray, John. *I & II Kings.* OTL. Philadelphia: Westminster, 1963.

Gross, K. "Hoseas Einfluss auf Jeremias Anschauungen." *NKZ* 42 (1931) 241–56, 327–43.

Halligan, J. M. "The Role of the Peasant in the Amarna Period." In *SBL Seminar Papers,* 155–71. Missoula, MT: Scholars, 1976. [Reprinted in *Palestine in Transition: The Emergence of Ancient Israel,* edited by David Noel Freedman and David F. Graf, 15–24. Social World of Biblical Antiquity Series 2. Sheffield: Almond, 1983.]

Halpern, Baruch. "Levitic Participation.in the Reform Cult of Jereboam I." *JBL* 95 (1976) 31–42.

Hanson, Paul D. *The Dawn of Apocalyptic: The Historical and Sociological Roots of Jewish Apocalyptic Eschatology*. Rev. ed. Philadelphia: Fortress, 1979.

Hermisson, Hans-Jürgen. *Studien zur israelitischen Spruchweisheit*. WMANT 28. Neukirchen-Vluyn: Neukirchener, 1968.

Herzog, Frederick. "Liberation Hermeneutic as Ideology Critique?" *Int* 28 (1974) 387–403.

Heschel, Abraham. *The Prophets*. New York: Harper & Row, 1962.

———. *Who Is Man?* Stanford: Stanford University Press, 1965.

Holladay, William L. *The Architecture of Jeremiah 1–20*. Lewisburg, PA: Bucknell University Press, 1976.

———. *Jeremiah: Spokesman Out of Time*. Philadelphia: United Church Press, 1974.

Huffman, Herbert B. "The Treaty Background of Hebrew *Yada'*." *BASOR* 181 (1966) 31–37.

Huffman, Herbert B., and Simon B. Parker. "A Further Note on the Treaty Background of Hebrew *Yada'*." *BASOR* 184 (1966) 36–38.

Katsh, Abraham. "The Religious Tradition or Traditions in a Traditionless Age.'" In *Christian Action and Openness to The World*, edited by Joseph Papen, 189–218. Villanova, PA: Villanova University Press, 1970.

Kovacs, Brian. "Is There a Class-Ethic in Proverbs?" In *Essays in Old Testament Ethics (J. Philip Hyatt, in Memoriam)*, edited by James L. Crenshaw and John T. Willis, 173–89. New York: Ktav, 1974.

Kraus, Hans-Joachim. "Geschichte als Erziehung." In *Probleme Biblischer Theologie: Gerhard von Rad zum 70. Geburtstag*, edited by Hans Walter Wolff, 267–71. Munich: Kaiser, 1971.

———. *Prophetie in der Krisis*. Biblische Studien 43. Neukirchen: Neukirchener, 1964.

Lemke, Werner. "Nebuchadnezzar, My Servant." *CBQ* 28 (1966) 45–50.

Lindblom, Johannes. "Wisdom in the Old Testament Prophets." In *Wisdom in Israel and in the Ancient Near East*, edited by Martin Noth and D. W. Thomas, 193–200. VTSup 3. Leiden: Brill, 1955.

Luckmann, Thomas. *The Invisible Religion: The Problem of Religion in Modern Society*. New York: Macmillan, 1967.

McBride, S. Dean, Jr. "Jeremiah and the 'Men of Anatot.'" Unpublished paper.

McKane, William. "Jeremiah 13:12–14: A Problematic Proverb." In *Israelite Wisdom: Theological and Literary Essays in Honor of Samuel Terrien*, edited by John G. Gammie et al., 107–20. Homage Series 3. Missoula, MT: Scholars, 1978.

———. *Prophets and Wise Men*. SBT 1/44. Naperville, IL: Allenson, 1965.

———. *Proverbs: A New Approach*. OTL. Philadelphia: Westminster, 1970.

Mendelsohn, I. "Samuel's Denunciation of Kingship in Light of the Akkadian Documents from Ugarit." *Bulletin of the American Schools of Oriental Research* 143 (1956) 17–22.

Mendenhall, George E. "The Hebrew Conquest of Palestine." *Biblical Archaeologist* 25 (1962) 66–87.

———. "The Monarchy." *Int* 29 (1975) 155–70.

———. "Samuel's Broken *Rib*." In *No Famine in the Land: Studies in Honor of John L. McKenzie*, edited by James W. Flanagan and Anita Robinson, 63–74. Missoula, MT: Scholars, 1975.

———. *The Tenth Generation: The Origins of the Biblical Tradition*. Baltimore: Johns Hopkins University Press, 1973.

Merton, Robert. *Social Theory and Social Structure*. Glencoe, IL: Free Press, 1957.

Miller, Patrick D., Jr. "The Divine Counsel and the Prophetic Call to War." *VT* 18 (1968) 100–107.

Miranda, José Porfirio. *Marx and the Bible: A Critique of the Philosophy of Oppression*. Translated by John Eagleson. 1974. Reprinted, Eugene, OR: Wipf & Stock, 2004.

Moltmann, Jürgen. *The Experiment Hope*. Translated by M. Douglas Meeks. Philadelphia: Fortress, 1975.

Mowinckel, Sigmund. "Psalms and Wisdom." In *Wisdom in Israel and in the Ancient Near East*, edited by Martin Noth and D. W. Thomas, 205–24. VTSup 3. Leiden: Brill, 1955.

Muilenburg, James. "Baruch the Scribe." In *Proclamation and Presence: Old Testament essays in honour of Gwynne Henton Davies*, edited by John I. Durham and J. R. Porter, 215–38. London: SCM, 1970.

———. "The Terminology of Adversity in Jeremiah." In *Translating and Understanding the Old Testament*, edited by H. T. Frank and W. L. Reed, 42–63. New York: Abingdon, 1970.

Mumford, Lewis. *The Myth of the Machine*. 2 vols. New York: Harcourt, 1967, 1970.

Murphy, Roland E. "A Consideration of the Classification 'Wisdom Psalms.'" In *Congress Volume: Bonn 1962*, 157–62. VTSup 9. Leiden: Brill, 1963.

———. "The Kerygma of Proverbs." *Int* 20 (1966) 3–14.

North, Francis S. "The Expression The Oracle of Yahweh as an Aid to Critical Analysis." *JBL* 71 (1952) x.

Overholt, Thomas W. "King Nebuchadnezzar in the Jeremiah Tradition." *CBQ* 30 (1968) 39–48.

———. *The Threat of Falsehood: A Study in the Theology of the Book of Jeremiah*. SBT 2/16. London: SCM, 1970.

Peake, A. S. *Jeremiah and Lamentations*. 2 vols. Century Bible. Edinburgh: Jack, 1910–11.

Rad, Gerhard von. *Old Testament Theology*. 2 vols. Translated by D. M. G. Stalker. New York: Harper & Bros., 1962.

———. *Wisdom in Israel*. Translated by James Martin. Nashville: Abingdon, 1972.

Rendtorff, Rolf. "Reflections on the Early History of Prophecy in Israel." In *History and Hermeneutic*, edited by Robert W. Funk, 14–34. Journal of Theology and Church 4. New York; Harper & Row, 1967.

———. "Zum Gebrauch der Formel 'ne'um Jahwe' im Jeremiabuch." *ZAW* 66 (1954) 27–37.

Reventlow, Henning Graf. *Liturgie und prophetisches Ich bei Jeremia*. Gütersloh: Mohn, 1963.

Rudolph, Wilhelm. *Jeremia*. 2nd ed. HAT 12. Tübingen: Mohr/Siebeck, 1958.

Sano, Roy. "Neo-Orthodoxy and Ethnic Liberation Theology." *Christianity and Crisis* 35 (1975) 258–64.

Schutz, Alfred, and Thomas Luckmann. *The Structures of the Life-World*. Translated by Richard M. Zaner and H. Tristram Engelhardt Jr. Northwestern University Studies in Phenomenology and Existential Philosophy. Evanston, IL: Northwestern University, 1973.

Scott, R. B. Y. *Proverbs and Ecclesiastes*. AB 18. Garden City, NY: Doubleday, 1965.

Skinner, B. F. *Beyond Freedom and Dignity*. New York: Knopf, 1971.

Sölle, Dorothee. *Suffering*. Philadelphia; Fortress, 1975.

Streane, A. W. *Jeremiah*. Cambridge Bible. Cambridge: Cambridge University Press, 1913.

Terrien, Samuel. "Amos and Wisdom." In *Israel's Prophetic Heritage: Essays in Honor of James Muilenburg*, edited by Bernhard W. Anderson and Walter Harrelson, 108–15. New York: Harper, 1962.

Underwood, K. *The Church, the University and Social Policy: The Danforth Study of Campus Ministries*. 2 vols. Middletown, CT: Wesleyan University, 1969.

Volz, Paul. *Der Prophet Jeremia*. KAT 10. Leipzig: Deichert, 1922.

Wanke, Gunther. *Untersuchungen zur sogenannten Baruchschrift*. BZAW 122. Berlin: de Gruyter, 1971.

Weinfeld, Moshe. *Deuteronomy and the Deuteronomic School*. 1972. Reprinted, Winona Lake, IN: Eisenbrauns, 1992.

Weiser, Artur. *Das Buch Jeremia*. Alte Testament Deutsch 20–21. Göttingen: Vandenhoeck & Ruprecht, 1960.

Westermann, Claus. *Jeremia*. Biblisches Seminar. Stuttgart: Calwer, 1967.

Whedbee, J. William. *Isaiah and Wisdom*. New York: Abingdon, 1971.

Whybray, R. N. *The Intellectual Tradition in the Old Testament*. BZAW 135. Berlin: de Gruyter, 1974.

Wildberger, Hans. *Jahwes Eigentumsvolk: Eine Studie zur Traditionsgeschichte und Theologie des Erwählungsgedankens*. Abhandlungen zur Theologie des Alten und Neuen Testaments 37. Zurich: Zwingli, 1960.

Williams, James. "What Does it Profit a Man?" In *Studies in Ancient Israelite Wisdom*, edited by James L. Crenshaw, 375–89. Library of Biblical Studies. New York: Ktav, 1976.

Wolff, Hans Walter. *Amos the Prophet: The Man and His Background*. Edited by John Reumann. Translated by Foster R. McCurley. Philadelphia: Fortress, 1973.

———. *Anthropology of the Old Testament*. Translated by Margaret Kohl. Philadelphia: Fortress, 1974.

———. "'Wissen um Gott' bei Hosea als Urform von Theologie." *EvTh* 12 (1952/53) 533–54. Reprinted in *Gesammelte Studien zum Alten Testament*, 182–205. ThBü 22. Munich: Kaiser, 1964.

Zimmerli, Walther. "Das Wort des göttlichen Selbsterweises (Erweiswort): Eine prophetische Gattung." In *Gottes Offenbarung: Gesammelte Aufsätze zum Alten Testament*, 120–32. ThBü 19. Munich: Kaiser, 1963. [ET = "The Word of Divine Self-Manifestation (Proof-saying): A Prophetic Genre." In Zimmerli, *I Am Yahweh*, edited by Walter Brueggemann, 99–100. Translated by Douglas W. Stott. Atlanta: John Knox, 1982.]

8

"Exodus" in the Plural

(Amos 9:7)

SINCE THE EMERGENCE OF a critical consensus in Old Testament study in the nineteenth century, it has been agreed that the prophecy of Amos, preserved as the book of Amos, provides the first clear, uncontested evidence that Israel had arrived at ethical monotheism.[1] Indeed, liberal developmentalism came to regard the words of Amos as the first utterance of "Israel's normative faith." This scholarly consensus concerning "ethical monotheism" was viewed in such interpretation as a great positive victory over (a) polytheism, which was primitive and ignoble, and (b) cultic religion, which smacked of magic and manipulation. That is, classical liberal scholarship, with its unabashed Christian commitments, wedded to a developmental notion of Israel's faith, viewed Amos as the clear emergence of what is right and good and noble, which would eventuate in Christianity. There could be no going back on this monotheism.[2]

---

1. Fosdick, *A Guide to Understanding the Bible*.

2. On the scholarly debate on monotheism, see especially M. S. Smith, *The Early History of God*; and Miller, "Israelite Religion." Particular attention should be paid to the work of Bernhard Lang, cited there. Sanders ("Adaptable for Life") has nicely used the phrase "monotheizing tendency," by which he means that Israel is "soft" on a full monotheism. I understand my comments here not to be opposed to those of Sanders but to state the other side of a dialectic that is critical of absolutism. There was as well a pluralizing tendency, albeit a minmity report among those who formulated canon.

One God, One People

It was not so readily recognized in nineteenth-century developmentalism that ethical monotheism, insofar as that is a correct judgment about Amos, not only constituted a great theological gain in the history of Israelite religion but also brought with it an enormous ideological temptation, a temptation most often readily accepted. It was proudly and doxologically affirmed that Yahweh was one or that Yahweh was the only one,[3] and, moreover, that this one and only Yahweh had as a partner a one and only people Israel, so that there was taken to be a complete commensurability between the "onlyness" of Yahweh and the "onlyness" of Israel.[4] And where the "onlyness" of Yahweh has, as an adjunct affirmation, namely the onlyness of Israel, it is self-evident that the ideological temptation to absolutize Israel along with an absolute Yahweh is almost irresistible.

We may consider two impetuses for this ideological extension of the "onlyness" of Yahweh to include the "onlyness" of Israel, which I shall term mono-ideology.[5] The first impetus, not at all surprising, is the Davidic-Solomonic, royal ideology that insisted upon a close connection between Yahweh and royal Israel, as a way of giving theological legitimation to political power. Indeed, Rainer Albertz has suggested that monotheism becomes an indispensable counterpart to the claims of monarchy and that monotheism in Israel emerges only as needed for monarchy.[6]

This ideological combination of one God and one people is evident in David's response to Yahweh's legitimating oracle uttered by Samuel in 2 Samuel 7. In the oracle, Yahweh through Samuel promises to David:

> I will raise up your offspring after you, who shall come forth from your body, and I will establish his kingdom. He shall build a house for my name, and I will establish the throne of his kingdom forever. I will be a father to him, and he shall be a son to me. When he commits iniquity, l will punish him with a rod such as mortals use, with blows inflicted by human beings. But I

---

3. The translation of Deut 6:4 concerning Yahweh as "one" or as "only" is not obvious. See Miller, *Deuteronomy*, 97–104; Janzen, "On the Most Important Word in the Shema"; and McBride, "The Yoke of the Kingdom."

4. I use the awkward term "onlyness" in order to flag that the use of monotheism is a particularly performative notion in scholarship.

5. I intend by this term to refer not only to theological monotheism but also to its allied claim of mono-people.

6. Albertz, *A History of Israelite Religion*, 1:105–38. See also Albertz, "Der Ort des Monotheismus in der israelitischen Religionsgeschichte."

will not take my steadfast love from him, as I took it from Saul, whom I put away from before you. Your house and your kingdom shall be made sure forever before me; your throne shall be established forever. (vv. 12b–16)

Yahweh makes an open-ended, unconditional promise to the dynasty.

In his reception of this oracle (vv. 18–29), David articulates due deference to Yahweh and his own unworthiness (vv. 18–21). But then David moves promptly to hold Yahweh to Yahweh's promise (vv. 28–29). In the middle of this affirmation, David breaks out in doxology concerning the incomparability of Yahweh:

Therefore you are great, O Yahweh God; for there is no one like you, and there is no God besides you, according to all that we have heard with our ears. (v. 22)[7]

This doxological assertion, however, is followed immediately by a parallel claim for Israel, that is, royal Israel:

Who is like your people, like Israel? Is there another nation on earth whose God went to redeem it as a people, and to make a name for himself, doing great and awesome things for them, by driving out before his people nations and their gods? And you established your people Israel for yourself to be your people forever; and you O Yahweh, became their God. (vv. 23–24)

There is no God like Yahweh. There is no people like Israel. Israel's incomparability is derivative from and shaped by the singular, irreversible, incomparable commitment of Yahweh to Israel. Thus we anive not only at mono-theism but also at mono-ethnism, or mono-people. The rhetorical question of v. 23,

Who is like your people, like Israel?
Is there another nation on earth . . . ?

requires a negative answer. There is none like Israel. There is not another nation on earth whose' God wants to redeem it as a people. The claim of Yahweh is now deeply and intimately tied to the claim ofisrael. There is not room on this horizon for any other people.

The second impetus for this remarkable mono-linkage is in Deuteronomic theology, likely the source of the exclusive covenantal relation

---

7. Labuschagne (*The Incomparability of Yahweh in the Old Testament*) has fully reviewed the formulae of incomparability.

between Yahweh and Israel and surely the proximate source of the "Yahweh alone" party in Israel.[8] The ideological intention of the Deuteronomic tradition is not so simple and straightforward as the royal ideology we have just cited, for it is at the same time rooted in the Mosaic covenant, and yet makes room for royal claims.[9] It is plausible that in the figure of Josiah, the model king of the Deuteronomists, we see the Deuteronomic hope for a Davidic king fully committed to the Mosaic Torah (cf. Deut 17:14–20), thus faithfully honoring both traditions.[10]

However that may be concerning the Deuteronomic theology, there is no doubt that the traditions of Deuteronomy also attached singular claims for Israel to the singular claims made for Yahweh. This is evident in the "centralizing" tendency of Deuteronomy, concerning the cult place in Jerusalem. Just as there is only one Yahweh, so there is only one right place of worship:

> But you shall seek the place that Yahweh your God will choose out of all your tribes as his habitation to put his name there. You shall go there, bringing there your burnt offerings and your sacrifices, your tithes and your donations, your votive gifts, your freewill offerings, and the firstlings of your herds and flocks. And you shall eat there in the presence of Yahweh your God, you and your households together, rejoicing in all the undertakings in which the Lord your God has blessed you . . . But only at the place that Yahweh will choose in one of your tribes—there you shall offer your burnt offerings and there you shall do everything I cqmmand you. (Deut 12:5–7, 14)

It is, of course, correct that the tradition of Deuteronomy tries to distance itself from the crass claims of presence made by high royal theology, by the device of "the name."[11] Thus it is not Yahweh, but Yahweh's "name"

8. On the "Yahweh alone" party, see M. Smith, *Palestinian Parties and the Politics That Shaped the Old Testament.* On the cruciality of Deuteronomy, see Perlitt, *Bundestheologie im Alten Testament,* and the summary of the discussion by Nicholson, *God and His People.*

9. Von Rad, *Studies in Deuteronomy,* 74–91. The same material is reiterated by von Rad, *Old Testament Theology,* 1:334–47.

10. Here I make no claim for the historicity of the account offered by the Deuteronomists of Josiah. Even if the account is fiction, it evidences the determination of this tradition to hold together Mosaic Torah and royal claims.

11. The peculiar function of "name theology" was first identified in contemporary scholarship by von Rad, *Studies in Deuteronomy,* 37–44. It has now been more fully explicated in relation to other theologies of presence by Mettinger, *The Dethronement*

that is in Jerusalem. Given that provision, however, it is unambiguous that the Deuteronomic traditions were powerful in generating the view that the one Yahweh must be worshiped only in the one place by the one people of Yahweh. And while the program of Deuteronomy may have been in the interest of purging theological deviations in the service of the purity of Yahwism, there is also no doubt that mono-place theology had an ideological dimension, in legitimating the royal–scribal–Levitical interpretive claims of Jerusalem.

In a somewhat later text from the same tradition, one can see this ideological claim that attaches Israel to Yahweh with considerable force:

> You must observe them diligently, for this will show your wisdom and discernment to the peoples, who, when they hear all these statutes, will say, "Surely this great nation is a wise and discerning people!" For what other great nation has a God so near to it as Yahweh our God is whenever we call to him? And what other great nation has statutes and ordinances as just as this entire law that I am setting before you today? (Deut 4:6–8)

The evident intention of this statement is to make a bid for obedience to the Torah. The subtext of the statement, however, is that only Israel has a God so near, and only Israel has a Torah so just; that is, only Israel can claim to be peculiarly privileged in the world of the nations. Thus what purports to be a theological affirmation of "only Yahweh" turns out to be a claim, in rather blatant ways, for "only Israel."

Now if "Israel" be understood simply as a theological entity bound in covenant to Yahweh and extant in history only to obey Torah, this singular and exclusive linkage to Yahweh is not a drastic problem. It yields something like a sound ecclesiology, albeit a triumphalist one. The inescapable problem, of course, is that Israel (and belatedly the church) is never simply a theological entity, but it is always a socioeconomic-political entity, alive to issues of power, and therefore endlessly capable of committing overt ideological claims for itself.

Thus it takes no great imagination to anticipate, that with royal claims that assert the Yahwistic oddity of Israel (as in 2 Sam 7:11–16) and Deuteronomic claims that assert the Yahwistic oddity of Israel (Deut 4:5–8; 12:5–7, 14) then Israel will be prepared, uncritically, to transpose

---

of Sabaoth, 38–79. One important example of name theology is evident in 1 Kings 8. In vv. 12–13, we are offered an unqualified notice of material presence in the temple, which is promptly protested in vv. 27–30, which are evidently an expression of the theology of name.

its theological claim of "ethical monotheism" into an ideological claim for the singularity, peculiarity, and privilege of Israel as a political entity in the world. This ideological claim, I propose, in the eighth century is not only an understandable outcome of emergent monotheism but also an outcome that was proposed, propelled, and driven by the needs of monarchy and by that rather gingerly support of monarchy, namely, the Deuteronomic school.

Thus while nineteenth-century scholarship, with its developmentalist inclination, would celebrate the emergence of ethical monotheism, ideology criticism at the end of the twentieth century can notice that what is a theological gain in Israel can be recognized, at the same instant, as a problematic and seductive assertion.[12] This assertion enabled Israel to imagine itself as privileged, in every sphere of life, as Yahweh's unrivaled and inalienable partner.

One God, Many Peoples

The problematic of emerging ethical monotheism in Israel is this: Is it possible to make a theological claim for Yahweh that is not shot through with ideological accoutrements for Israel? We are wont to answer, "Yes, it is possible." The evidence in the Old Testament is not that it is impossible but that it is exceedingly improbable. In any case, on the ground, monotheism is problematic as a social practice because it invites all kinds of reductionisms that are taken to be equated with or commensurate with or in any case inevitably derived from Yahweh's singleness.

It is into such a situation that the prophet Amos apparently uttered his word.[13] The problem be addressed is not that the Israelites did not believe in Yahweh but that they believed too much. They believed not only that Yahweh alone is God but also that Israel alone is Yahweh's people. A consequence of this ideological linkage is that Israel became self-satisfied

---

12. I take the terms developmental and ideological to contrast in a specific and accurate way the dominant horizons of classical nineteenth-century scholarship and our present situation. Part of the work of Old Testament theology is now to move our understanding of texts out of a developmental pattern and into an awareness of the ideological dimension of texts.

13. Here I make no historical assumptions about Amos but seek to work with the text as it comes to us. See n. 10 above.

in its ethics and in its worship, so that its very "orthodoxy" became a warrant for self-indulgence (cf. Amos 4:4–5; 6:1–6).[14]

In countering this distortion of Yahwism (which passed for orthodoxy in context), the strategy of Amos is to accept the high claims of Yahwism and then to turn those claims against Israel.[15] Thus in the oracles against the nations (1:3—2:16), Amos speaks Yahweh's harsh judgment against the nations, only to circle Israel's geographical environment and then to deliver the harshest judgment against Judah (2:4–5) and Israel (2:6–26).[16] In the succinct statement of Amos 3:2, the poet, in the first two lines, accepts Israel's exclusive claim upon Yahweh, apparently alluding back to the ancestral traditions of Genesis (Gen 12:3; 18:19). Indeed, the introduction of 3:1 appeals precisely to the exodus, the primal "electing" deed of Yahweh. But those appeals to the tradition are utilized by the poet as a rhetorical setup for the harsh judgment of the second half of the verse:

> therefore I will punish you for all your iniquities. (3:2b)

The "therefore" ('al-ken) of this phrase suggests that the very tradition of chosenness (here "known") is the ground and the reason for severe judgment. Thus Amos must struggle with an ethical, monotheistic Yahwism that has been drawn too tightly into self-confidence and that has issued in a distorting self-sufficiency.

In this chapter, I propose to deal with only one verse, which presents the poet as struggling precisely against the settled orthodoxy that is problematic. The poetic lines of 9:7 seem to stand alone, without a connection to what precedes or follows them:

> Are you not like the Ethiopians to me,
>> O people of Israel? says Yahweh.
> Did I not bring Israel up from the land of Egypt,
>> and the Philistines from Caphtor and the Arameans from Kir?

---

14. Of course the term orthodoxy is an anachronism here. But the confrontation in Amos 7:10–17, between the prophet and the priest who is the chaplain of the king, suggests that there was an authorized interpretation of matters that would tolerate no deviation. Thus the term is not remote from the actual conflict. On the text in Amos 7:10–17, see Ackroyd, "A Judgment Narrative between Kings and Chronicles?"

15. On this strategy in Amos, see Dell, "The Misuse of Forms in Amos."

16. The oracle against Judah is often regarded as late in the text. This judgment, however, has no bearing on the argument I am seeking to make.

Andersen and Freedman treat the verse in connection with v. 8, so that v. 7 functions for v. 8, by giving the warrant for the judgment, in the same way that the two parts of 3:2 relate to each other.[17] That connection may be correct, but it is not required by the text and in any case falls beyond the scope of my concern here. It is my suggestion that Amos seeks to undermine the assured mono-ideology of Israel-mono-Yahweh, mono-Israel, perhaps mono-Jerusalem[18]—by introducing a radical pluralism into the character of Yahwism, a pluralism thatsubverts Israel's self-confident mono-faith.

The four-line utterance of 9:7 is organized into two rhetorical questions, broken only by the authorizing formula "says Yahweh." The first question ends in a vocative, "people of Israel,"[19] so that this is a direct and intimate appeal, acknowledging Yahweh's attentiveness to Israel. It is to those who are fully self-conscious about their identity as the Israel of God that this question is addressed. The question posed is about the likeness, comparability, and similarity of Israel and the Ethiopians (Cushites). The formulation in Hebrew is even more shocking than our usual reading, because "Ethiopians" precedes "you": "Are not the Ethiopians like you?"

The question is not clear about its expected answer. At our distance, we are prepared to assume that the answer is yes. "Yes," the Ethiopians are like us. But the entire ideological development ofIsrael, royal and Deuteronomic, had prepared the answer "no." No, the Ethiopians are not like us. No, no one is like us.[20] The question is made more demanding by the indirect object, "to me," that is, to Yahweh. Now the comparison of Israel and Cush is not territorial or political or ethnic or linguistic. It is Yahwistic: alike to Yahweh.

Israel, of course, does not answer. The poet does not seem to have waited for an answer. It might have been wise for Israel to anticipate the ploy of Ezekiel, who, when asked an equally demanding question, answered, "O Lord Yahweh, you know" (Ezek 37:3). But, of course, Israel, in the face of Amos, could not beg off as did the later prophet. Because

17. Anderson and Freedman, *Amos*, 867–70.

18. Polley (*Amos and the Davidic Empire*), in part following John Mauchline, has proposed that the book of Amos is committed to a Davidic political vision of reality.

19. The text, of course, reads "sons," but the inclusive rendering does not at all change the intention of those who are addressed.

20. It is not clear that the contrast means to accent the matter of race; that is, the Ethiopians are blacks. If this dimension is intended, then, of course, the radicality of the contrast is even more powerful.

Israel did know the answer in its self-congratulatory mono-faith; Israel was clear that there is no other such God, no other such people, with a God so near and a Torah so righteous. Clearly the putting of the question throws all such uncritical confidence into confusion.[21] The "to me" of the question means that Yahweh stands outside the cozy reductions of certitude and confidence that marked Israel's theo-politics.

The second question of our text, introduced by the same interrogative particle with a negative, is more complex. It falls into two parts, except that the two parts cannot be separated. The first part is easy enough: "Did I not bring Israel up from the land of Egypt?" Of course! Amos has already affirmed that (2:10; 3:1).[22] Israel has affirmed that claim since Moses. The problem, of course, is that the question does not end there. If it did, it could be easily answered. It continues uninterrupted, with a simple conjunction "and," without a new or even reiterated verb. The same verb, "bring up," still functions and governs the second half of the question. Only now the object of this good and familiar verb, the Exodus verb, consists in two (bad!) peoples, never before linked to Israel's exodus verb or to Israel's theological discourse. The question permits an oxymoron:

> bring up . . . Philistines,
>
> bring up . . . Arameans.

How can Amos use a perfectly good, salvific verb with Yahweh as subject, related to enemies? (Notice that, in geopolitical terms, nothing has changed about these enemies; it is still Palestinians in the Gaza Strip and Syrians in the Golan Heights).

The listeners to Amos surely wanted to answer the first line of the second question with a resounding yes and the second with a militant no. The problem for such an inclination is that it is only one question and it admits of only one answer. To answer no is to give up, in the first line, the identity-giving claim of tradition. To answer yes is to give up the mono-claim of Yahwistic "ethical monotheism," as understood in royal and Deuteronomic traditions. So Israel (wisely? cf. Amos 5:13) does not answer. Israel does not answer no, because it will not give up its positive claim upon the God of the exodus. It will not answer yes, because that answer would destroy the

21. Dell comments: "Here again Amos is taking a familiar formulation and filling it with a surprising and devastating new content in a fresh context" ("The Misuse of Forms in Amos," 58–59).

22. Barton (*Amos's Oracles against the Nations*, 37) following Hans Walter Wolff, takes the phrasing as a quotation of a familiar formula of Israel.

ideological "mono" and open Yahweh up to a plurality of exoduses beyond Israel, which Israel cannot countenance. John Barton comments upon the harshness of this option: "When everybody is somebody, then no one's anybody."[23] Israel had become somebody by its singular, exclusivist claim, which in four quick lines is placed into deep jeopardy.

Yahweh, God of Many Peoples

But, of course, the question is answered yes. It is answered yes by the literary force of the entire Amos tradition. It is answered yes, moreover, by Yahweh, the asker of the question, who will not be contained in or domesticated by Israel's exclusivist ideology. It is possible, as developmentalists have done, to take this as a statement of Yahweh's monotheism; that is, Yahweh governs all nations as Yahweh's scope of governance expands. I wish, however, to move in a counter-direction, that the text wished to expose and subvert Israel's mono-faith into a radical pluralism that resists every ideological containment.

Consider first what happens to Yahweh in this odd and threatening utterance. Yahweh attests, here in Yahweh's own words, to have many client peoples to whom Yahweh attends in powerful, intervening ways, client peoples who are Israel's long-standing enemies. There is, according to this, no single "salvation history," no fixed line of "God's mighty deeds," for such "mighty deeds" happen in many places, many of which are beyond the purview of Israel's orthodoxy. That much seems unarguable, if Yahweh's double question requires a twofold yes, as seems evident in the rhetoric.

Let me, however, venture beyond that conclusion about Yahweh that is inescapable in order to extrapolate more from what we know of the exodus. The exodus event, as given us in the liberation liturgy of Exodus 1–15, concerns a community of Israelite-Hebrew slaves who, so far as we know, know nothing of Genesis.[24] All we are told of them, in the narrative itself, is that they were in slavery of an oppressive kind, for the Bible prefers to operate narratively in medias res.

The account in the book of Exodus concerns "*a new king*" who oppressed (Exod 1:8), midwives who "feared God" (notice, not Yahweh) and so outwitted Pharaoh (1:17), and the birth of *baby Moses* (2:1–10),

23. Ibid., 37.

24. On the relation of Genesis to Exodus, see Moberly, *The Old Testament of the Old Testament.*

who promptly becomes a terrorist and a fugitive (12:11–22). The narrative oddly proceeds this far without reference to Yahweh.

The concluding preliminary comment in Exod 2:23–25 concerns the death of the harsh king and the reactive effect upon Israel, who "groaned . . . and cried out."[25] What strikes me about this narrative is that without any theological self-awareness and without any explicit reference to Yahweh, the exodus narrative is set in motion by slaves who seize a moment of social upheaval (the death of the king) and cry out. They bring their pain to speech; they do not cry out because they are believers but only because they hurt. They do not cry out because they know the book of Genesis and the promises of God but because they face the irreducible human datum of unbearable suffering. That is all. The rest is the response of Yahweh who "heard . . . remembered . . . looked . . . and took notice" (2:24–25). Israel voiced its unbearable situation, to which Yahweh is drawn like a moth to the light. And thus exodus.

Now between this full, well-known account of Israel's liberation and the sparse reference to the Philistines and Arameans in the utterance of Amos, there is not much that is comparable. One is situated in a complete narrative; the other receives only a terse mention. More than that we must imagine. The prophet Amos, by his ideology-shattering rhetorical questions, invites us to imagine that these two traditional enemies of Israel, the Philistines and the Arameans, have a history with Yahweh not unlike Israel's history with Yahweh, even though that history is not known to Israel. We may, of course, wonder how Amos knows and alludes to such a history, to which Israel has no access. The answer to that question is that Amos's vigorous capacity to imagine the pluralistic propensity of Yahweh permits him to know and imagine facets of lived reality from which Israel is blocked by its mono-ideology.

Thus, here I imagine that the "hidden history" of the Philistines and the Arameans is, *mutatis mutandis*, closely parallel to the liberated history of Israel.[26]

1. Like Israel, the Philistines and the Arameans found themselves in an oppressive situation, though the references to Caphtor and Kir tell us little that we can understand about their past. From Israel's life with

25. See my more extended comments on this passage in Brueggemann, "Exodus," 705–7.

26. There are many accounts of various "hidden histories." The one with which I am most familiar is Zigmund, ed., *Hidden Histories in the United Church of Christ*, vols. 1 and 2.

Yahweh, it is evident that all peoples live in such a zone of abusiveness, sometimes as victims, sometimes as perpetrators.

2. Like Israel, the Philistines and tbe Arameans were hopelessly embedded in a situation of oppressiveness, where for a long period they could only endure in silence the demanding power of the overlord. Many peoples are like Israel in this season of powerlessness, powerless until a moment of rupture.

3. Like Israel, the Philistines and Arameans were deeply in touch with their history-denying pain, and they watched for a moment when the silence could be broken. When the time came, we may imagine, they groaned and cried out, as the oppressed are wont to do, when the cry and the groan are thought to be worth the risk.

4. Like Israel, the cry of the Philistines and the Arameans "rose up to God." Note well, they did not cry outto Yahweh, for they were not Yahwists. Indeed, like Israel, they did not even cry out "to God." But as the cry of Israel "rose up to God," so we may imagine the cry of these restive neighbors "rose up to God," for this God is oddly and characteristically attentive to the cry of the bandaged who find enough voice to risk selfannouncement, that is, who become agents of their own history.[27]

5. The rest, as they say, is history. Israel understood that God "heard, saw, knew, remembered, and came down to save," out of which came a new people in history. In parallel fashion, so Amos proposes, Yahweh did the same for these other peoples, who emerged in history, liberated by the work of Yahweh, the God of Israel and the God of many oppressed client peoples.

Of course, we have no data for this scenario. I suggest only that Amos's succinct utterance requires some such scenario. It may be that we are permitted to generalize, to say that the Philistines and the Arameans are representative communities, so that all of human history is offered by Amos as a scenario of Yahwistic liberation. Or, if we refuse such generalization, we may only say that Amos offers two such parallels to Israel, or three if we include the Ethiopians in the second question. Either way, the story line of the exodus has substance outside the scope oflsrael's life and liturgy.

---

27. The first step in such an initiative is voicing pain that then turns to energy, precisely what the slaves in Egypt did. On that process in contemporary life, see Chopp, *The Power to Speak*; Herman, *Trauma and Recovery*; and Scarry, *The Body in Pain*.

Yahweh in Many Histories

Now it is clear that Amos's utterance has no special concern for the Philistines or the Arameans (cf. 1:3–5), except to assert that they also are under the governance of Yahweh's sovereign intentionality. It is beyond doubt that the utterance of Amos intends to have its primary effect upon Israel, to jar Israel's mono-ideology and to defeat Israel's sense of exceptionalism.

When Amos finishes this double question, Israel is left without its illusion that it monopolizes Yahweh. Israel is disabused of its self-congratulatory indifference and self-confidence, which issue in a cult of satiation and an ethic of aggrandizement. Amos does not deny Israel's self-identity as a people of the exodus. He denies only the monopolistic claim made as the only exodus subject of the only exodus event by the only exodus God.

Beyond this remarkable assault upon Israel's claim to preference and privilege, which surely is the intent of the utterance, we may suggest that something happens to Yahweh as well in the process of this utterance, as an inescapable by-product of shattering Israel's mono-ideology. There is no doubt that the main claim of that mono-ideology pertains not only to Israel but also to Yahweh, so that the claim of exclusive commitment may apply in both directions. That is, it is not only affirmed in the stylized utterance of Yahweh,

> I shall be your God, that is, no other God,
> > but it is also affirmed,
> You shall be my people, that is, the only people of Yahweh.[28]

Given the hidden histories of the Philistines and the Arameans, however, we are given a glimpse of Yahweh's hidden history, that is, Yahweh's long term interaction with other peoples, about which Israel knows nothing and wants to know nothing.

Yahweh, it turns out in this utterance, has other partners who are subjects of Yahweh's propensity to liberation. Presumably these other peoples groaned and cried out in their own language, and Yahweh responded. We may, moreover, wonder if perhaps these other peoples had behind their exoduses a promissory Genesis, and if perhaps the exodus of these other peoples issues in a form of covenant, commandment, and obedience. We are told none of that, and we are lacking in any such evidence. But Amos does clearly require his listeners to entertain the subversive notion that Yahweh is at work in other ways, in other histories, in order to effect other

28. On this formula, see Smend, *Die Bundesformel*.

liberations. There is to Yahweh, in this imaginative reading, an identifiable core of coherence.[29] Yahweh's self-presentation is everywhere as an exodus God. That is who Yahweh is, and that is what Yahweh does. "History" is a series of exodus narratives of which Israel's is one, but not the only one.

Beyond that powerful mark of coherence as a subject, everything else about Yahweh, in this brief utterance, may take many forms, so that Yahweh may be a character in Philistine history or in Syrian history, surely a treasonable shock to those in the mono-ideology that Amos subverts. Moreover, this action of Yahweh, from what we have in this utterance, did not convert these peoples to Yahwism, did not require them to speak Hebrew, and did not submerge their histories as subsets of Israel's history. The liberation wrought by Yahweh left each of these peoples, so much as we know, free to live out and develop their own sense of cultural identity and of freedom. Thus it is fair to imagine that Yahweh, as the exodus God who generated the Philistines, came to be known, if at all, in Philistine modes. And Yahweh, as the exodus God who evoked the Syrians to freedom, came to be known, if at all, in Syrian modes. Beyond the coherent, pervading mark of exodus intentionality, we may as a consequence imagine that Yahweh is enormously pliable and supple as a participant in the histories of many peoples, not all of which are exact replicas of Israel's narrative or subsets of Israel's self-discernment.

Emancipation in the Plural

To be sure, this is only one brief text in a prophetic collection that does in many places assume Israel's exceptionalism, so that too much must not be made of this one verse. Moreover, Amos is only one brief collection in Israel's text that became canonized, and there is no doubt that Amos was situated in the midst of the powerful mono-ideology of the Deuteronomists.[30] Thus I do not waut to overstate the case.

Nonetheless, in a book addressing the crisis of pluralism, I offer this single verse in the context of the Amos collection and in the larger context of Israel's seductive mono-ideology as evidence that pluralism is voiced as a critique of reductive mono-ideology. Amos resituates Israel, Yahweh,

29. On the cruciality of a core of constancy in the character of Yahweh, see Patrick, *The Rendering of God in the Old Testament*.

30. On a characteristic tension between the Deuteronomists and Amos, see Crüsemann, "Kritik an Amos im deuteronomistischen Geschichtswerk."

and the nations by asserting that what is true concerning Yahweh cannot be contained or domesticated into Israel's favorite slogans, categories, or claims. The actual concrete happenedness of Yahweh in the world is much more comprehensive than that, even if mostly kept hidden.

It is now conventional, both in the U.S. church and in current cultural confusions of U.S. society, to value, with nostalgia, the good days of "coherence," when the church "willed one thing," and when all of society was ordered around stable, broadly accepted coherences.[31] Conversely, given such a view, which is immune to the thought that such coherence was constituted by an imposition of hegemony, it is held that more recent pluralism is a terrible demise and collapse of all that is good. Recovery, moreover, will mean an overcoming of pluralism and the reasseriion of an ordered hegemony.

There may be some truth in that claim—even though it is not going to happen. But truth or no, I propose that this one verse from Amos must stick in the throat of our nostalgic sense of loss and yearning, as it must have stuck in the throat of the mono-ideologues in Israel. If we take this succinct utterance seriously, the pluriform nature of Yahweh is a truth that is not negative. It is rather a truth that can emancipate Israel from its deluding mono-ideology, in which what had been a Yahwistically enacted gift of truth (the actual exodus) had become a possession and property legitimating imagined self-importance and autonomy. Thus pluriform Yahwism may be seen as a healthy resituation of Israel's life in the world that affirms that there are facets of Yahweh's life not subject to Israel's definition and facets of the life of the world not to be placed under Israel's mono-ideological umbrella. There is a deep, dense otherness to Yahweh in human history, which stands as an invitation and principle of criticism when Israel's faith becomes self-serving ideology. Amos clearly has no fear of pluriform Yahwism but sees it as a stance from which Israel may re-vision itself more faithfully and more realistically.

The Ideology of Yes

From this reflection on this single verse in Amos, I wish to draw three concluding reflections:

---

31. For one example of such an exercise in nostalgia, see Bloom, *The Closing of the American Mind.*

1. There is, in this subversion of the mono-ideology of ancient Israel, an important critique and warning against a notion of "God's elect people" as it pertains both to Jews and Christians. It is clear that Amos was addressing neither Judaism nor Christianity, but the antecedent of both. And because the ancient Israel addressed by Amos is the antecedent of both derivative communities of faith, the subversive warning applies no more to Judaism than it does to Christianity.

As concerns Judaism, in my judgment, one may draw a warning and critique from Amos concerning the "mystery of Israel," where it is drawn too tightly toward an ethnic Jewishness. I do not cite this verse, in the horizon of Judaism, to suggest anything like Christian supersessionism but only to assert, even in the face of Judaism's unrivaled formal claim as the people of Yahweh, that the density and majesty of Yahweh cannot be contained in any ideological Judaism that weds Yahweh to an ethnic community.

While this warning to and critique of Judaism are not my concern here (nor my proper business as a Christian), the visionary utterance of Amos can be related to two recent Jewish statements concerning Judaism. First, Jon Levenson, apropos of liberation theology, resists any notion of God's "preferential option" for the marginated that removes the essential Jewishness of God's preference.[32] In the end, however, even Levenson, in his insistence on Jewish focus, acknowledges that the exodus narrative may be paradigmatic for other communities awaiting God's emancipation.[33] This seems to me congruent with the utterance of Amos.

Second, Jacob Neusner, in a recent argument, has insisted that the definitional mark of Judaism as God's people is simply, singularly, and only adherence to the Torah.[34] Neusner is alert to Christian misconstruals of Judaism as ethnic Jewishness but is much more concerned with the misconstrual of Judaism among Jews who confuse a community embedded in the mystery of Torah with ethnic or cultural markings of Jewishness. In a way even more direct than the comment of Levenson, Neusner seems to me precisely aimed at the concern of Amos, even though, to be sure, Amos focuses upon the exodus and not the Torah.

2. In a book concerned with Christianity and pluralism and perhaps more precisely Calvinism and pluralism, our interest here has to do with the Christian spin-offs from the utterance of Amos. As Deuteronomy is

32. Levenson, "Exodus and Liberation."
33. Ibid., 159.
34. Neusner, *Children of the Flesh, Children of the Promise*.

a main force for mono-ideology in ancient Judaism, so it is possible to conclude that Calvinism has been a primary force for mono-ideology in modern Christian history because of its insistence upon God's sovereignty, which is very often allied with socioeconomic-political hegemony.

Given that propensity of Western Christendom in general and Calvinism in particular, if pluralism is not perceived as a threat (as it is in many quarters), it is at least a demanding challenge that a characteristic tilt toward mono-ideology be radically reconsidered. As pluralism in a variety of forms flourishes among us, there is a sharp tendency to want to take refuge in an old coherence against pluralism, an old coherence that is variously seen to be theological orthodoxy but seems always to. be accompanied by a certain kind of sociopolitical hegemony.

Here my concern is not the relation of Christianity to other "Great Religions" but the internal life of Christianity. The utterance of Amos has voiced in a forceful way that Yahweh (the God we confess to be fully known in Jesus Christ) is not unilaterally attached to our preferred formulas, practices, or self-identity. There is a profound otherness in Yahweh that is incommensurate with the church, as with Israel. It is my hunch that ours is a time in the church when retrenching into mono-ideology is a severe temptation, but a recognition of the history of Yahweh's otherness, which is fearful and problematic, may he an embrace of prophetic faith. If such a quality in Yahweh's life be embraced, it may be that our preferred theological formulations, liturgic inclinations, and cultural assumptions may be incongruous with the oddness of Yahweh, whose liberating intentions may be allied with and attached to many forms of human life other than our own. The mono-propensities that sound most orthodox may be desperate attempts to reduce Yahweh to a safer proportion. Of course, I do not know how far this pluriform reality should be extrapolated to our circumstance. One such extreme extrapolation is the conclusion of Maurice Wiles, in his comment on the reality of divine forgiveness and divine presence apprehended in the cross and in the church: "Calvary and the institutional church are not necessarily their only instantiations in history."[35]

3. I am sure there is need for "mono-izing" that arises from time to time in the church. But it is not a given that mono-izing is, in every circumstance, the proper work of the church. There are also occasions when it is an act of disobedience, when in God's time pluralizing is required. If both practices on occasion are congruent with God's will and purpose,

---

35. Wiles, *Christian Theology and Interreligious Dialogue*, 76.

theu we may now (and in any time) have a conversation about which is our appropriate posture, without mono-izers assuming that they automatically hold the high ground, high gronnd that seems almost always to be congruent with vested interest.[36]

What better way, in a chapter offered to Shirley Guthrie, to conclude than with a quote from Barth? In thinking, early on, about the relationship between Christian faith and culture, Barth fully affirms that the position of right faith is genuinely open and dialectical. In commenting on the relation of Christianity to society and the need to be flexible to the right and to the left, Barth writes:

> Without being disturbed by the inconsistent appearance of it we shall then enjoy the freedom of saying now Yes and now No, and of saying both not as a result of outward change or inward caprice but because we are so moved by the will of God, which has been abundantly proved "good, and acceptable, and perfect" (Rom. 12:2).[37]

Of course much of "Barthianism" has taken a moment of Barth and hardened it into a principle. But not so Barth.

In commenting upon the work of Barth, Gogarten, and others in this regard, Klaus Scholder comments:

> It is to this freedom to which the Word of God is a summons that Karl Barth was referring at the end of his Tambach lecture . . . There is no need to say anything in support of the justification and the significance of this approach; they are evident. But the question now is whether in the struggle against binding the Word of God to any ideologies a new ideology did not to some extent creep in through the back door, namely the ideology of crisis . . . the absolute No replaces the absolute Yes.[38]

Scholder is explicit in exempting Barth from the tendency to make "No" a new ideology, which he associates especially with Gogarten.

---

36. Thus in the right moment, both activities are proper and indispensable. One can see a parallel in the presentation of Ballas, *Cracking Up*. He writes: "This freedom is found in the necessary opposition between the part of us that finds truth by uniting disparate ideas (i.e., 'condensation') and the part of us that finds the truth by breaking up these unities" (ibid., 3). This seems to me a close parallel to monotheizing and pluralizing.

37. Barth, *The Word of God and the Word of Man*, 325–26.

38. Scholder, *A Requiem for Hitler and Other New Perspectives on the German Church Struggle*, 44.

In this regard, the refusal of an ideology of No as much as an ideology of Yes, which I here transpose into mono-ideology and an ideology of pluralism, Barth echoes the radical view of Amos. Neither is always and everywhere an act of obedience.

At the end of the Old Testament, prophetic faith knows that Yahwism runs well beyond Israel. Indeed, Yahweh, in the end, has more than one chosen people:

> On that day Israel will be the third with Egypt and Assyria, a blessing in the midst of the earth, whom Yahweh of hosts has blessed, saying, "Blessed be Egypt my people, and Assyria the work of my hands, and Israel my heritage." (Isa 19:24–25)

In our struggle with the matters that preoccupied Amos, it may be important to ease our desperate need for control enough to be dazzled at the Holy One of Israel, a dazzling that outruns our need or capacity for our particular mode of coherence. It is more important, as James Robinson has observed, that Israel should be endlessly amazed and grateful for its own existence:

> For the wonder of Israel is, rather than not being at all, is the basic experience of Israel in all its history. The reference to the living God . . . "answers" the question precisely by pointing to the God before whom this wonder at being is constant and inescapable.[39]

The rest may be left to God.

Bibliography

Ackroyd, Peter R. "A Judgment Narrative between Kings and Chronicles? An Approach to Amos 7:9–17." In *Canon and Authority: Essays in Old Testament Religion and Theology*, edited by George W. Coats and Burke O. Long, 71–87. Philadelphia: Fortress, 1977.

Albertz, Rainer. *A History of Israelite Religion in the Old Testament Period*. Vol. 1, *From the Beginnings to the End of the Monarchy*. Translated by John Bowden. OTL. Louisville: Westminster John Knox, 1994.

———. "Der Ort des Monotheismus in der israelitischen Religionsgeschichte." In *Ein Gott Allein? JHWH-Verehrung und biblischer Monotheismus im Kontext der israelitischen und altorientalischen Religionsgeschichte*, edited by Walter Dietrich and M. A. Klopfenstein, 77–96. Orbis biblicus et orientalis 139. Göttingen: Vandenhoeck & Ruprecht, 1994.

---

39. Robinson, "The Historicality of Biblical Language," 156.

Andersen, Francis I., and David Noel Freedman. *Amos.* AB 15A. New York: Doubleday, 1989.

Ballas, Christopher. *Cracking Up: The Work of Unconscious Experience.* London: Routlege & Kegan Paul, 1995.

Barth, Karl. *The Word of God and the Word of Man.* Translated by Douglas Horton. London: Hodder & Stoughton, 1928.

Barton, John. *Amos's Oracles against the Nations: A Study of Amos 1:3—2:5.* Society for Old Testament Study Monograph Series 6. Cambridge: Cambridge University Press, 1980.

Bloom, Allan. *The Closing of the American Mind: How Higher Education Has Failed Democracy and Impoverished the Souls of Today's Students.* New York: Simon & Schuster, 1987.

Brueggemann, Walter. "Exodus." In *The New Interpreter's Bible,* vol. 1. ed. Leander E. Keck et al. Nashville: Abingdon Press, 1994.

Chopp, Rebecca S. *The Power to Speak: Feminism, Language and God.* New York: Crossroad, 1991.

Crüsemann, Frank. "Kritik an Amos im deuteronomistischen Geschichtswerk: Erwägungen zu 2. Konige 14:27." In *Probleme biblischer Theologie: Gerhard von Rad zum 70. Geburtstag,* edited by Hans Walter Wolff, 57–63. Munich: Kaiser, 1971.

Dell, Katherine J. "The Misuse of Forms in Amos." *VT* 45 (1995) 45–61.

Fosdick, Harry Emerson. *A Guide to Understanding the Bible: The Development of Ideas within the Old and New Testaments.* London: SCM, 1938.

Herman, Judith. *Trauma and Recovery: The Aftermath of Violence—From Domestic Abuse to Political Terror.* New York: Basic Books, 1993.

Janzen, J. Gerald. "On the Most Important Word in the *Shema.*" *VT* 37 (1987) 280–300.

Labuschagne, C. J. *The Incomparability of Yahweh in the Old Testament.* Pretoria Oriental Series 5. Leiden: Brill, 1966.

Levenson, Jon D. "Exodus and Liberation." In *The Hebrew Bible, The Old Testament, and Historical Criticism: Jews and Christians in Biblical Studies,* 127–59. Louisville: Westminster John Knox, 1993.

McBride, S. Dean, Jr. "The Yoke of the Kingdom: Exposition of Deuteronomy 6:4–5." *Int* 27 (1973) 273–306.

Mettinger, Tryggve N. D. *The Dethronement of Sabaoth: Studies in the Shem and Kabod Theologies.* Coniectanea Biblica, Old Testament Series 18. Lund: Gleerup, 1982.

Miller, Patrick D. *Deuteronomy.* Interpretation. Louisville: John Knox, 1990.

———. "Israelite Religion." In *The Hebrew Bible and Its Modern Interpreters,* ed. Douglas A. Knight and Gene M. Tucker, 210–37. Philadelphia: Fortress, 1985.

Moberly, R. W. L. *The Old Testament of the Old Testament: Patriarchal Narratives and Mosaic Yahwism.* OBT. Minneapolis: Fortress, 1992.

Neusner, Jacob. *Children of the Flesh, Children of the Promise: A Rabbi Talks with Paul.* Cleveland: Pilgrim, 1995.

Nicholson, Ernest W. *God and His People: Covenant and Theology in the Old Testament.* Oxford: Clarendon, 1986.

Patrick, Dale. *The Rendering of God in the Old Testament.* OBT. Philadelphia: Fortress, 1981.

Perlitt, Lothar. *Bundestheologie im Alten Testament.* WMANT 36. Neukirchen-Vluyn: Neukirchener, 1969.

Polley, Max E. *Amos and the Davidic Empire: A Socio-Historical Approach*. New York: Oxford University Press, 1989.

Rad, Gerhard von. *Old Testament Theology*. Vol. 1, *The Theology of Israel's Historical Tradition*. Translated by D. M. G. Stalker. San Francisco: Harper & Row, 1962.

———. *Studies in Deuteronomy*. Translated by David Stalker. SBT 1/9. London: SCM, 1953.

Robinson, James M. "The Historicality of Biblical Language." In *The Old Testament and Christian Faith: Essays by Rudolf Bultmann and Others*, edited by Bernhard W. Anderson, 124–58. New York: Harper, 1963.

Sanders, James A. "Adaptable for Life: The Nature and Function of Canon." In *From Sacred Story to Sacred Text: Canon as Paradigm*, 9–39. Philadelphia: Fortress, 1987.

Scarry, Elaine. *The Body in Pain: The Making and Unmaking of the World*. New York: Oxford University Press, 1987.

Scholder, Klaus. *A Requiem for Hitler and Other New Perspectives on the German Church Struggle*. London: SCM, 1989.

Smend, Rudolf. *Die Bundesformel*. Theologische Studien 68. Zurich: EVZ, 1963. ET = "The Covenant Formula." In Smend, *'The Unconquered Land' and Other Essays: Selected Studies*, edited by Edward Ball and Margaret Barker, 41–72. Translated by Margaret Kohl. Society for Old Testament Study. Burlington, VT: Ashgate, 2013.

Smith, Mark S. *The Early History of God: Yahweh and the Other Deities in Ancient Israel*. San Francisco: Harper & Row, 1990. 2nd ed., Grand Rapids: Eerdmans, 2002.

Smith, Morton. *Palestinian Parties and the Politics That Shaped the Old Testament*. New York: Columbia University Press, 1971.

Wiles, Maurice. *Christian Theology and Interreligious Dialogue*. Philadelphia: Trinity, 1992.

Zigmund, Barbara Brown. *Hidden Histories in the United Church of Christ*. 2 vols. New York: Pilgrim, 1984, 1989.

9

Theology of the Old Testament
A Prompt Retrospect

No one can doubt that theological interpretation of the Bible—most especially in the context of a Christian reading—is in a quite new, quite different, and quite demanding interpretive situation. It does not matter to me if that new circumstance is termed "postmodern," though I have used that term to describe it. What counts is a *pluralistic* interpretive community that permits us to see the polyphonic character of the text, and the *deprivileged* circumstance whereby theological interpretation in a Christian context is no longer allied with or supported by dominant epistemological or political-ideological forces. So long as Christian interpretation was dominant and normative, it could count on "intellectual reasonableness" to sustain it. That supportive alliance no longer pertains. Learning to do biblical theology outside the Western hegemony is demanding work, in order that Christian interpretation may come to know something of what Jewish interpreters have long known how to negotiate. Or more briefly, hermeneutical problematics and possibilities have now displaced positivistic claims—historical or theological—as the matrix of theological reflection.

Continuity and Discontinuity

As a consequence of that changed contextual reality, theological reflection concerning the Old Testament/Hebrew Bible must perforce move beyond the great twentieth-century achievements of Walther Eichrodt and Gerhard von Rad. Indeed, reading those works now strikes one as remarkably dated and as largely innocent of the interpretive problems and possibilities that one now must face.

Having said that, however, I must add that no serious interpretive enterprise ever begins *de novo*, and certainly biblical theological work stands in important and grateful continuity with those contributions. Thus it is my intention to have worked carefully at issues of continuity and discontinuity with that scholarship, though it is likely that my appropriation and borrowing are more pervasive than I am aware. Eichrodt's effort to organize around the single conceptual frame of covenant was, in his time, an immense gain. It is unfortunate, moreover, that the theological grid of covenant got carried away into historical-critical matters with Klaus Baltzer, George Mendenhall, and Dennis McCarthy, because Eichrodt's governing theological insight—namely, that the God of Israel is characteristically a God in relation—was better than any of that. That insight, rooted for him in the Christian interpretation of John Calvin, is what Eichrodt sought to exposit.

It is clear that von Rad's work has been much more decisive for me, and indeed my opening section in my *Theology of the Old Testament* on "core testimony" is willfully von Radian. Von Rad's thesis of recital as a fundamental dynamic behind the Old Testament permitted a sense of openness, an acknowledgment of variation and plurality, and an accent upon "the said." All of that I have appropriated, though I have gone further than von Rad with the rhetorical, and have sought to avoid the morass of positivistic history from which von Rad was unable to escape. Thus the continuities with this scholarly work are important to me, and I have the sense that the thesis of an alternative world voiced in Israel's testimony is indeed a Barthian impulse on my part, which echoes G. Ernest Wright's thesis of "against."

Moving beyond Dominant Models

Having said that and having acknowledged debts and continuities with gratitude, I want to suggest now the ways in which I have tried to move beyond those dominant models of the twentieth century, hopefully to contribute in a way congruent with our own interpretive context that is outside hegemony, pluralistic, and deprivileged. I will suggest six elements of my exposition that I consider to be contributions to our ongoing work.

History

At the outset it has seemed clear to me that a theology of the Old Testament cannot appeal to "history," as evidenced by von Rad's inability to hold together "critically assured minimum" and "theological maximum":[1] "But our final comment on it should not be that it is obviously an 'unhistorical' picture, because what is in question here is a picture fashioned throughout by faith. Unlike any ordinary historical document, it does not have its centre in itself; it is intended to tell the beholder about Jahweh, that is, how Jahweh led his people and got himself glory."[2] I do not for one instant mean to suggest, following Rudolf Bultmann, that there is nothing of "happenedness"; rather, the "happening" is not subject to the measure of modern positivistic categories.[3] The "happenedness" of the theological claims made for Israel's God is in, with, and under Israel's attestation; critical positivistic—and now nihilistic—judgments do not touch those claims. Indeed, Israel's recital and attestation at many points consciously assert a memory and a claim that is counter to dominant history, and our interpretation must attend to that impulse to counter. Thus the problematic is not Israel's claim made for its God, but the flattened criticism that refuses in principle to host such claims.

The issue, then, is not at all a particular claim that should be dissolved into universal assertion, for I have insisted everywhere on the particular and have refused a groundless universalism. The issue rather is particularity that has confidence in its own utterance and that refuses to submit its claim to any universal norm.

Rhetoric

The counterside of eschewing modernist historical categories is to appeal to the practice of rhetoric. I understand Old Testament theology

1. Von Rad, *Old Testament Theology*, 1:108.
2. Ibid., 302.
3. See Brueggemann, *Abiding Astonishment*.

to be reflection upon the uttered faith claims of Israel concerning the God who is given to us precisely in and through those claims. In this regard, the focus upon utterance is congruent with von Rad's approach, which was unfortunately complicated by his appeal to critical history. Beyond von Rad, moreover, I am much influenced by Paul Ricoeur's awareness that utterance is an act of imagination that produces worlds and/or counterworlds.[4] More closely than Ricoeur, I am inescapably instructed by my teacher, James Muilenburg, who understood best about faith and rhetoric, so that in some general way Old Testament theology is "rhetorical criticism." Such a focus upon rhetoric, in a context outside hegemony—pluralistic and deprivileged—is an effort at nonfoundationalism, an attempt to trade neither upon the stable claims of the Western theological-ontological tradition nor upon the claims of Western positivistic history, either in its maximal or now in its exceedingly minimalist tendency. Israel's rhetoric mediates a God not held in thrall by either mode of Western certitude or control.

Interactionism

I have increasingly found thematic approaches to biblical theology wanting, not only because they are inescapably reductionist, but because they are characteristically boring and fail to communicate the open-ended vitality of the text. It is for that reason that I decided, early on, to focus not on substantive themes, but on verbal processes that allow for dynamism, contradiction, tension, ambiguity, and incongruity—all those habits that belong peculiarly to interactionism.[5] What I hope I have offered is an interactionist model of theological exposition congruent with this believing community that is endlessly engaged with God, a God who is available for the extremities of praise and complaint, which are Israel's characteristic modes of speech in this conflictual engagement. The importance of this move from theme(s) to process cannot be overstated for me, because the interactive process seems crucial both to the Subject of Old Testament theology and to the pluralistic, deprivileged context of our own work.

4. On the production of worlds, see Berger and Luckmann, *The Social Construction of Reality*; and Wilder, "Story and Story-World." More directly pertinent for us, see Kort, *"Take, Read,"* 9 and passim.

5. On the remarkable emergence of such interactionism in the twentieth century as a theological and philosophical perspective, see von Balthasar, *Theo-Drama*, 1:626.

Juridical Language of Testimony

More specifically, it is the focus upon juridical language of testimony that I hope will be the major gain of my work. I understand that "testimony" as a theme can be as reductionist as any other theme, but I intend it not as a theme but as a process whereby Israel endlessly gives an account of reality featuring the God of Israel as decisive, whether in presence and action or in absence and hiddenness.

It may be that the notion is reductionist because one can, I am sure, claim that not everything is testimony. Except that I think a case can be made that Israel, in all its utterances and writings, stays roughly fixed upon that single and defining claim for Yahweh.[6] Testimony about a single and defining claim permits two maneuvers that are important. There is, on the one hand, immense variation (as one would expect) in the detailed accounts offered the court by witnesses who nevertheless agree on the main point. On the other hand, there is a significant core of agreement among these witnesses, when heard in the presence of other accounts of reality that construe without reference to Yahweh.

It strikes me as odd that the genres of disputatiousness, given often in litigious tone, have not more centrally occupied theological interpreters. I would focus, for many reasons, on Second Isaiah wherein the poetry disputes about other gods. But the "speech of judgment" is dominant in the preexilic prophets.[7] The Deuteronomistic history, informed as it may be by Deuteronomy 32, proceeds as an extended narrative speech of judgment. The psalms of complaint, culminating in the book of Job, proceed in similar fashion. I believe, moreover, that it is legitimate to conclude from such a core of material that even where the genre is not visible, Israel characteristically makes a case for a Yahwistic construal of reality against other construals of reality. Where the case is not disputatious, it is even there a lesser or softer advocacy for this rather than that. Thus I want to offer this focus on testimony as a gain, as long as it is taken as metaphor and not pressed too hard to a conclusion.

---

6. See the comprehensive perspective on "testimony" by Ricoeur, *Essays on Biblical Interpretation*, 119–54.

7. See Westermann, *Basic Forms of Prophetic Speech*.

Juxtaposing Core Testimony and Countertestimony

The process of litigation that gives great maneuverability allows for a paradigmatic juxtaposition of core testimony and countertestimony, a juxtaposition that I count as a major gain of my study. While Israel's utterances make a sustained case for a Yahweh-focused world, and in the face of rivals speak with one voice on the matter (acknowledging many traces of religious phenomenology not fully incorporated into that dominant voice), yet there is vigorous dispute with that unified claim among these advocates. It is my insistence that the counterclaims must be taken seriously as a datum of theological utterance.[8] My impression is that heretofore a coherent way has not been found for such an interface. Even von Rad's "answer" really did not exhibit the remarkable dynamic of that text.[9]

I take the countertestimony to be powerful evidence that Israel is resolved to tell the truth, to tell the truth of its own life, and to tell that truth even if it crowds the large claims made for Yahweh. This is no small matter, for it means that Israel's faith has little patience for religious softness or prettiness or cover-up in the interest of protecting or enhancing God. I am drawn to Jacques Derrida's verdict that, finally, justice is undeconstructible.[10] Or in another mode, Israel's faith will not compromise the undeniable givenness of bodily reality, especially bodily pain or pain in the body politic.

Such a procedure of claim and counterclaim is, in my judgment, definitional for theology in this tradition. This procedure appears to be deeply and endlessly open and unresolved, so that finally "claim" will not silence "counterclaim," nor, conversely, can "counterclaim" ever nullify "claim." This disputatious dialectic seems of absolute importance for the character of Yahweh rendered in this text, and consequently for the character of this people that renders and responds to Yahweh.

The refusal to give closure is a defining point of the data. This is a very different read from Bultmann's sorry verdict that the Old Testament is a failure, because the openness is not failure but a rigorous willingness

---

8. Fackenheim, *To Mend the World*, 11, refers to the Holocaust as "the most radical countertestimony to both Judaism and Christianity."

9. I refer to von Rad's rubric, "Israel before Jahweh (Israel's Answer)," as his title for the discussion of the wisdom traditions (*Old Testament Theology*, 1:355).

10. Derrida, "Force of Law," 945, has famously averred, "Justice in itself, if such a thing exists, outside or beyond the law, is not deconstructible. No more than deconstruction, if such a thing exists. Deconstruction is justice." Such a verdict seems to me to be quintessentially Jewish in its claim.

to speak in dispute.[11] Christians exhibit an endless propensity to give closure to the matter in Jesus of Nazareth. I am, however, instructed by Jürgen Moltmann's suggestion that Friday and Sunday constitute a "dialectic
of reconciliation," that is, both parts enduring and in force, so that the
claim of Easter does not silence the counterclaim of Friday. The dynamic
belongs to the process of faith and therefore inescapably to the parties in
the process, Yahweh and Israel.

The Relatedness of Yahweh

Finally, I have tried to extrapolate beyond Eichrodt's covenant the definitional relatedness of Yahweh, which I have voiced under the rubric of
"Unsolicited Testimony." That is, everything said about Yahweh is said
about Yahweh in relation. Yahweh is characteristically embedded in sentences with active verbs that have direct objects for whom the agency of
Yahweh matters decisively.

I have, moreover, tried to make the case in some detail that what
is said of Yahweh is, *mutatis mutandis*, characteristically said of Israel as
well. Derivatively what is said of Israel as Yahweh's defining partner is
said of all partners, so that Yahweh vis-à-vis Israel becomes the model
for Yahweh vis-à-vis creation, nations, and human persons. This parallelism that I have suggested is in no way a move away from the privilege
and particularity of Israel's status with Yahweh, but is the matrix through
which all else is to be understood vis-à-vis Yahweh.

This relatedness that we subsume under covenant is crucial, because
it not only draws the human-historical side of reality into the orbit of
Yahweh's rule and reality—a point decisive in Calvinist theology since
the first pages of the *Institutes*—but the relatedness bespeaks the truth of
Yahweh as much as it voices the truth of Israel or any of Yahweh's derivative partners. That is, Israel can entertain the claim that this relatedness is
not always a one-way deal: it does not always move from Yahweh to Israel
(and the other partners). Nor is it adequate to suggest, as scholarship has
done, that the relation is "bilateral." On occasion, so it seems to me, there
is role reversal, so that Israel (or other partners) can take the initiative

11. Bultmann, "Prophecy and Fulfillment," 75, has devastatingly expressed trjum-
phalist Christian interpretation: "In the same way faith requires the backward glance
into Old Testament history as a history of failure and so of promise, in order to know
that the situation of the justified man arises only on the basis of this miscarriage."

over against Yahweh, in complaint and in praise.[12] This prospect of role reversal, whereby the lesser party becomes provisionally the dominant party, seems to me a question for further probing, even though the possibility is beyond the horizon of conventional Christian understanding. This possibility is a learning that Christian interpretation may recover from Jewish tradition. It is an evidence of how radical and daring Israel is prepared to be in its dissent from Yahweh, as well as how capable it is in resisting the conventions of perennial Western philosophy.

This sense of relatedness is true to the text in broad outline. In parallel fashion, this construal of holiness represents a powerful alternative to Cartesian reductionism. Thus the interactionist model of holiness offered by Martin Buber and Franz Rosenzweig, and now voiced afresh by Emmanuel Lévinas, seems to be thoroughly rooted in the Bible, though it entails a drastic relearning for the dominant theological tradition of Western Christianity.[13] It will be evident that all of these elements I regard as gains are interrelated and of a piece in an interactionist model that refuses to take God either as a fixed object or as an empty cipher. Everything about this theological tradition insists, in the utterances of Israel, that there is Someone on the other end of the transaction who is decisive—even if absent, hidden, or in eclipse.

Acknowledged Vulnerabilities

The gains that I suggest are commensurate with what will surely emerge as points of contention and continued dispute. I do not imagine that I have been able to see things convincingly through to the end. So I am glad to acknowledge at least four points where the argument is vulnerable, though other such points will surface in our discussion. I regard these as vulnerable points because they propose fresh perspectives for which we lack adequate categories. I incline to think that the vulnerability is only because things are not carried through, not because they are wrongheaded. It remains to be seen, of course, whether that judgment turns out to be acceptable to my colleagues.

12. On the prospect of role reversal, see Brueggemann, "Prerequisites for Genuine Obedience (Theses and Conclusions)."

13. It is important to recognize that the entire interpretive trajectory from Buber, given new voice by Lévinas, is designed precisely to counter the Cartesian claim of autonomy. It is important that this counteroffer is Jewish, but it is equally important that it is a public claim not addressed simply to Jewish faith.

A Nonfoundationalist Perspective

There is now available a huge literature moving in this direction.[14] But no one in the biblical field known to me has tried to make the case as directly as have I. Thus my formulation of the matter leaves me with some considerable uneasiness.

A nonfoundationalist approach is open to criticism from two perspectives. First, it will not satisfy conventional theologians who have cast matters in categories of Hellenistic ontology with the assumption that God is a stable, fixed point. But the insistences out of ancient Israel cannot concede this point, because to do so is to conform the oddity of Yahweh to settled generic categories, a maneuver that is both an epistemological accommodation and an excessive political compromise. Anyone who reflects theologically on this text knows that the God of Abraham, Isaac, and Jacob, to say nothing of the God of Moses and Job, is not easily confused with the God of the philosophers.[15] Second, and more difficult, is my urging that the rhetorical claims for Yahweh in ancient Israel are not fully linked to the happenedness of history as it has been understood in positivistic categories. The current rage of historical minimalism (nihilism?), on the basis of positivistic claims, would love to nullify theological claims for Yahweh on the basis of the negation of historical data. But that is to fall into von Rad's dilemma. I prefer to insist that history follows rhetoric, so that the memory uttered is the memory trusted. This is, in my judgment, how it works in a reciting, testifying, confessing community, except that acceptance of the testimony creates a circle of affirmation in which it can be subsequently claimed that the rhetoric derives from the history. The difficulties are acute. I suppose I am more aware of the problem of "history behind rhetoric" than I am skilled at articulating the countercase against that long-standing Western assumption. Rhetoric is indeed "the weapon of the weak."[16] To the extent that ancient Israel lives its life and practices its faith "outside," to that extent its rhetoric is and must be profoundly originary, the only recourse held by "the weak" to remain outside hegemonic assumptions.

14. See the brief expression by Thiel, *Nonfoundationalism*.

15. This claim in the twentieth century has been especially voiced by Barth, "The Strange New World within the Bible." See also Buber, "The Man of Today and the Jewish Bible."

16. The phrase is from Scott, *Weapons of the Weak*.

Historical Criticism

The previous point leads to the question of historical criticism, which Brevard Childs has identified as the crisis point for doing biblical theology. I am sure that I have not done well in articulating the delicate relationship between historical criticism and theological exposition. Part of the problem is that I am so deeply situated in historical criticism that it is likely that I appeal much more to such categories than I am aware. And part of the problem is that it is increasingly difficult to say with precision what it is that constitutes historical criticism, given the eruption of methodological alternatives. What now is taken as historical criticism is certainly very different from what it was in ancient days when I was in graduate school.

But the real issue is neither of these two preliminary matters; the real issue is the work and import of such criticism. We must think critically about the Bible, because we live in an inquiring intellectual world. Taken on that basis, criticism is simply being intellectually responsible. A case is readily made, however, that what has passed for historical criticism has in fact been a commitment to something like Enlightenment rationality, whereby criticism has had the negative task of eliminating whatever offended reason and the positive task of rendering the claims of the text compatible with autonomous reason. That way of understanding criticism is supported by the so-called historical minimalists who have made a virtue out of skepticism, thus pushing criticism toward skepticism that is endlessly dismissive of the claims of the text.

The issue is nicely represented in Old Testament theological scholarship by comparing the work of Childs with that of James Barr. Childs has indicated that historical criticism is largely a deficit operation for theological exposition. But Barr, fearing authoritarian obscurantism, will insist that any credible theological claim from the text must be cast in the environs of critical categories. I suspect that what is made of historical criticism depends on what one most fears in the project of interpretation: a debilitating fragmentation (Childs) or an excessive fideism (Barr). It may be then that we do best to say that criticism is to be assessed dialectically in terms of the interpretive context. I have sought to occupy a mediating position. My sympathies are with Childs, but I do not want to follow him—as I shall clarify in a moment—toward his notion of "canonical," which strikes me as unfortunately reductionist. The issue, in the end, is how the odd claims of this text make their way in an intellectual environment inclined toward domestication and resistant to the scandal of particularity, a particularity that refuses the flattening that becomes predictable and replicatable.

Jewish and Christian Reading

Biblical theology in a conventional Christian context is often deeply supersessionist.[17] The assumption too often is that the Old Testament moves directly and singularly toward the New Testament and its christological claims, so that any other interpretive trajectory is excluded in principle.[18] There is no doubt that this is a deeply vexed question beyond my capacity to address, and that such conventional supersessionist interpretations have contributed powerfully, even if indirectly, to the anti-Jewish barbarism of the recent past. But it seems clear that exclusionary reading toward Christology is morally intolerable as well as theologically problematic.

I suspect that I do not know enough to deal adequately with the issue. My take on it, while waiting for further instruction, is that as a Christian I will by conviction and by habit read toward the New Testament. But because the text is endlessly polyvalent and because its Subject is endlessly elusive and beyond domestication, it is impossible, in my judgment, to pretend a monopolistic reading. Thus my reading toward the New Testament is done in the midst of other legitimate and valued readings—primarily Jewish—to which I must attend and by which I may expect to be instructed. It is my expectation that in the long run Jewish reading may also be open to the (not exclusive) validity of Christian reading, though clearly the issues are not symmetrical because of the long history of Christian hegemony and abusiveness. While I do not imagine any easy convergence in these readings, neither will I accept the verdict shared by Childs and Jon Levenson that we read different Bibles.[19] Rather we must read together as far as we can read and, beyond that, read attentively in each other's presence. Such a strategy, to be sure, has much to unlearn and to undo, but we must begin somewhere. I am encouraged that N. T. Wright has made a powerful case that the New Testament gos-

17. See the analysis of Soulen, *The God of Israel and Christian Theology*.

18. This perspective has been powerfully advocated by Watson, *Text, Church and World*; and Watson, *Text and Truth*.

19. See Levenson, *The Hebrew Bible, the Old Testament, and Historical Criticism*, 76–81.

pel is the retelling of the story of Israel through the life of Jesus, a retelling that does not preempt.[20] In all such common reading the particularity and primacy of Jewish claims are to be affirmed, and whatever else follows must follow from that primal affirmation. As I have indicated in my comments on the "Partners" for God, Israel is the defining partner, and whatever else is to be said of other partners is derived from and informed by that claim and relationship. My sense, therefore, is that Christian reading must be done very differently from what we have done heretofore. The barbarism of the twentieth century is not an irrelevance, but is rather a primary datum that requires learning to read (and believe) differently.

Toward the Church

The Christian enterprise of biblical theology, and specifically Old Testament theology insofar as it is Christian, has important responsibilities and limitations. This point is the counterside of my last point concerning the interface between Jewish and Christian modes of theological exposition.

There is now an important insistence, especially by Childs (and, from the side of systematic theology, by Francis Watson), that Old Testament theology must be deeply and exclusively linked to the New Testament because, in Childs's terms, the two testaments are "two witnesses to Jesus Christ."[21] This tendency (i.e., to assume that Christian interpretation of the Old Testament is distinctively and closely focused upon the church's claim for Jesus) assures that no competing or complementary interpretation— even Jewish—warrants any consideration. The several schemes of relation of Old Testament and New Testament—law–gospel, promise–fulfillment, salvation history—may all be utilized, but the common assumption is that the Old Testament awaits the New for a compelling reading.[22] The accent is completely upon the continuity between the testaments.

A student of the Old Testament, however, cannot help but notice the disjunction and disconnection from one testament to the other, so that the theological claims of the Old Testament do not obviously or readily

20. Wright, *The New Testament and the People of God*; and Wright, *Jesus and the Victory of God*. In a very different way and from a Jewish perspective, Levenson, "The Universal Horizon of Biblical Particularism," has offered a fresh scenario of an extent to which Jews and Christians may read together in a way that is seriously theological.

21. From this perspective, see also Peter Stuhlmacher, *How to Do Biblical Theology*.

22. The issues are summarized in a quite conventional way by Gunneweg, *Understanding the Old Testament*.

or smoothly or without problem move to the New Testament. Indeed, if we are to claim some kind of continuity—as any Christian reading surely must—it is a continuity that is deeply hidden and endlessly problematic. For that reason, and given the intensely and consistently iconoclastic propensity of the Old Testament text, it may be suggested that the Old Testament stands as a critical principle over against any easy claims of New Testament faith, so that the God of Israel is not easily reduced to or encompassed by Christian claims.[23] After all of the adjustments from the faith of Israel to the faith of the church there is yet a deep "otherwise," which is uncontained and undomesticated, that must be acknowledged.

If the issue is to struggle with the ill fit between the two testaments, the problem is even more acute when one moves from the claims closely linked to Jesus in the New Testament to the developed dogmatic tradition of the church. It is well known that over the course of his long engagement with the intractable problem of canon, "canon" has meant several different things to Childs. In his *Biblical Theology of the Old and New Testaments*, surely his most mature articulation, the term canon has come to refer to the "rule of faith" (whereby Childs seems to mean the christological-trinitarian formula) as the way in which biblical theology is to be done.[24] Such perspective seems to me, in the end, both reductionist and excessively ideational, because it must gloss over the characteristic disjunctions of Old Testament rhetoric that mediate the disjunctive God of Israel. This same inclination is present in the essays collected by Carl Braaten and Robert Jenson in response to Childs.[25]

It seems to me that such a reductionist reading remains in the service of the hegemonic, triumphalist claims of the church, without at the same time recognizing the endlessly subversive intention of the text that is endlessly restless with every interpretive closure, whether Jewish or Christian. My own inclination is more congruent with the recent proposals of Wesley Kort—who considers Calvin's theory of reading as informed by *sicut*, "as if"—to read against every given conviction, to an unfounded (nonfoundational?) alternative that is given only in the text.[26] From Cal-

23. I take this, in a different voice, to be the point of Johnson, *The Mystery of God*, an insistence that in Barth God's mystery is not finally reduced to theological control.

24. Childs, *Biblical Theology of the Old and New Testaments*, 67 and passim. A closely parallel argument is made by Stuhlmacher, *How To Do Biblical Theology*, 61 and passim.

25. Braaten and Jenson, eds., *Reclaiming the Bible for the Church*.

26. Kort, "Take, Read," 25–36 and passim.

vin, Kort's sense of Scripture in a postmodern context is that Scripture is too elemental, too primal, and too originary to be administered and shaped by established interpretation and doctrine:

> This is not to say that institution and doctrine are unimportant. The question is one of relative status. Reading the Bible as scripture must lead to an exit from them. For theology this means, first of all, freeing reading from theological determinations, particularly the substitution of doctrines of scripture for reading the Bible . . . But unity and stability in the church are not necessarily good things, and certainly imposed or abstract unity and stability are not . . . But reading the Bible as scripture involves first of all movement away from self and world and toward their divestment and abjection.[27]

It is my sense that Christian reading, long hegemonic in the West, must now face *divestment and abjection* of a social-political-economic kind that is best—perhaps inevitably—matched by a theological divestment as well. Although Israel has long understood that the force of the Holy One requires the exposure of the idols, any long triumphalist interpretation characteristically does not regard its own triumphalism as idolatrous.

Kort is against the stream in much current theological conviction. I think he has it proximately right and am reassured that he finds this guiding motif at the center of Calvin's own perspective. It is Calvin's (and Kort's) "as scripture" to which we must attend, in a phrasing parallel to that of Childs that comes to mean something very different. It is this "as scripture" that is *originary* and *undetermined by institutional force* that may help us face the demands of interpretation, for both the wounded and the wounder.

It is evident that such a stance toward church claims, a stance critical but not dismissive, is a complement to my suggestion concerning Christian theology vis-à-vis Jewish faith. The claim of Scripture, endlessly problematic in the history of Christian reading and made poignant for our time by Karl Barth, is that the Holy One of Israel will not be held in church claims any more than in the temple claims of Solomon, for "Even heaven and the highest heaven cannot contain you, much less this house that I have built!" (1 Kgs 8:27).

---

27. Ibid., 124, 128.

Conclusion

It will be evident that I have opted for a *process* of testimony, dispute, and advocacy; I trust it will be equally evident why I have done so. The process of adjudication is not formal and vacuous, but endlessly implies *content* about the Subject of that testimony, dispute, and advocacy. The emphasis on the process, however, seems crucial to me because: (a) Israel presented its most daring utterance in disputatious process; (b) the God of Israel characteristically engages in precisely such dispute; and (c) such ongoing, respectful disputation is the only interpretive option, in my judgment, in a pluralistic, deprivileged interpretive environment. I do not believe for a minute that deprivileged environment should itself dictate the terms of our exposition; I am, however, convinced that the shape of our interpretive environment is oddly congruent with Israel's preferred way to voice its faith. I have suggested, in *Theology of the Old Testament*, that the endless negotiation of core testimony and countertestimony, in Christian mode, takes the form of the dialectic of Friday and Sunday.[28] I have, moreover, been deeply moved and informed by the judgment of George Steiner that "ours is a long day's journey of the Saturday."[29] A Christian dynamic of Friday–Sunday regards post-Easter Monday as still under the aegis of Easter joy. In Christian perspective, Monday is very different from Saturday. But serious Christian discernment also knows that the problems of Saturday must continue to be faced on Monday, better faced with Jews who also wait. My attempt at theological interpretation is to engage the reading of our common calling, Saturday issues even on Monday.

Bibliography

Balthasar, Hans Urs von. *Theo-Drama: Theological Dramatic Theory*. Translated by Graham Harrison. San Francisco: Ignatius, 1988.

Barth, Karl. "The Strange New World within the Bible." In *The Word of God and the Word of Man*, 28–50. Translated by Douglas Horton. 1928. Reprinted, New York: Harper & Brothers, 1957.

Berger, Peter L., and Thomas Luckmann. *The Social Construction of Reality: A Treatise in the Sociology of Knowledge*. Anchor Books. Garden City, NY: Doubleday, 1967.

Braaten, Carl E., and Robert W. Jenson, editors. *Reclaiming the Bible for the Church*. Grand Rapids: Eerdmans, 1995.

28. Brueggemann, *Theology of the Old Testament*, 400–403.

29. Steiner, *Real Presences*, 232.

Brueggemann, Walter. *Abiding Astonishment: Psalms, Modernity, and the Making of History*. Literary Currents in Biblical Interpretation. Louisville: Westminster John Knox, 1991.

———. "Prerequisites for Genuine Obedience (Theses and Conclusions)." *Calvin Theological Journal* 36 (2001) 34–41.

———. *Theology of the Old Testament: Testimony, Dispute, Advocacy*. Minneapolis: Fortress, 1997.

Buber, Martin. "The Man of Today and the Jewish Bible." In *On the Bible: Eighteen Studies*, edited by Nahum N. Glatzer, 1–13. New York: Schocken, 1968.

Bultmann, Rudolf. "Prophecy and Fulfillment." Translated by James C. G. Greig. In *Essays on Old Testament Hermeneutics*, edited by Claus Westermann, 50–75. Richmond: John Knox, 1963.

Childs, Brevard S. *Biblical Theology of the Old and New Testaments: Theological Reflection on the Christian Bible*. Minneapolis: Fortress, 1993.

Derrida, Jacques. "Force of Law: The 'Mystical Foundations of Authority.'" *Cardozo Law Review* 11.5–6 (1990) 919–1046. Reprinted in *Deconstruction and the Possibility of Justice*, edited by Drucila Cornell et al., 3–67. New York: Routledge, 1992.

Fackenheim, Emil. *To Mend the World: Foundations of Post-Holocaust Thought*. New York: Schocken, 1989.

Gunneweg, A. H. J. *Understanding the Old Testament*. Translated by John Bowden. OTL. Philadelphia: Westminster, 1978.

Johnson, William Stacy. *The Mystery of God: Karl Barth and the Postmodern Foundations of Theology*. Louisville: Westminster John Knox, 1997.

Kort, Wesley A. *"Take, Read": Scripture, Textuality, and Cultural Practice*. University Park: Pennsylvania State University Press, 1996.

Levenson, Jon D. *The Hebrew Bible, the Old Testament, and Historical Criticism: Jews and Christians in Bible Studies*. Louisville: Westminster John Knox, 1993.

———. "The Universal Horizon of Biblical Particularism." In *Ethnicity and the Bible*, edited by Mark G. Brett, 143–69. Biblical Interpretation Series 19. Leiden: Brill, 1996.

Rad, Gerhard von. *Old Testament Theology*. Vol. 1, *The Theology of Israel's Historical Traditions*. Translated by David M. G. Stalker. New York: Harper & Row, 1962.

Ricoeur, Paul. *Essays on Biblical Interpretation*. Edited by Lewis S. Mudge. Philadelphia: Fortress, 1980.

Scott, James C. *Weapons of the Weak: Everyday Forms of Peasant Resistance*. New Haven: Yale University Press, 1985.

Soulen, R. Kendall. *The God of Israel and Christian Theology*. Minneapolis: Fortress, 1996.

Steiner, George. *Real Presences*. Chicago: University of Chicago Press, 1989.

Stuhlmacher, Peter. *How to Do Biblical Theology*. Pittsburgh Theological Monograph Series 38. Allison Park, PA: Pickwick, 1995.

Thiel, John E. *Nonfoundationalism*. Guides to Theological Inquiry. Minneapolis: Fortress, 1991.

Watson, Francis. *Text and Truth: Redefining Biblical Theology*. Grand Rapids: Eerdmans, 1997.

———. *Text, Church and World: Biblical Interpretation in Theological Perspective*. Grand Rapids: Eerdmans, 1994.

Westermann, Claus. *Basic Forms of Prophetic Speech*. Translated by Hugh Clayton White. Philadelphia: Westminster, 1967.

Wilder, Amos N. "Story and Story-World." *Int* 37 (1983) 353–64.

Wright, N. T. *Jesus and the Victory of God*. Christian Origins and the Question of God 2. Minneapolis: Fortress, 1996.

———. *The New Testament and the People of God*. Christian Origins and the Question of God 1. Minneapolis: Fortress, 1992.

Scripture Index

Old Testament

Genesis

2–3	35
8:1	103
8:20–22	106
8:21–22	103
8:21	55
9:8–17	106
9:11	55, 103
12:3	148
18:14	73, 80
18:19	148
32:29	10

Exodus

1–15	151
1:8	151
1:17	151
2:1–10	151
2:23–25	152
2:24–25	152
3:14	10
6:2	10
12:11–22	152
15	72
33:5	100
34:6–7	23, 35, 76, 106
34:6a	76

34:7	133
34:7b	76–77
34:9	24
34:10	24

Leviticus

26:19–20	43

Numbers

14:18	24
14:19	24
14:20–23	24

Deuteronomy

4	106
4:5–8	146
4:6–8	146
4:7–8	18
4:23–31	97–98
4:23–28	97
4:24	97–98
4:25–26	97
4:26	97
4:27	97
4:29–31	33, 97
4:29	97
4:31	98

6:4	143
7:7	33
10:12–13	126
10:15	33
12:5–7	145–46
12:14	145–46
17:14–20	145
28:23–24	43
29:18–19	25
29:20—30:20	24, 33
29:20–28	24–25
29:20	25–28, 33
29:24	29
29:29—30:14	24–25
30:1–10	26–28, 30–33
30:1	25
30:11–14	22
30:15–20	24–27
32	167

Judges

12:23	136

1 Samuel

2:6–8	41

181

New Testament

Index of Names

Ackroyd, Peter R., 92–96, 110, 148, 160
Albertz, Rainer, 143, 160
Albrektson, Bertil, 52, 68
Alter, Robert, 66, 68, 73, 87
Anderson, Bernhard W., 103, 110, 141, 162
Andersen, Francis I., 149, 161

Bach, Robert, 120, 136, 138
Bailey, Kenneth E., 137, 138
Balentine, Samuel E., 74, 87, 99, 110
Ball, Edward, vii, 89
Ballas, Christopher, 159, 161
Balthasar, Hans Urs von, 60, 68, 166, 177
Baltzer, Klaus, 164
Barker, Margaret, 89
Barr, James, 5, 18, 63, 172
Barth, Karl, 3–7, 9, 18, 35, 39, 47–49, 100, 110, 159–61, 171, 175–77
Barton, John, 150–51, 161
Batto, Bernard F., 103, 110
Beal, Timothy K., viii
Beker, Christiaan, 96, 109–10
Bellah, Robert, 16, 18
Berger, Peter, 114, 138, 166, 177
Bloom, Allan, 156, 161
Blumenthal, David R., 9, 18, 64–65, 67–68
Bogaert, P.-M., 111
Bowen, Nancy R., vii
Braaten, Carl E., 10, 18, 175, 177

Bracke, John Martin, 83, 87
Braulik, Georg, 97, 110
Brett, Mark G., 178
Bright, John, 90, 110, 121, 131, 138
Brooks, Roger, 14, 18
Brueggemann, Walter, xi, 4, 6–8, 10, 18–19, 23, 31, 38, 50, 54, 60, 63, 68, 71–73, 79, 87, 105, 110, 112, 123, 138, 141, 152, 161, 165, 170, 177–78
Buber, Martin, 9, 51, 107, 170–71, 178
Bultmann, Rudolf, 39, 49, 165, 168–69, 178
Butler, James T., 20

Calvin, John, 57, 68, 99–100, 102, 105, 111, 164, 175–76
Campbell, Charles L., 15, 19, 63, 69
Carroll, Robert P., 31–32, 34, 38, 72, 74, 87, 104, 111
Childs, Brevard S., 5, 9, 11, 14, 19, 58, 60–61, 63–65, 67, 69, 126, 138, 172–76, 178
Chopp, Rebecca S., 153, 161
Clines, David J. A., 69
Coats, George W., 160
Cobb, John B. Jr., 16, 19
Collins, John J., 14, 18, 85, 87
Conrad, Edgar W., 20
Crenshaw, James L., 50, 55, 62, 68, 69, 75, 88, 113–15, 124, 138–39, 141